THE WORLD GOT AWAY

MUSIC IN AMERICAN LIFE

The Music in American Life series documents and celebrates the dynamic and multifaceted relationship between music and American culture. From its first publication in 1972 through its half-century mark and beyond, the series has embraced a wide variety of methodologies, from biography and memoir to history and musical analysis, and spans the full range of musical forms, from classical through all types of vernacular music. The series showcases the wealth of musical practice and expression that characterizes American music, as well as the rich diversity of its stylistic, regional, racial, ethnic, and gendered contexts. Characterized by a firm grounding in material culture, whether archival or ethnographic, and by work that honors the musical activities of ordinary people and their communities, Music in American Life continually redefines and expands the very definition of what constitutes music in American culture, whose voices are heard, and how music and musical practices are understood and valued.

For a list of books in the series, please see our website at www.press.uillinois.edu.

THE WORLD GOT AWAY

A Memoir

MIKEL ROUSE

Foreword by Kyle Gann

UNIVERSITY OF ILLINOIS PRESS
Urbana, Chicago, and Springfield

Manufactured in the United States of America
1 2 3 4 5 C P 5 4 3 2 1
∞ This book is printed on acid-free paper.

Library of Congress Cataloging-in-Publication Data
Names: Rouse, Mikel, author. | Gann, Kyle, writer of foreword.
Title: The world got away : a memoir / Mikel Rouse ; foreword
    by Kyle Gann.
Description: Urbana : University of Illinois Press, 2024. |
    Includes index.
Identifiers: LCCN 2023043787 (print) | LCCN 2023043788
    (ebook) | ISBN 9780252045813 (hardcover) | ISBN
    9780252087912 (paperback) | ISBN 9780252056697 (ebook)
Subjects: LCSH: Rouse, Mikel. | Composers—United States—
    Biography. | LCGFT: Autobiographies.
Classification: LCC ML410.R854 A3 2024 (print) | LCC ML410.
    R854 (ebook) | DDC 780.92 [B]—dc23/eng/20230918
LC record available at https://lccn.loc.gov/2023043787
LC ebook record available at https://lccn.loc.gov/2023043788

To MSR and JJR for HK

Contents

Foreword by Kyle Gann	ix
Preface	xxiii
Dennis Cleveland (1996): Part 1	1
Dennis Cleveland (1996): Part 2	12
Recordings (1980–2020): Part 1	24
Quorum (1984)	48
Failing Kansas (1995)	55
Cage/Cunningham (1997–2013)	64
The End of Cinematics (1998): Part 1	82
The End of Cinematics (1998): Part 2	92
Bars & Restaurants (1965–2021)	101
Luminato Trilogy (2008)	114
Gravity Radio (2009)	128
The Demo (2015)	142
Recordings (1980–2020): Part 2	154
One Boy's Day (2014–?)	188
Acknowledgments	197
Illustration Credits	203
Index	205

Foreword

I have long considered Mikel Rouse the most phenomenal composer of my generation. I want to put that right up front—because, if you skip this introduction, you may not find much support or rationale for that opinion in what Mikel has written. This book is no artist's explanation of his work, no treatise on his personal aesthetics, no self-justification. This is a jaunty, rollicking memoir of an artist who's had a busy, wide-ranging career, and even if he's had a lot of ups and downs (the ups deliriously exciting, the downs pretty penurious), he always knew how to have fun, and he wants to tell you about the fun. I would say it's a self-portrait of an amazing character, but perhaps what's most amazing about Mikel is how many characters he can attract around him. He's released dozens of recordings, and he's performed and toured his works through Spain, France, the Netherlands, Brazil, Canada, United Kingdom, Australia, Ireland, New Zealand, and around every corner of the US. He brought opera, technologically, into the twenty-first century. He's a songwriter of astonishing imagination and invention, with a range of idioms that rivals the Beatles. But he's also a connoisseur of truck stop food and Southern barbecue, and he's just as happy to talk about that.

Let's start with the basics, not all of which Rouse reveals on his own (although he tells some poignant stories about his childhood in the interludes of the final chapter, so don't miss that). He was born in St. Louis in 1957 and grew up in a little town called Poplar Bluff in the southeast "boot-heel" area of Missouri. His father was a state trooper, and a pretty tough character. In third grade Rouse decided that Michael was a counterintuitive spelling for his name and changed it to Mikel (still pronounced the same). He grew up so rural that jumping from a running horse onto a moving train was a boy's pastime. As a teenager he once ran away from home to join a carnival. But he loved to draw and play guitar and piano, and he got degrees in both art and music from the Kansas City Art Institute and the Conservatory of Music at the University of Missouri at Kansas City.

Rouse's musical beginnings were pure rock and roll. In Kansas City he formed a band called Tirez Tirez, which was the only local band progressive enough to open for Talking Heads when the latter played there in 1978. But pop music wasn't the only genre in Rouse's bloodstream. In 1979 he moved to New York City, where he studied Schillinger technique with Jerome Walman. Joseph Schillinger (1895–1943) was a composer and theorist who believed that the basis for all artistic beauty was mathematical. His system, which only those certified were (and still are) allowed to teach, was based on repeated rhythms or pulses going out of phase with each other, and mathematical structures governing pitches and chords. George Gershwin studied with Schillinger (as passages in *Porgy and Bess* attest), as did other Tin Pan Alley songwriters; no less an avant-gardist than Henry Cowell wrote the intro to Schillinger's book, and the aleatory composer Earle Brown started out in Schillinger technique as well. At the same time, Rouse studied the complexities of African rhythm from A.M. Jones's groundbreaking, then-new *Studies in African Music.*

And so Rouse developed what one might call a geometrical musical imagination based in systems and patterns. Along with his rock songs, he also composed instrumental pieces for piano, string quartet, orchestra, and an instrumental rock band he formed called Broken Consort. An early drum-machine piece called *Quorum* (1984, later choreographed by Ulysses Dove, and kept in the Alvin Ailey company repertoire for thirty years) crammed all of his ideas about rhythm into one ambitious tour de force, which, despite its sonic austerity, has remained an inspiration for his musical ideas ever since. His 1984 album *Jade Tiger* and its 1993 successor *Soul Menu*, both for Broken Consort, introduced Schillinger-type rhythmic complexity into minimalism, spearheading a new style that would come to be called totalism. The first time I heard Rouse's music, at a Broken Consort concert in a Manhattan rock club in 1989, he blew me away with a twelve-tone piece called "Quick Thrust." Every note was based on a row of all twelve pitches repeating against itself in variously slow and fast cycles, in rhythms all based on the Fibonacci series. And yet, in the free-wheeling, pop-and-classical mixing of the New York 1980s, the piece seemed perfectly at home in a rock club.

That's one of the things I find so phenomenal about Rouse. The generation of composers who matured in the 1980s often had roots in rock, jazz, and the classical avant-garde, and they were tired of everything being so separated. They wanted to smash those walls between genres and be allowed to express all their influences at once. No one went further in that direction than Rouse. As a pop performer, he has made a lifelong study of pop record production, and no other classically trained musician has become so sophisticated at placing lines and layers in a transparent audio space in a way that you can hear so many things going on at once. I play his CDs for my students, and at first they think it's just pop music. Then they listen into his textures and begin to hear intricate polyrhythms, polytonalities, unobtrusive odd meters, layers of nonsynchronized lines, samples quoted from song to song, and get drawn into complexities that no merely vernacular pop music can provide. (For instance, if you want to hear an overt result of the African rhythm studies, listen to "My Love's Gone" from *Love at Twenty*, which winds up a bunch of mismatched repeated tunes in different meters and lets them run as your brain struggles to keep track of them.)

In a December 1782 letter to his father, Mozart wrote about the piano concertos he had just finished: "There are parts here and there from which *connoisseurs alone* can derive satisfaction, but these passages are written in such a way that the less learned cannot fail to be pleased, albeit without knowing why." *That's* what happens in Rouse's music.

For an early, formative example, in the song "Never Forget a Face" from the album *Living Inside Design* (1994), a six-syllable phrase "Shaking the tree of God" gets repeated over and over, but the rhythm repeats every seven notes, so the word-rhythm is a little different every time. It's hard to perform (I've watched Rouse surreptitiously count on his fingers while doing it) and brings into a pop setting a clever variation on the phase-shifting that Steve Reich had made famous in his early minimalist scores. The second scene of *Failing Kansas* (1995) has a hymn spoken in 12/8 meter, but the rock background beneath it is in 4/4, the eighth-note being equal, so you're subliminally hearing two meters at once, with different measure lengths. "Soul Train" from *Dennis Cleveland* (1996) has canons made from spoken phrases at different lengths; chart it out, as I have, and it looks like a geometric graph from the wilder passages of *The Rite of Spring*. One of his tricks is to start a five-beat repeating pattern going at the same time as a four-beat pattern, so that you can't tell whether it's in 4/4 or 5/4. You can tap your foot to the music, but sometimes you have to decide which tempo to follow. And as Mozart points out, you don't have to be able to recognize these complexities to find the music lively and mysterious and engrossing—you cannot fail to be pleased, albeit without knowing why.

That's the low-level, technical side of Rouse's music that classical music nerds like me love ferreting out. There's a whole lot more creativity going on above that basis, because Rouse is breaking barriers in all directions. In *Living Inside Design* he pioneered a technique he called "counterpoetry," because he uses poetry in the manner of counterpoint. Overdubbing his smoothly crooning voice, he'll have several texts going on at once, so carefully organized and insistently repeated that you catch every word.

The counterpoetry continued and turned into opera. One of Rouse's heroes (and the dedicate of *Dennis Cleveland*) is Robert Ashley (1930–2014), who rethought opera as a television medium, but had trouble getting his operas produced in video format. Rouse, while sticking to the performance format, has gone even further, using new technologies to rethink the operatic stage. In *Failing Kansas* he wrote an opera he could perform by himself (the economics of New York City have forced many composers to become self-sufficient), with a film, a background tape, his own voice, and a virtuosically played harmonica. He took texts associated with the Clutter family murders that Truman Capote wrote about in his explosive 1966 novel *In Cold Blood* and created impressionistic pictures of the events through the thoughts and words of the murderers, Dick and Perry.

His next, exponentially more ambitious opera *Dennis Cleveland* is the work in which Rouse broke through to fame and a wider audience. It's been called "an opera in the form of a talk show," but I experience it the other way around: a talk show in the form of an opera. Always an exhaustive researcher, he sat in the audiences of talk shows like those of Geraldo Rivera, Ricki Lake, Gordon Elliott, and others to soak up the weirdly manipulative behavior that turns people talking about their problems into a circus atmosphere. *Dennis Cleveland* turned New York's premiere avant-garde space The Kitchen, where it was premiered, into a TV studio with big cameras wheeling around. Rouse played the eponymous host, and his onstage guests wove counterpoetry from actual phrases quoted from talk shows. But periodically Dennis would swoop down into the audience, where many of his singers were unobtrusively placed, stick a mike in front of them, and they'd start singing. It was a scary feeling for me when once he did it to the woman sitting next to me and she rose and started telling her story; would he do it to me next?

Rarely has the theater's fourth wall been so startlingly broken down.

Next, *The End of Cinematics* (1997, which Rouse considers the last in a trilogy with *Failing Kansas* and *Dennis Cleveland*) took place on a three-tiered stage, on which performers moved in front of films in which they also took part. The piece also exists as a film opera, in which the images (filmed in Paris) tell a story in counterpoint with the songs. *Funding* (2001) was a second opera-as-film, in which the songs alternate with monologues in English, French, and Portuguese, the same passages of text sometimes cycling through different languages. Again, the images of street life—filmed in New York City, Beirut, Barcelona, and Vienna—often have no clear relation to the texts, but both illustrate the social degradation that gentrification brings to people just trying to make a living. Rouse's ultimate grand opera that we're still waiting for—its production was delayed by the 2020 pandemic—is *One Boy's Day*, a thirteen-hour immersive installation based on a description by 1940s psychologists of every single minute of an average boy's day. He gives us a foretaste in the last chapter of his memoir.

Even outside opera, every major new Rouse work has come up with some big innovation. *International Cloud Atlas* (2006) was a score commissioned for the Merce Cunningham Dance company, and in accordance with the Cunningham/John Cage tradition of combining music and dance by chance methods, every audience member viewed the dance and heard the music in different combinations. Each audience member was given an iPod upon entering, with the music set to shuffle mode, and so the various songs, heard through ear buds, accompanied the dance differently for each viewer. One of Rouse's contributions to the John Cage Trust was to record all the various sounds of Cage's prepared piano (with bolts, screws, erasers, and other objects between the strings) for commercial sale as samples, based on the preparations of Cage's prepared-piano magnum opus *Sonatas and Interludes*. Rouse used those samples himself in his 2004 album *Love at Twenty* (and later albums as well), extending the use of Cage's inimitable timbres into a pop arena. *Gravity Radio* (2009) included live radio reports of the news that wove the day's headlines into the musical dialogue.

A relatively low-profile Rouse album I have a soft spot for is *Return* (1999). A decade earlier he had written a group of pieces for string quartet based on Schillinger methods. By 1999 he had moved on, but he liked those quartets and decided to go back and do something else with them (thus the title *Return*)—namely, layer other instruments and vocals over them. Beneath the foregrounded drums, saxophone, and vocals, you can often still hear the original string quartets evoking a rather different ambience. The number of lines you're listening to at once in that album rivals the huge orchestra pieces of the serialist 1960s (think Stockhausen), and yet every element is so carefully positioned in audio space that you can always catch any piece your ear wants to focus on. No other composer has achieved that level of complexity with results so audible and immediately ingratiating.

Speaking of *Return* brings up Rouse's lyrics, which represent a whole other layer of creativity. "Dammit Bikini" starts out:

> *I got good looks, I do declare(!)*
> *To take apart the ones that stare*
> *Into the void; their afternoon*
> *When comes a time to make more room*
>
> *When the misery says to me, "All-y All-y All Outs In Free,"*
> *Take a line out of history: dammit bikini!*

In the next song, "You Know Why I'm Here," Rouse is singing "I am your guide / I see your face" in a languidly unmetered tempo, while also singing a faster refrain over it:

> *You don't mind it, you don't wind it,*
> *You don't stop 'cause you're never going to find it,*
> *You're all over, you're in clover,*
> *You're uptown and you're in a Range Rover.*

They're vivid, memorable lyrics, but as one critic mentioned, sometimes they "stubbornly refuse to make sense."

On the other hand, "Drop the Ball" from *The End of Cinematics* is definitely describing something, though it's hard to say what:

> You could say you caused my head to spin
> But you don't get to do that again
> You could say the writing on the wall
> Was the kindest letdown of them all
>
> You could say your love was Heaven sent
> But that don't explain the money spent
> You could say my life was something
> To believe in till I fell for you.
>
> My intake on love is briefly:
> Take a number, float upstreamly
> Be awake and try to have it all
>
> Clear out of the office early
> Break for dinner and a movie
> Make up for mistakes and drop the ball

Some relationship has gone bad. There's a story here, and we're not told what it is, but the enumeration of feeling responses is enough; we've all been there, or close enough. Money is involved: "The missing bank books is a reason to look up," he sings in the same disc's "Be More Really." Sometimes Rouse's texts resemble Robert Ashley's, in that there's a backstory alluded to, only part of which appears in the music's frame. But one could say that Ashley's enigmatic texts are more about the facts of the story, while Rouse's are about the feelings they inspire.

On which point, take "Where Are Those Girls" from *Music for Minorities* (2003):

> Don't worry 'bout the good life
> That's already been taken
> Don't worry 'bout your bad dreams
> Those bad dreams will awaken
> The photos you'll remember
>
> And where are those girls?
> They're safe in your mind
> That goes for the one
> That left you behind
> And where are those girls?
> Those two of a kind

"Don't worry 'bout the good life / That's already been taken." Ouch. It starts out so comforting, but what a sad message. Will you awaken from those bad dreams, or will the bad dreams awaken to become reality? More impressively, the first four lines sound like a typical stanza, and the fifth line seems to be the beginning of a similar stanza. But suddenly, on the sixth line the bass shifts down to E-flat (in F major) on the poignantly nostalgic line "Where are those girls?," with a smooth triplet breaking the rhythm. I always melt at that point, even though I can anticipate it after hundreds of listenings. It's so simple, almost embarrassing to parse technically, but it's a magic moment—and magic moments require an intelligent setup. Who else writes a song in eleven-line verses?

The lyrics often sound like sound bites from a love song, as in "Roseland" from *Return*:

> And when you were crying at Roseland
> And I could not reach out to you
> Yea, when you were crying at Roseland
> A moment of history flew

Or "I Loved that Too" from *Love at Twenty*:

> I was loved and I was left
> I was loved and I was left
> I was left, left by you
> I loved that too

The phrases never add up to a love song, their apparent sentimentality never finds an object. The lines are *signifiers* of sentiment, they make us feel the way love songs make us feel, but they turn into a collage of feelings without a narrative. The singer (Rouse) is pushing our emotional buttons, drawing up random memories helter-skelter, but without the maudlin sincerity of a real pop song. "I collect these memories in hopes that they'll add up to a life," Rouse says in *Funding*, and similarly the feelings alluded to in his texts might add up to a song.

That said, it would not do to portray Rouse as some kind of Dadaist Gertrude Stein putting words together without meaning. While the faux love-song phrases occupy most of the foreground, they take place within a widespread critique of capitalism, corporate greed, and escapist entertainment that often creeps from the periphery into the foreground. *Dennis Cleveland* resulted partly from Rouse having his political outlook focused by *Voltaire's Bastards* by the Canadian author John Ralston Saul, a brilliant book that diagnosed the ills of Western society as an overreliance on reason, method, and management techniques at the expense of emotion, spirituality, humanitarianism, and common sense. The opera is an apparent celebration, but implies condemnation, of how entertainment by celebrities both alienates us from our lives and helps us avoid noticing our alienation. Dennis, the talk show host, starts out talking about "the conformity that passes for individualism," and continues,

> *"One lacks form, desire, zest for life,*
> *A set of principles to live by,*
> *But most disturbing,*
> *Lacks the ability to make money.*
> *In this highly charged atmosphere*
> *Decisions are made,*
> *Faults are flaunted, dishonesty looms*
> *And in the pocket of every free man: The Bottle."*

The "Beautiful Murders" scene has an engaging but dark refrain:

> *This time the finger that I put into the pie*
> *'Sgonna be a gold retriever, not just pointing at the sky.*
> *This time the mystery, the questioning of life*
> *Will surrender to addiction, the celebrity of hype.*
>
> *This time the mandate that you passed off on the world*
> *Will be shuffling the money leaving nothing left to earn . . .*
> *This time the finger that I put into the pie*
> *'Sgonna be the last reminder of the simple corporate lie.*

Rouse broadly returned to this theme in the 2019 album *Swingers Castle*, with songs like "Hollywood and Sons," "The Pop Machine," and "The Edges of Entertainment":

> *Basic freedom basic income*
> *Basically your frozen sitcom*
> *Nothing left to reason with*
> *So settle for new season myth*
> *Recycling the garbage bin*
> *Billboards in the bullpen*
> *Hollywood Reporter*
> *Psycho image sorter*
> *Welcome to the status quo*
> *As far as entertainments go . . .*

Words that you can't say
Put those fucking words away

Everybody benefits from
The PC condiments
To feel good about yourself
Maybe dream of Uber wealth . . .

That's entertainment
That's entertainment
No one can blame it
No one can tame it

Funding is a sharper meditation on the gentrification of New York City over a twenty-year period, and monologues by the characters make Rouse's concerns even more explicit. In the first, actress Veanne Cox expresses (the words unsynchronized with footage of her talking) the thoughts of many a New York artist caught in a financial vise:

And if you knew you were never in it for the money, well good for you. But guess what?
Now you're really not in it for the money.
And there's this Ferris wheel of everyone else you know
and they're on the ride of a lifetime—
money pouring out of their ears. Popping out babies.
Building homes on Fire Island . . .
I guess I thank God for a fiscal crisis.
That as much as anything else brought me here . . .
And if life on Surf Avenue was bumpy, life on Fourteenth Street was better.
Sitting on the fire escape, watching all the cons go by.
Three-card Monte and mystery meat.
Knowing you are entry level but so happy to be in the game at last.
Where did I get the idea that innovation was a criteria for funding?
Didn't Marshall McLuhan say "A successful book cannot afford to be more than ten percent new?"
At what point did I think I should get paid for what I do?
"Nothing rankles as much as the undeserved success of contemporaries."
I didn't make that up. I think some astronaut said it—Isaac Asimov or Peter Usinov—someone like that.
Anyway, it's true. I live it every day. That slip and slide.
And waiting to get paid, that gets in the way of everything.
While most people are paying mortgages and funding Time Warner,
I'm juggling a phone bill versus a slice of pizza.

And as I curse Wall Street week and the dot-comers, because I know I'm smarter than they are, they've just gotten off another round.

And as the smoke clears you see that the bar has been raised yet again. Corporate gods are so excited. And there's little ole me surrounded by friends in sheep's clothing. And they're all saying, "Lighten up, the city is cleaner and I'm doing better."

And the mayor gives each one of them their own personal city block to demolish.

But no one plays music on the street corner anymore. And that's one of the reasons I came here. And nobody sits around in coffee shops and argues about things like they matter. I mean besides investment planners. . . .

Well, the good news is that you can't smell Wall Street from up here. Not yet anyway . . .

It would take an enormous effort of bad taste to turn this one oasis of urban blight into a rerun of middle America.

Typically, rather than preach, Rouse obliquely illustrates the mindsets that rampant capitalism pushes people into, the sad thoughts we have without assigning a concrete cause to them.

After the financial crash of 2008, organizations no longer had the money needed to stage Rouse's large operas, and for a while he retreated into a series of song cycles in which his reflections on politics sometimes took center stage. In "Albany Handshake" from *False Doors* (2012) he sings,

> From canvasser to lobbyist
> The ethics bills agreed
> The public face of leadership
> Is flawed but never freed . . .
>
> What's left around to lie about
> The dungeons of the day
> Imagining through government
> Party's arrest to play
> And even untold Washington
> Will cower and agree
> There's no greater inspiration
> Than the skirt of Albany.

The cycle's final song "Come from Money" has a recurring refrain: "It doesn't hurt to come from money."

And in 2020, during the pandemic, Rouse put out basically a rap album (a genre he'd been edging closer to) called *~/Library/Mouth/*

Congress, in which he gave fuller voice to protesting the ills that were rankling American society. Here's "I Broke":

> *Like if Christ was fer reals*
> *Second comings "you feel?"*
> *You might be Kanye-stupid*
> *Is that a thing?*
> *It should've been in 2016*
> *But that brain trust won't go away*
> *Break your jaw, call it a day*
> *Take Hillsong for holy foreplay*
> *MAGA your ass to Judgement Day . . .*
> *I'll give you 2 to 1 Ronald Reagan's to blame*
> *It seems the GOP likes toddlers with atrophied brains . . .*

Yet in this rap style he will also break down his lyrics into fragmented units that are basically sound poetry, as in "Pick It Up, Audrey":

> *Work work*
> *Just work like this*
> *Hit me quick*
> *Hit me run*
> *It gotta holler*
> *Beat that beats*
>
> *In your spectrum*
> *Beat beep beep*
> *But I still run*
> *But I live*
> *In outdoor in out*

I have sometimes characterized Rouse's overall musical aims as a postmodern simulation of normalcy. That is, he takes techniques associated with the musical avant-garde—Schillinger rhythmic layering, information overload, Cage's prepared piano, hypertextual superimposition—and works them into the background, while the foreground offers the combination of qualities—simple tonality, a steady, articulated beat, rhyming and regular lyrics, timbres common to the rock vernacular—which create the superficial impression of a kind of "normal" music. The mechanisms of musical modernism provide the foundation, and over them are laid the signifiers of a pop vernacular.

And where better for modernism to have ended up? Those complexities created a vast and oft-noted gulf between "art music," composed music, and the mass audience, splitting audiences into mutually contemptuous camps. Rouse's music acknowledges that all those rhythmic, tonal, textural, and textual complexities are fascinating to hear, but also that they're not enough by themselves to engage a large audience. Or—to reverse it—he knows that what attracts most listeners are poignant lyrics and a rhythmic groove, but also that those by themselves don't provide enough depth to keep people mystified and coming back for more. The cerebral serialist Milton Babbitt used to claim that he was "simply trying to make music all it can be," but it is Rouse who has let us have our cake and eat it too (thus the origin of the musical movement he's been associated with, totalism).

Ultimately, that's what's so astounding about Rouse's music. It isn't (only) pop. It isn't (only) classical. It isn't (only) experimental. It isn't (only) multimedia. It stands above and aloof from such classifications, though it maintains connections to each genre. It's the music my generation of musicians thought we were eventually headed for, beyond classifications ("beyond category," to quote what Duke Ellington said was the highest compliment). This is why, for me, Rouse has been *the* composer of our time, the modernist, minimalist, totalist songwriter who took all the streams and fused them into a joyous and engaging postmodern unity. His style is immediately recognizable, and he has remained remarkably true to his original vision for more than four decades, no matter how much deeper, more sophisticated, and wide-ranging his projects have become. He hasn't made anything I get tired of hearing, and I've listened to some of his discs hundreds of times (though he puts out records in such profusion that I have trouble keeping up).

Now, to say a word about the memoir you're about to read: as someone who has known Mikel for thirty-three years, I can assure you that reading it is just like hearing him talk at the bar over vodka tonics. (When I met him, he still had a day job playing background piano on a tourist boat that circled Manhattan.) His *joie de vivre* colors every page. He can take as much pleasure in a good meal as in a brilliant premiere, and I could never manage to match his grand enthusiasm for the hot dogs from the hot dog rollers at Rudy's bar. Disappointments, some of which I know touched him deeply, are dismissed in a blithe sentence or two, and remarkable successes, like the notoriety he received from a controversy over *Failing Kansas* in New Zealand, he describes as preposterous bits of luck that surprised him as much as anyone else. He makes friends everywhere he goes, and everyone he's ever worked with or who even saved his day with a free sandwich gets a shout-out, in glowing terms. The history of music has afforded no more generous soul. No musician has ever worked harder on his art, yet he treats every accolade and prestigious gig as a windfall that a poor kid from Poplar Bluff had no right to expect. I would love to have known Oscar Wilde, or Cole Porter, or Groucho Marx, but I can't envy anyone: I've known Mikel Rouse. In these pages, you'll come to know him too.

Kyle Gann

Preface

The World Got Away is a snapshot of a life. Well, my life. But the essential thing is it could be anyone's life. What I mean is, every life is uniquely singular. And by writing about the ups and downs, warts and all, I'm reminded that each of us has a journey. Leonard Cohen was once asked, "What's your idea of an important achievement?" He answered, "There is only one achievement in life, and that's the acceptance of your lot."

The World Got Away is structured around "the work" over the last forty-five years. I've always wanted to focus only on the work. If I'd wanted to focus on me, I'd have become a celebrity. As some pieces had a touring life of ten or twelve years, organizing this book around individual works seemed like a good way to cover territory. Similar to my score *International Cloud Atlas* for the Merce Cunningham Dance Company, this approach can be likened to an autobiographical composition. Chapters are intentionally placed out of chronological order; they can be read in any combination, as they are self-contained essays with references to other sections of the book. However, because recordings are the mainstay of my life, chapters concerning them tend to be a bit more chronological in the narrative. I stumbled on the idea of the final section, *One Boy's Day*, as a way to mirror the end with the beginning: childhood appears at the end, hopefully expressing the idea that we all end up where we started.

THE WORLD GOT AWAY

Dennis Cleveland (1996)

I'm sitting in the middle booth of Rudy's, a 1919-era bar around the corner from me in Hell's Kitchen. The booths have seen better days. They used to be red naugahyde, but in the '80s they started repairing tears in the surface with red duct tape. Now all the booths are completely covered in duct tape and make a squishy sound when you move around on them. I first started coming here when a saint of a fellow named Ernie Schroeder began managing four bars in HK. He started at the original Holland Bar, which in the '70s and early '80s was under the Holland Hotel, a welfare hotel on Forty-Second Street. The Holland is where a number of traditions started: free hot dogs, free Thanksgiving and Christmas dinners, folks selling stolen meat and tube socks. Ernie catered to the old-school boozers in HK. He brought all of these traditions to Rudy's. (Ernie used to bring White Castle hamburgers to the Holland and Rudy's, but this was before they sold them in stores; he got busted for transporting and selling food across state lines.) Before Ernie took over Rudy's, it was a scary country and western bar. It had a very strange clientele. I once asked Ernie how he changed that, and he said he only needed to do one thing: change the jukebox from country to jazz and blues.

I spent a lot of time there with fellow artists and friends. Vickie, one of the bartenders, would take pictures every day and give you one, or as she said, "One for you, one for the wall." At one time, there was an entire gallery of pics. This would eventually become untenable as I brought more dates to Rudy's. I would bring scores to work on in the middle booth in the mornings when my place was too hot. Rudy's has supreme air-conditioning. They didn't serve coffee, but Ernie would make me a cup. A great memory from the early '90s was when Kyle Gann, the polymath music critic for the *Village Voice*, wrote an article about a new music movement called totalism. When Kyle mentioned in the article that he first heard the term at Rudy's, I guess the editor at the *Voice* thought it would be good to have a picture of the bar where a possible music movement started. The article was dense with technical music jargon, and I remember Ernie saying happily, "I don't know what the fuck it means, but I love it." He loved it so much that he made hundreds of copies on multicolored paper and hired a clown to pass them out in front of the bar. In some ways, that article put Rudy's on the map. Young musicians would come and ask the bartenders Steve and George (who were also the curators of the jukebox) about what totalism was, and they'd point to the booth where I was gathered with friends. I became good at making up answers for free drinks. I also remember dancing to "The Girl from Ipanema" with Astrud Gilberto on her birthday. So many memories. So many hot dogs.

Ernie had some health issues in the early '90s, so he moved to Florida and turned over the day-to-day operation to his brother, Johnny Dirt. Johnny had run the Dirt Club in New Jersey and was a true character. The Dirt Club was kind of on a circuit of East Coast clubs like CBGB in New York, Maxwell's in Hoboken, and the Rat in Boston. Johnny's trademark move was to go onstage when a band was playing and stand on his head. Johnny and I got along immediately. He liked it when I brought my National guitar and played in the back garden. I put him in my film *Music for Minorities*, shooting him at Rudy's waxing philosophical as only he could. His wife, Marnie, was a sweetheart who adored him even though he could be a challenge. Johnny and Marnie both loved Lisa Boudreau, my wife in those days. When we would go out for dinner together, it always amused me to see Johnny try to relate to Lisa's dance career with Merce Cunningham by talking about the dancers (strippers) at the various clubs he had managed over the years. Now Rudy's is in the capable hands of Danny, another saint of a fellow, supported by Yolanda, Judy, and Nils.

Anyway, I'm sitting with Johnny in 1996, after The Kitchen premiere of the talk show opera *Dennis Cleveland*. I always liked the sound of that phrase, *talk show opera*. We're sitting here talking about the sensation it has caused and the great press it has received. I know it was a tremendous success because I'm $50K in debt and the creditors are hounding me daily. Sitting here fretting about money is normal, and in my angst, I simply can't imagine the twelve-year journey this piece would launch. But I guess a little background is in order.

I started writing the music for *Dennis Cleveland* around 1994 while I was finishing the music and staging for my first opera, *Failing Kansas*. *Failing Kansas* had taken five years to write, so I was itching to write something quickly, but I also wanted it to be big. Forced to do solo work after the 1987 crash, I missed working with other artists and musicians, and I was feeling like I might be able to pull off a larger show. I knew the themes I wanted to focus on: mass culture hypnosis, consumerism, advertising, and ritual. Kyle, who would often venture far and wide outside of music to hammer home ideas and theories, had written an article on an equally compelling polymath, John Ralston Saul. Because of Kyle's coverage, Saul's book *Voltaire's Bastards: The Dictatorship of Reason in the West* garnered a lot of attention from music enthusiasts (it was already required reading for anyone interested in connecting the dots of history to see how we got to our rationalist consumer society). I was transfixed by this book and saw parallels to my own interest in and critique of popular culture. This interest truly peaked during the late '80s and early '90s with the advent of the TV talk show.

I'd done a deep dive into researching the phenomenon of the TV talk show, learning that one fascinating reason it came about was because local stations discovered that it was actually cheaper to produce their own low-budget talk shows than to pay the exorbitant licensing fees of sitcom reruns. And if the viewing numbers didn't change and they didn't lose ad dollars, why not? This led me to an almost addictive fascination with the shows, especially as they got more and more surreal. A remarkable example of the absurdist approach was *The Richard Bey Show* on WWOR-TV in New Jersey. Bey had turned the format on its head with all kinds of competitive events, from the "Miss Big Butt" contest to the "Mr. Punyverse" contest to the "Country Drag Queens versus City Drag Queens" to the "Dysfunctional Family Feud." A staple was the "Wheel of Torture," where busted cheating spouses were strapped to a large wheel on the floor and spun around while the "victimized" spouse poured food on them. Think Karen Finley, but with an audience of one to two million. I drove a few of my high-brow artist friends crazy when

I would call them in the middle of their studio work, begging them to drop everything and turn on Bey's show. I knew the general themes I wanted to address.

I knew I wanted it to be about TV and TV culture. I also wanted to explore Saul's idea of how television had become secular society's replacement for the ritual normally found in religion. I was drawing designs that were wild and explicitly intended to saturate: full-court basketball with an accompanying chorus of singers, advertising bombardments with manipulative musical arrangements (see "*Gravity Radio* (2010)"). I had written and recorded sketches for almost half of the music when I had one of the few actual epiphanies of my life. I was walking through Central Park, thinking about the piece and how it would unfold. I stopped dead in my tracks as it occurred to me: it isn't about television. It *is* television. And at that moment, I had every answer I was looking for. (And in another serendipitous moment, I would wake up from a fever dream with the words "Dennis Cleveland, Dennis Cleveland" in my foggy brain. As I slowly awoke, I said, "That's the name of my opera!" I woke up long enough to write it down and go back to sleep.) It would be staged as a talk show, with both camera crew and audience under relentless studio lighting. I was literally shaking with excitement. I could hardly move. It seems silly now, but around this time there were arguments about the Metropolitan Opera's use of subtitles. *Dennis Cleveland* would use rollovers to stream the libretto, as they did on talk shows. The chorus would be the talk show guests, and there would be singers and performers placed among the audience. And I would have the ridiculous job of playing the talk show host (because I'd also need to conduct the chorus and guests), possibly making a complete fool of myself.

So, unexpectedly in research mode once again (see "*Failing Kansas* (1995)"), I started going to the talk shows that were taped in Times Square, which is a couple of blocks from my place, and around Midtown. *Geraldo, Sally Jessy Raphael, Montel Williams* (sadly, I never got to see *The Richard Bey Show* live, as it was canceled in 1996). I got a crash course in crowd manipulation, prerecorded sound design, and TV studio lighting. I did many set drawings and decided on a minimum three-camera setup, eventually adding a fourth, roving camera. I also gained insight into the character of the talk show host by going to numerous tapings. Geraldo Rivera would actually flirt with women in the audience during breaks. Given his trajectory, I guess that's not such a surprise.

After the success of my opera *Failing Kansas*, I decided to pitch *Dennis Cleveland* to Ben Neill, the music director at The Kitchen, who had supported the premiere of *Failing Kansas*. He suggested a meeting with Executive Director Lauren Amazeen and Producing Director John Maxwell Hobbs. While both seemed interested, I think Ben was ultimately the catalyst for moving the idea forward. He was doing some pretty progressive programming at The Kitchen, and I think he saw *Dennis Cleveland* as an extension of that aesthetic direction. I can't remember how I came to meet John Jesurun, but I think he might have been suggested as a set designer for the show. John had done a serial play called *Chang in a Void Moon* at the Pyramid Club, where I had done some shows with Mikel Rouse Broken Consort. (After The Kitchen's *Dennis Cleveland* run, John cast me as the patriarch, Antonio, a part originally played by performance artist Frank Maya, in Episodes 51 and 52 of *Chang*. I had the good fortune of singing "Caroline, No" by the Beach Boys and nervously playing opposite Steve Buscemi as he forgot his lines. This proved even more significant because on opening night of *Dennis Cleveland*, the fire marshal came and threatened to shut down the production. John was able to call Steve, a former firefighter, and a crisis was averted.)

John seemed to like my idea, and we agreed on a live switching approach to the cameras similar to a normal TV talk show. In his earlier years John had worked on the *The Dick Cavett Show*, so I think placing that setting in a theatrical context made sense to him. Say what you will about the content of talk shows, they represented the full spectrum of race, gender, and the melting pot of America. I wanted that diversity reflected in the cast, as well as to enlist talent from a wide range of the musical spectrum: hip-hop, rock, opera, classical. I also wanted to replicate the loudspeaker sound of talk shows, so I knew I'd need to use a combination of live singing and prerecorded (canned) music. With all of this in mind, I had completed large sections of the piece, sampling talk show snippets *(If you don't love me the way I am, then you can go; She feels that you let her down, though; When I get my sex on, I like to position; If I can't position, then I ain't enjoyin' it)* and looping them in metric combinations. All that remained was to write the confessionals that the audience members would tell Dennis; like a Greek chorus, they would be revealing Dennis Cleveland's own story.

As luck would have it, I found the perfect place to write this dialog. I had never been interested in artist colonies. For composers, they were usually set up with a piano and didn't reflect the way I was working. By this time, I'd built my own studio, so I had all I needed to work. But I read about the Edward F. Albee Foundation in Montauk, a kind of colony that had something I could use: a beach. I applied in March of 1996 for the month of August, which would be two months before the premiere. I was accepted and, after arranging a sublet for my place (which would turn out badly), I headed to the colony. It was an old barn named after William Flanagan, a composer and former partner of Albee's. I had a small room, but since I was traveling with DAT tapes and a portable player, it was all I needed. I met Albee early on. He had bought several bicycles for the five of us at the colony that month so we could descend the hill to the center of town and to the beach. I would bike to the beach every day to write, often stopping at the Shagwong restaurant, which had a chalkboard sign in the window that sums up the life of many musicians: "Piano player wanted. Must have knowledge of opening clams."

To say that this was one of the greatest months of my life would be an understatement. The artists I met each left a big impression. There was Jan Baracz, a sculptor who quietly brought me a vodka with lemon while I was on the phone finding out my stepgrandfather had died. He was also there with unbridled enthusiasm when I learned my sister had come out as gay. And Larry Kunofsky, a young and gifted writer who was only a little annoyed when Edward paid me the most attention at a picnic we invited him to (I think this had more to do with the fact that, like Flanagan, I was a composer). I remember Edward telling me that stopping drinking was a choice he made to keep writing; it had to be one or the other. But the most unexpected artist was the sculptor Ryuji Noda, who would make the group elaborate dinners after shopping for fresh seafood and vegetables. One afternoon, I could hear some blues music coming from his studio, but something also sounded live. Thinking it was likely the acoustics of the barn, I leaned into his studio to discover him wailing away on a blues harmonica. He seemed very shy and apologized if it was disturbing me. I said, "Are you kidding? You're fantastic." Remembering the sideshow quality of some of the talk shows, I immediately asked him if he'd consider being in my upcoming show. And that's how I got a Japanese, harmonica-playing, Hawaiian shirt–wearing audience member for *Dennis Cleveland*. Over the twelve years we did the show, casts changed (especially with all audience cast members being cast locally from town to town), but Ryuji did every show in every country it played.

Because of the commercial references in *Dennis Cleveland*, and wanting the piece to comment on corporate culture, I decided I wanted a logo and consistent branding images, something high art would frown upon. Fast-forward to twenty years later and you'll find new music ensembles and artists focused on branding without any sense of irony. Anyhow, I set up a photo shoot at The Kitchen and, with a few friends posing as audience members, the photographer Susan San Giovanni was able to grab a classic shot. I not only had my branding image, but the cover of the CD—or so I thought. In 1995 I had released *Failing Kansas* through the New Tone Records label in Italy. But given the American-centric approach in *Dennis Cleveland,* I thought it best to find a US label. I can't remember how I came to New World Records, but they were a traditional classical/new music label, and I was surprised when they wanted to release the record. I was happy that I would have a CD release to coincide with the premiere. I worked with Mark Kingsley, of Greenberg Kingsley, on the cover design. I met Mark through the composer William Duckworth. Mark is one of those infuriating people who are as smart and talented as they think they are (Mark even performed in a few of the shows as an audience prompter, a dedicated designer to the end). When I showed the muckety-mucks (Johnny Dirt term) at New World the cover photo, they said they couldn't use it. I asked why. They answered, "Because we don't put pictures of composers on our releases." I tried to explain that the picture was of the character Dennis Cleveland. They weren't persuaded. So we were forced to do a lame redesign and live with it. (Fortunately I've always signed licensing deals, so when the rights reverted back to me, I released the record on my own label, Exit-Music Recordings, and reinstated the original cover.)

In September, back from the Albee colony, I got a call from Lauren and John at The Kitchen. They needed to see me. I went for the meeting, and they told me the good news was that The Kitchen would be honoring their 1996–97 season. The bad news was there was no money. I was basically on my own with a raw space. I'd already spent a considerable sum on preproduction, and now I had to decide whether to keep going or cut my considerable losses. And as usual I thought, "in for a dime, in for a dollar." I think Thomas Buckner (who was in Robert Ashley's ensemble) learned of my work from the press. He ran the *Interpretations* music series and offered me a decent fee for a solo performance. I wondered if he'd consider helping with *Dennis Cleveland* instead, so I invited him to my studio to discuss it. He agreed and I was relieved, and I think he was as well. He came to the premiere and was pleasant enough, but I think the piece was a bridge too far for him. So this was a start, but I would need way more funding to do the show I wanted. The good news is that several of the local talk shows provided a low-budget, low-quality example of what could be passable. I never collected baseball cards as a kid, but you wouldn't know it based on the way I was collecting credit cards. I literally had a deck of them and, of course, I lost track of which was which. I would not recommend this approach to anyone.

But I was obsessed and already working on the third opera of the trilogy (see "*The End of Cinematics* (1998)"). I remember conversations with Blaine Reininger in the early '80s when we collaborated and toured our EP *Colorado Suite* (I met him as an expat when I moved to Brussels; he was an inspiration). He had racked up huge debt and would plead with the credit card companies that continually tried to offer him a new card, "Please! You don't want me!" But I felt like I was in a zeitgeist moment, and I was all in (during the premiere at The Kitchen, my great friend and artist Rob Shepperson would fax me updates from the Jenny Jones trial (look it up—or don't), confirming that whatever I thought I was doing, it was, at the very least, of the moment. Another feature of the piece was having the "audience plants" mingle with the real audience waiting for the doors to open, thus ensuring a believable ruse.

During rehearsals of *Dennis Cleveland,* we would always make a composite VHS tape of the "live edit" of the show, and I would take these tapes back to review them and make notes for the next rehearsal. This process continued for years, but the first time I went home to review the VHS was memorable. I had done it! It looked and felt like the real thing, not an "art version." I remember calling my friend Mark Lambert, who lived down the street and was in the cast. It was 2:00 a.m., but I was so excited to share the news: it works!

So the big day comes, and it's a huge success. I heard there were scalpers for tickets for the first time in The Kitchen's history. I guess it's true, but it might be that due to the dire financial constraints of The Kitchen, they had little experience with an extended run; there was no way to know. I had invited John Ralston Saul to come, and to my surprise he did come and brought along his partner, Adrienne Clarkson, whom I knew from her Canadian arts program *Adrienne Clarkson Presents*. Maybe the best moment of the run was sitting with them on a very late night at the Empire Diner, just a few blocks from The Kitchen. We had the kind of post-show conversation I'd always dreamed of. So smart and so human. John is maybe the smartest person I've ever met, but he has never come across as arrogant. I remember a conversation we had in a cab on the way to an interview in Toronto when I was doing the entire trilogy of operas at the Luminato Festival in 2008 and his inclusion of the cabby in the convo. I truly think he learned more from listening to others, never caring if people knew how brilliant he was. Looking at photos of us together from that period, I'm reminded that I lost twenty-five pounds from the stress of mounting the show. I had debilitating back pain at the time, and I remember calling the Texas Back Institute to get advice. They said they currently don't know the reason for 85% of back pain. I felt better until the person on the other end of the line added, "Unless it comes with rapid weight loss. Then it might be a tumor." Good times.

Sônia Braga (who was dating cast member Mark Lambert) threw a cast party for *Dennis Cleveland* in her swank Tribeca apartment. I remember Ryuji making sushi with the same culinary skill he had displayed at the Albee colony. Cast members Napua Davoy, Andrea Weber, Eric Smith, and Levensky Smith were there. Mark Kingsley remembers kissing Sônia goodbye after the party. My mom hadn't seen the show but had come for a visit and slowly began to realize this had turned out to be a big deal. The piece got great notices in the *New York Times* ("Surreal Talk-Show Host Roams Through an Opera"), *New York Magazine* ("Rouse has fashioned a stunning ninety-minute musical drama"), Toronto's *Globe and Mail* ("gripping and hypnotic"), and the *Village Voice* ("the most exciting and innovative new opera since *Einstein on the Beach*), to name a few. The gamble had seemingly paid off, though it didn't occur to me how much I might have been risking until I had lunch with Ben a week or so later. He laughed and said, "I believed in the piece, but I was also afraid for you." I asked him what he meant, and he replied, "I thought you risked flushing an entire career down the toilet." It was only at that moment that I realized what a risk I had taken. But for now, I was basking in the glow of a huge success, and I would just wait for the offers to start pouring in.

It turned out to be a very long wait.

Dennis Cleveland, Luminato Festival, 2008.

Dennis Cleveland, Lincoln Center, 2002.

Dennis Cleveland. Krannert Center for the Performing Arts, 2001.

Dennis Cleveland (1996)

Part 2

The show probably looked bigger than it was. The Kitchen was a black-box theater that I believe was once used to shoot TV shows. The space lent itself to this particular approach. Still, with a cast and crew of about twenty five people, it wasn't cheap. I remember changing bulbs myself in the light grid when a couple blew out. Folks had wondered how I pulled it off. One publicist asked me if I had a trust fund. But I knew I just had a bunch of credit cards. The issue got even more confusing when Jon Pareles—a great writer and supporter of progressive music—stated in a largely positive review in the *New York Times* that I had been a recipient of a MacArthur grant. Although this was an honest mistake, it caused me great anxiety, as I didn't want anyone to think I had anything to do with the news of my having received a "genius" grant (I didn't; it was a misreading of the program). But the more difficult effect was that many people assumed I had gotten the award and that's how I financed the production. A correction was later printed, but the damage was done. I was on my own and probably wasn't gonna see a return on my investment for a while. At one point I pulled out the (predigital) press clippings just to make sure the success had actually happened. I hadn't imagined it.

Scrambling to pay my rent and the bare minimum on my credit card collection, I decided to hold a fundraiser to offset some of the production costs. I managed to reprise the solo show *Living Inside Design* and, with Cliff Baldwin's help, remounted the piece with his digital films. This event was held around the block from me at the theater in St. Clement's Episcopal Church. John Jesurun was the emcee for the evening and ruffled some feathers by dissing The Kitchen and their staff. But a bunch of folks consented to be on the steering committee, including several art and music luminaries. This might have helped to bring out a full house for those who had read about *Dennis Cleveland* but didn't get to see the show. Laurie Anderson, the performance artist, Fran Richards, head of the concert division of ASCAP, and Laura Kuhn, director of the John Cage Trust (see "*Cage/Cunningham* (1997–2013)") all made an appearance. I remember after the reception sitting in my apartment with Sue Devine, head of Film and Television at ASCAP, ruffling through the $3,000 or so in cash.

I recall a morning call on my (pre-cell 1997) landline from composer Steve Reich. I think Fran at ASCAP had told him about my financial distress. He said, "I hear you're suffering from your success." I laughed and what followed was a kind and supportive talk. He revealed he had lost a considerable sum on *The Cave*. He then asked how old I was, and I replied I had recently turned 40. He thought for a moment, then said, "That sounds about right." I asked him what he meant, and he said, "That's when I wrote *Music for 18 Musicians*, Phil [Glass] wrote *Einstein* [meaning *Einstein on the Beach*], and Górecki wrote his *Symphony No. 3*." Not wanting to miss the point, I asked, "Meaning?" He replied, "That's about the time you get your shit together." He also said he was nominating me for the Academy of Arts and Letters but added wryly, "I don't think there's a chance in hell that you'll get in." I somehow took that as a compliment. In the '80s and early '90s, I had kept up a correspondence with Steve and he had sent a postcard praising the recording of *Dennis Cleveland*. On the call, he asked where I had recorded it, and I sheepishly replied, "In my Hell's Kitchen apartment." He seemed even more impressed when he heard that.

Margaret Selby, a producer (see "*Quorum* (1984)"), had come to see *Dennis Cleveland* and seemed blown away. She expressed a real interest, but around the same time I got a note from Fred Zollo, who had produced David Mamet's plays on Broadway as well as several Eric Bogosian solo shows. Oddly he became interested in my work from reading a negative review of *Failing Kansas* in the *New York Times* that, while not being favorable, did an OK job of describing the piece. Fred seemed keen on producing an off-Broadway run, and after a couple of cigar smoking sessions in his office, we agreed to move forward. Also, around this time, Rosemary Holland, who worked at Sony Classical, brought me to meet Peter Gelb (now general manager of the Metropolitan Opera), who was the head honcho there. We agreed to try to move forward with Fred and do a group project. This started a yearlong wait-and-see game that was ultimately derailed by the arrival of Jonathan Larson's *Rent*. Even though we had signed agreements and were ready to go, the success of *Rent* made music theater cool again and theaters were now double- and triple-booked. Fred said he'd never seen anything like this. Fred was producing the Wooster Group's production of Eugene O'Neill's *The Hairy Ape* with Willem Defoe at the old Selwyn Theatre on Forty-Second Street. They had reconfigured the inside with metal bleacher seating, and he wondered if I thought the theater would work for *Dennis Cleveland*. I went to the show and thought it would work fine, especially considering the theater's seedy past as a porn palace. But as luck would have it, the theater closed again only to await a new renovation, becoming the American Airlines Theatre (insert irony here). We also investigated the Variety Arts Theatre in my old hood below Fourteenth Street and the Orpheum Theatre, where *Stomp* had moved in and seemed would never leave. In other words, nada.

After a dressing down by Margaret about wasting a year of time (hard to dispute that), she offered to help produce another performance and set up a meeting for me to meet an agent named Michael Mushalla. Michael worked with several performers as a booking agent at Columbia Artists Management (CAMI). I had met Joe Melillo (see "*The End of Cinematics* (1998)") a few times and he'd come to be a supportive confidant, sharing drinks at the iconic Peter McManus pub just down the street from Dance Theater Workshop. He encouraged me to move forward with Michael, so together with Margaret we booked a weeklong run with Dean Corey and the Philharmonic Society of Orange County. I made a few preproduction trips to LA, often staying at the Hotel Del Capri on Wilshire. The motel was run by a grand lady named Marion, who catered to artists and misfits like me. So many interesting times were had there, with Merce and the *Alphabet* crew (see "*Cage/Cunningham* (1997–2013)") and with the Cunningham company. I was pleased to do a feature interview on *Dennis Cleveland* for the *Los Angeles Times* at the Del Capri.

When we arrived in October 1999 to start to build the show, it was a reality check for me: while I'd stayed busy with other projects, three long years had passed since the New York premiere. The build did not go smoothly. Margaret and John did not get along. The camera crew would be willing but underwhelming students from a school, and the small theater wouldn't have the capabilities to meet the technical requirements I'd spent so long conceiving at The Kitchen. Morale was low and the struggle seemed even harder than when I was doing it all on my own. Perhaps the turning point came when Sue Devine brought 100 hot dogs from the LA institution Pink's Hot Dogs and the entire cast and crew dined on picnic tables outside of the loading dock of the theater. Maybe it's my karma with hot dogs, but even John commented that the afternoon brought a necessary shift in everyone's attitude.

Many of the original cast members joined for the second incarnation of the show, such as the talented Levensky Smith, Eric Smith, Napua Davoy, and David Masenheimer. But I will never forget original cast member Kate Sullivan and her commitment to her life and art. Kate had been diagnosed with cancer and was undergoing chemo before the West Coast run had begun. She was concerned about her hair loss and my feelings about her being in the show. I made clear that the role was hers and she had nothing to fear. Then she totally shocked me with the ingenious suggestion that at a certain climactic-reveal moment in the show, her partner could tear off her wig and throw it across the stage. I was flabbergasted by the suggestion and secretly hoping she would be OK doing it. It turned out to be a sensation. Another wonderful performer was Andrea Weber, who was also a trapeze artist. She wore a midriff T-shirt and John had to constantly tell one of the students to stop spending so much camera time on her navel.

Despite technical issues, a low-rent set, lousy sound, and many interpersonal conflicts, the reviews were nearly unanimous. *Variety*: "The considerable and delightful triumph of Mikel Rouse's *Dennis Cleveland*"; *Los Angeles Times*: "Every barrier you can possibly think of has been broken down—between audience and actors, between pop and art music, between fantasy life and harsh reality, between naturalist theater and surreal poetry"; *LA Weekly*: "Maybe it's an opera, maybe something else for which no name has yet been coined; whatever, I found the sheer energy in *Cleveland* irresistible, exhilarating." I will always be grateful to Dean Corey for his courage in booking the show for the Philharmonic

Society's Eclectic Orange Festival (along with the Luminato Festival, Dean mounted all three operas in my trilogy, *Dennis Cleveland*, *Failing Kansas*, and *The End of Cinematics*, in that order). I was excited for the response, but I truly felt as though we had dodged a bullet, and I didn't think I'd be given another pass unless I brought the show to a higher production level. Timothy Mangan of the *Orange County Register* had written a great preview piece on the opera. But he was underwhelmed with the production, and I felt he was correct. I left Los Angeles exhilarated and exhausted, fairly certain I wouldn't be working with this production team again.

A few weeks later, I got a call from Michael Mushalla, who said, "That was fun. Wanna do it again?" We met and agreed to continue to work together, and this started a fourteen-year run that would be a roller coaster of shows and commissions. Next stop: Perth Arts Festival. I met Séan Doran, the artistic director of the festival, through Michael. Michael was leaving CAMI and starting his own company, Double M Arts & Events. He had made quite a few connections over the years with other artists he represented, including the Mark Morris Dance Group. Séan is Irish, and over many beers at McSorley's Old Ale House in New York (his favorite pub outside of Ireland), we hatched a number of ideas. He would present *Dennis Cleveland* at the 800-seat Octagon Theatre for two weeks starting January 25, 2001. Along with the Merce Cunningham Dance Company, we would be the main stage headliners. And the Australian Broadcasting Company (ABC) would film a documentary about the build of the show from start to finish.

At around the same time in 1999, Michael also introduced me to Mike Ross, the director of the Krannert Center for the Performing Arts in Urbana, Illinois. I remember we met at Gallaghers Steakhouse in Midtown a couple of blocks from my apartment. Mike and I hit it off immediately, and we have remained great friends and collaborators for over twenty years. Mike had previously been at the Miller Theatre in New York and wanted to bring cutting-edge work to Krannert. He was fascinated by the concept, and we set about trying to figure out how to keep the intimate set of a talk show while expanding to 1,000-seat theaters (in order to at least break even financially). This would need to be figured out because later, Jon Nakagawa wanted to bring *Dennis Cleveland* to the Great Performers series at Lincoln Center.

I arrived in Perth in early January 2001 to do local casting, a ton of advance press, and meet and greets with the ABC to discuss the documentary. I remember doing laundry in a local laundromat when I saw two full-page ads side by side, one for *Dennis Cleveland* and the other for Merce Cunningham, and I thought, "I have arrived." The New York cast flew in about ten days later, and we had a gathering in the lobby of the Rydges Hotel, where the company and various artists were staying for the festival. I remember the gathering of over thirty people and the gratitude I felt. I expressed to my good friend and cast member Mark Lambert that I thought, after all the trials and tribulations, I'd be jaded and bitter. But here I was, happy to see the larger implications of the piece: so many folks from different backgrounds were here for a common purpose. And remembering my curmudgeonly personality, Mark humorously said, "And just think, you of all people made it happen." On January 26, my birthday, fireworks went off all over the city. It was for Australia Day; at least that's what they told me.

Opening night was memorable, to say the least. January is summer in Australia and the theater was always hard to keep cool during rehearsals (there are lights over the audience as well as the stage). I remember requesting that they start cooling the hall in the early afternoon because once the theater was full, it could be very uncomfortable. They agreed to do so, but something went wrong and there was no air at all through the entire opening night performance. There's nothing quite like seeing an entire audience on camera trying to desperately fan themselves with their programs. I was completely soaked in sweat through my suit coat, but John Jesurun laughed later and said it looked amazing—like a true televangelist! In a kind gesture, Michael had gifted me a massage before the big opening. It was great, but with the heat, I was totally wiped out. The entire local cast was marvelous, and two local cast members, Melissa Madden Gray and Gibson Nolte, went on to do the 2002 Lincoln Center performances as well. We were the buzz of the festival, and when I met opera director Peter Sellars in the hotel lobby, he said *Dennis Cleveland* was what everyone was talking about. Once the Cunningham Company arrived (the Cunningham performances on Bondi Beach, with the sun setting as a backdrop, were spectacular), Lisa and I were photographed for a daily paper (her luggage was lost, but she had asked if I could pack one dress and heels. It was lucky I did).

On completion of the Perth run, I made a number of trips to the Krannert Center for preproduction and marketing meetings. These were grand times, and I remember getting the marketing folks very excited about the idea that the marketing and branding were actually part of the show, not just a way to sell the show. This resulted in two large billboards in Champaign-Urbana. (I also had a huge billboard in Ruston, Louisiana, to announce my three-year Meet the Composer Residency [MTC] in 2002; two states down, forty-eight to go.) We also worked out a video conferencing system with Lincoln Center so we could share solutions on building a truss over the audience for lights and TV monitors. Today this form of video conferencing doesn't sound like a big deal, but at the time it felt like the future. We also held auditions for the local cast rolls, mostly compiled of students from the theater department. Some of these performers would also be included in the Lincoln Center shows. Activity was intense. I was planning for the upcoming three-year MTC residency, and we were also screening the rough cut of the ABC doc. In the early Krannert days, they would put me up at Jumer's Castle Lodge, which was a Bavarian-style lodge that you either loved or hated. I loved it! It was like a setting for an Agatha Christie novel. When the New York cast arrived, we would eat breakfast in the opulent but very dusty dining hall. I always expected Lurch from *The Addams Family* to show up as our waiter. When cast member Ryuji Noda sent back the "fresh-squeezed" orange juice he had ordered, he stated, "Some kind of no taste."

Dennis Cleveland began a prodigious twenty-year relationship with Mike Ross and the Krannert Center. They would go on to be a lead commissioner (see "*The End of Cinematics* (1998)"), as well as present numerous works. And because the training program for grad students was so remarkable, I would go on to give many stage managers and sound and lighting designers their first tours. Along with Mike, I was fortunate to become close with Senior Associate Director Rebecca McBride, who is a constant inspiration. Tammey Kikta, the assistant director of Artistic Services, always managed to do her high-stress job with kindness and a smile. And Karen Quisenberry, who was director of New Work at Krannert as well as of Level 21, was a joy to work with. The first student I snatched from Krannert was Carolyn Cubit-Tsutsui, who continued to be my stage manager for several years. The great thing about Krannert was that any time I was there in the prairie, I knew I could see a production as good as anything in New York, a true testament to Mike's vision and to the entire Krannert team.

We would be back at Krannert in the same year, just weeks after the 9/11 attacks, to perform a theatrical version of John Cage's *James Joyce, Marcel Duchamp, Erik Satie: An Alphabet* (see "*Cage/Cunningham* (1997–2013)"). It was the first stop back in the states after being stuck in Europe for weeks with the *Alphabet* company. But the early 2002 Lincoln Center performances of *Dennis Cleveland* were on my mind. Theaters in New York were canceling shows, and many Broadway shows were only at half capacity. I hoped *Dennis Cleveland* would still happen, but I was prepared for the worst. We would be converting the Gerald W. Lynch Theater at John Jay College into a TV studio using the same kind of truss system we devised at Krannert. But the recent events would make everything a challenge. Mark Lambert and his wife, Susana Ribeiro, had both been in the Krannert cast, but now Susana, who is Brazilian, was locked out of the country due to former president and current portrait artist George W. Bush. As important as the Lincoln Center shows were, my commitment to my cast was stronger. I waited until the last minute before I recast Susana's role (the only bright side to this fiasco was casting the multitalented Sylver Logan Sharp, of Chic fame).

I worked on some set redesign, and we copied the rear projection idea from the Krannert show (basically using the stage as a rear projection area and moving the "guest" performers down to the audience level). We also had better DVCAM cameras and tripods, which gave the show an even more realistic look. John was never great with technology, and fortunately for me he introduced Video Designer/Switcher Jeff Sugg and Director of Photography Richard Connors into the mix. It was refreshing to work with folks who understood the elements of video and live switching. I would happily get to work with Jeff on various shows for the next thirteen years, and Richard would be an essential player with my third opera, *The End of Cinematics.* I knew from Jon Nakagawa that the *New York Times* was planning on a feature in its Sunday Arts & Leisure section, but I was thrilled when I learned Kyle Gann would write the full-page article. He was one of the most versatile classical critics in New York and was more familiar with my approach than most conventional classical writers. Other features and preview pieces followed, and I was starting to feel that maybe the show would have a decent turnout.

A lot had changed in the seven years since I premiered the piece at The Kitchen. For one, you could now buy White Castle in the frozen food section. For another, Adrienne Clarkson had become the Governor General of Canada and she and John Ralston Saul were now married. I wanted to extend the courtesy of inviting them, even though they had generously come for the 1996 premiere, and I had to believe they would be too busy. But John said they must come. I was happy about this and moved on to the next issue until I was woken one morning at 7 a.m. by a brigadier general inquiring about Her and His Excellencies' details. I stammered, "Um, can I call you right back?" I immediately called Michael, who could barely contain his laughter and assured me that he and Jon had it under control. I later heard that the Secret Service from Canada had come in advance to make sure the theater was secure and were later shocked and scrambling to discover that, during the actual performance, the entire audience was visible and being photographed in real time. Oops. I remember after the show we all casually walked to a nearby place for dinner escorted by Secret Service agents, as one does in New York. Adrienne and John later invited Lisa and me to a fiftieth anniversary of the governor general Position at Rideau Hall, sort of the White House of Canada. John gave me the tour and I got to play the piano Glenn Gould donated. We dined with dignitaries and leaders of Canadian politics, religion, and business. The ice in our ice bucket was always refreshed. And when we woke up the day of a concert celebration (hearing Gordon Lightfoot rehearsing down the hall), Lisa, who is Canadian, waved her hand across the expansive suite and said, "Welcome to my country." It was gonna rain the day of the concert, so we were all taken to Canadian Tire to get rain boots. It was funny to see them all stacked together in a hallway. There were parties including a large one after the concert, and I remember saying to Lisa as the guests left that we just had to stroll upstairs.

Dennis Cleveland always attracted celebrities. Keanu Reeves and Michael Cerveris attended the West Coast shows. I told Michael Cerveris that I thought he'd be great in the role of *Dennis Cleveland*, and when he replied that he couldn't imagine anyone other than me doing it, I said, "Imagine harder." But the Lincoln Center shows had a who's who of artists and talk show hosts all revealed on camera to the live audience: Steve Reich, David Byrne, Merce Cunningham (dozing), Sally Jessy Raphael; it was a hoot. The shows were well received by most outlets. *New York Magazine*'s Peter Davis had reviewed the 1996 pre-miere and found even more to like in the new production: "The musical fabric of the work is carefully organized from the many different sources that have influenced composers of Rouse's generation: rock, serialism, rhythmic phasing, rap, a variety of world musics, jazz, minimalism, heavy metal, you name it. Rouse has added his own voice to the mix, a technique involving multiple unpitched voices moving in strict met-ric counterpoint. Listening to it all come together is fascinating as an abstract musical experience, but the total package never loses sight of its theatrical mission—a real opera, in other words, and one that takes the form to a new place." Similar praise came from *Billboard* magazine, the *Village Voice*, and the *New Yorker*. I had decided to stop following the press in 2002 (see "*Failing Kansas* (1995)" for a twist to this approach), but I heard that the review by the *Times*'s classical critic missed a beat or two. I will leave Kyle Gann's response as a proper riposte: "As for cogno-scenti who might be expected to hear the subtleties and couldn't, well, many of New York's fine music schools offer remedial ear training."

There would be one more incarnation of *Dennis Cleveland* (see "Luminato Trilogy (2008)"), but for now we end where this all began, in the early to mid-'90s. At Rudy's, where we celebrated our Lincoln Center run by renting the place for the closing cast party. It was great to see Jon Nakagawa there, slightly out of his element but proud of our achieve-ments. I thanked him profusely for following through when so many venues had to cancel shows. I will always remember his kind and confi-dent reply: "Mikel, this is what we do." A better reminder of the human spirit I cannot imagine. The cast party resembled the scrappy aspects of the show: Sylver selling her handmade jewelry, Johnny Dirt mingling with the muckety-mucks, Michael trading shots with Jeff Sugg. Lisa had come to all the shows including the final one but could only make a brief appearance before heading directly to the airport for her next tour with Merce in Dublin. This was our understood life, and we were both grate-ful for it, but I missed her not being there.

On the other hand, Rudy's was just around the corner from me and still is, and I was surprised when Johnny handed me a twelve-pack of frozen White Castle hamburgers. Johnny knew I missed them from the old days, so he got some for the occasion, forgetting that he'd need a microwave. So I strolled home with White Castle, and all seemed right with the world.

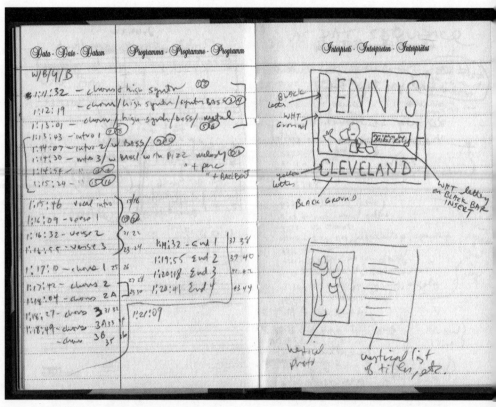

Dennis Cleveland Sketchbook 1.

got no point in the middle & life
stay so you take all the love
in one night

STAGING
— smaller venue – "Kitch's" or "LA MAMA"
* full show scenario — *
I go through audience —
"interview" guest singers —
"choons" – or stage

Dennis Cleveland

[figures sketch]

"soloists", "interviews" in
audience — I am up & is to "soloist"
— we "banter" – back & forth dialog

"confessional" — sections can be
done by "panel" members or "audience"
members

Billygoat don't know
the difference from whole sale
gonna be two prominent mobile up scale

it's the real thing
in the pocket to burn
to stand in line & take your turn
to motion sickness, to mothers milk
at the turn of the century
its the models will

And the safety in numbers
that you get from TV
that you got from the movie
that you got from maybe ...

is the line to the oven
where mother spells 'lovin'
like the planks that you walked
when you gave up the faith

the momentum
its a given
that there's nothing gonna be left around
for this person;
when the time was there
you build another hotel

Dennis Cleveland Sketchbook 2.

Recordings (1980–2020)

I grew up with records. It was the most stabilizing part of childhood. Records were tactile and the perfect way to process music, side by side in fifteen-to-twenty-minute increments. When I was in high school, I would listen to records before the bus came. I could see the bus winding from street to street in my rural neighborhood. As it got closer, I would manually fade out the song I was listening to, so sacred was the sound that I couldn't just cut it off. This brief overview of my recordings makes the biographical task easier, because no matter what show or large-scale piece I might be working on, my obsession with making records was always there.

Etudes 1980. Tirez Tirez was formed in Kansas City, Missouri. Rob Shepperson and I had been friends since meeting at the Kansas City Art Institute (KCAI) in 1975. We would sneak drums into the piano rooms of the Conservatory of Music across the street (where I would do a double major) and bang away together. Rob did a transfer-student thing in 1977, attending the Richmond School of Art in the UK, and returned having absorbed the punk scene there. We set out to form a band and found bassist Jeff Burk, I think from an ad he posted. He was a photographer studying at KCAI. We would rehearse at Epperson Auditorium at the school. Our first show in front of an audience would be opening for Talking Heads at One Block West. They were touring their second album *More Songs About Buildings and Food*. I think Rob may have landed the gig through a phone call. The Talking Heads felt like the epitome of what new wave music should be. They couldn't have been kinder to us, and when bassist Tina Weymouth saw my $30 thrift-store guitar (lovingly named Red Dog from one of our early songs), she insisted I use her Fender Mustang instead. So now the only reason I was out of tune was my ears. We were awful, but we weren't the rock of ages past. Tina told us we were the only opening act thus far that wasn't booed off the stage; most of the other acts were still mining '70s arena rock excess. A year later, before we headed to New York, the Heads came back to a much larger arena; David Byrne actually remembered my phone number and called to invite us to their show supporting their new album *Fear of Music*. We went back to their hotel to hang out. A class act.

We became the premiere punk/new wave band of KC solely for the fact that we were the only one. We played shows at the Falcon Club, Bette's Too (where we did our farewell show before heading to New York, playing our anthemic song "Reflections" for so long that Jeff simply couldn't hold mother nature's call), and Epperson (having our first rock moment when the packed crowd shouted out the lyrics to the "KCAI Fight Song" back at us onstage). That song was from one of two records we released in very limited runs. I'd purchased a TEAC 4-track reel-to-reel that I delighted in experimenting with and was heartbroken when it was stolen out of my first-floor apartment. We were ambitious but we weren't ready to make records yet. But by the time we got to New York (driving cross-country in a VW van named Betsy), we had amassed a number of songs and played well together. After landing in Patterson, New Jersey, and almost getting killed, we headed to the suburbs of East Brunswick. This is where we'd rehearse for *Etudes*. I think our manager at the time, Tom Cochran, might have found the studio Downtown Sound in New York on Christopher Street. I believe Tom's girlfriend, Julie Hair (of 3 Teens Kill 4 fame) fronted the studio costs. Our engineer was James Mason, who was responsible for the classic 1977 album *Rhythm of Life*. He brought a smooth '70s sound to the tracking and mixing, which made *Etudes* stand out in a field of rougher-sounding records. This was our first time in a real studio, and we tracked the album as a trio, adding vocals and overdubs. I played B3 organ on a couple of tracks. We climbed into the grand piano and made sound effects. The first track, "Radiation Dance," was a slow groove, with Jeff riffing melodically on bass. He's one of the most tuneful players, all the while maintaining a solid locked-in groove. The song was in E, but I suggested he tune the low E string down to E-flat while continuing to riff in E. This, along with the dreamlike Fender Rhodes I was playing, made for an unsettling sound, suitable for opening the album.

There were Dadaist ideas, like automatic writing and lifting lyrics from a daily bridge newspaper column, West Led the Diamond King. Once tracking and overdubs were finished, it was time to mix the album. I remember driving from New Jersey to the radio strains of "Funky Town." One particularly stressful day was when we were set to finish the final mixes. Jeff and Rob were already in the city. Mark Grimm (our roadie and sound man) and I were set to head in from Jersey when Betsy wouldn't start. Mark had a VW manual for dummies, and I anxiously watched as he started taking the engine apart. After an hour or so, I had a ton of parts sitting in my lap. At that point, he closed the manual and said we were ready. I asked him about the lap full of parts; he looked through the manual again and confirmed his original diagnosis. Sure enough, the van started, and we were on our way. Betsy would eventually be torched on the Lower East Side as a way for Mark to avoid the hundreds of dollars of traffic fines he'd collected, a common approach back in the day. Tom had found an independent label in the UK called Object Music, and the record came out to good reviews. David Bither wrote in *New York Rocker*, "It's got heart, and that's ultimately what it's all about. This is a good record." And one reviewer compared the record to Tim Buckley, which I loved.

The cover was an optimistic collage of four-leaf clovers. Object Music didn't have great distribution, so Tom found another label called Aura, also in the UK. We all anxiously waited for news on the second release. One day I was browsing through LPs at the classic Village record store Bleecker Bob's when, unexpectedly, I saw a hideous black-and-white cover with a—typical for the time—man in a "new wave" robotic position. The title of the record was Tirez Tirez–*Etudes*. My stomach sunk and I was heartbroken. When I confronted Tom, he admitted he'd approved this. I think Aura might have been a tax shelter operation, but whatever it was, the guy who ran it was unfazed by my disappointment. I eventually got the rights back and hope to release *Etudes* again soon.

We found a loft at 60 West Fourteenth Street, just east of Sixth Avenue. Our first show in New York was at CBGB and David Byrne was kind enough to come, which created a buzz for the show. It was enlightening talking with him backstage and getting some insights into the *Fear of Music* record. We originally had a front loft, and I enjoyed wailing on guitar on the fire escape and hearing the sound bounce off the building across Fourteenth Street. Then we got an offer to move to another, larger space on the same floor. We set up a recording room in that loft and had two large spaces, one for rehearsal and one for painting and art projects, plus four bedrooms. All for $500. We would sometimes open the space up for art happenings and concerts. I premiered a chamber opera called *Balboa* and was excited that the legendary Gil Evans came and loved it. We were booted out in 1982, a mere three months before the loft law passed.

I also started itching to bring some of my more complex rhythmic ideas into the music and expanded Tirez Tirez into a five-piece band including sax and keyboard. We played all the clubs, from Max's Kansas City to TR3 to Danceteria to the Peppermint Lounge. So many clubs and all original music. And an exciting time of no categories. I saw Phil Glass's ensemble nearly raise the roof at Danceteria with a rock volume performance of "Spaceship" from *Einstein on the Beach*. I also saw Robert Ashley do parts of his groundbreaking *Perfect Lives* there as well. James Chance, Sonny Sharrock, Glenn Branca, and Jules Baptiste and his band Red Decade were all around. Arto Lindsay and DNA did a farewell show at CBGB, ending with a wild rendition of Led Zeppelin's "Whole Lotta Love."

My first friends in New York were Tom Lee and his partner, Arthur Russell. Arthur was also combining classical structures with pop ideas, and he and I were supportive of each other's efforts. I think he was fired as music director of the avant-garde space The Kitchen for booking Jonathan Richmond and the Modern Lovers. Both Tom and Arthur would come by the loft to hear us rehearse. It was an exciting time when anything could happen. But maybe a year and a half after moving to the loft, Jeff decided to leave the band and I put an ad up at Juilliard. I was looking for a new bass player for Tirez Tirez, but I also wanted a bass player for a new chamber group that would become Mikel Rouse Broken Consort. Also, around this time, I had an idea about acquiring perfect pitch through hypnosis. After scouring the Yellow Pages, I found a gentleman named Jerome Walman, who said it was possible and that he was the only person in the city who could do it. I was game and went for several sessions, and during one session, I noticed that the Bach fugue playing in the background was rotating around the metronome he also had playing. I commented on how this was similar to one of my music approaches, and that's when I learned he taught the Schillinger System of Musical Composition, something my theory teacher had mentioned but I'd forgotten. I started studying with him and devoured the two-volume set of Schillinger's work.

Jade Tiger 1984 and *Story of the Year* 1983. As a five piece, Tirez Tirez headed to 39th Street Music Studio with James Mason and recorded an album that was a combination of instrumentals and pop songs. The album would have been called *Shield '81,* and it was mixed and sequenced as such. But it sat on the shelf for a while. Months later, after doing several shows with Mikel Rouse Broken Consort (playing at The Kitchen when it was still in Soho, the Pyramid Club, and all sorts of loft concerts), we headed to Secret Sound Studio, again with James Mason, to record the Mikel Rouse Broken Consort album *Jade Tiger* and six pop songs from Tirez Tirez. In addition to Rob on drums and Jim Bergman on bass, we were joined by Phillip Johnston, an avant-garde jazz saxophonist who fronted the venerable New York combo the Microscopic Septet. Mark Kamins was an A&R guy at Island Records, best known for discovering Madonna. But he was a fan and tried to bring me to Island. I always found it remarkable that he had all these posters of Tirez Tirez and MRBC on the wall in his office. One day I joked that I thought maybe he just put them up when I was coming for a meeting. He sheepishly admitted that that was indeed the case.

At any rate, he introduced me to Michael Shamberg, who had a connection with a label in Belgium called Les Disques du Crepuscule (Shamberg would go on to be a successful film producer). Crepuscule was run by a funny guy named Michel Duval and, along with Annik Honoré, they also formed Factory Benelux. Michel (whom Tuxedo-moon's Blaine Reininger called "the prince of darkness") was interested in both Broken Consort and Tirez Tirez. So I took the pop songs off of *Shield '81* and combined them with the six newer songs from the *Jade Tiger* sessions to produce *Story of the Year.* Both albums came out on Crepuscule in 1982, and I moved to Brussels for a year or two to support the records. Rob did the cover painting for *Story of the Year*, I think a watercolor of Midtown Manhattan viewed from the studio. And I did the number-oriented cover for *Jade Tiger* and did the silk screen with Tom Lee, who helped Rob and me land our first job in Manhattan at a silk screen company that focused on tax shelter art.

Broken Consort was one of the early rock-influenced classical ensembles, but with a twist: I viewed the early ensemble as more of a jazz lineup with sax, keyboard, bass, and drums. I also fully scored the drums and used the piano as more of a rhythm device, kind of reversing the traditional roles. While a couple of the tracks have a minimalist vibe (which is offset by the jazz ensemble instrumentation), the title track is a buoyant, joyful theme and variation composition. It received a ton of great reviews. Dean Suzuki, in *Vogue*, said the record is "so strong, so aggressively ebullient, that joy jumps off the record." *Village Voice* critic Greg Sandow, writing for the Jazz Short Takes column in *Musician*, said, "[Rouse is] young and he's one hell of a musician." He'd assumed I was an older accomplished jazz musician who'd heard minimalism and thought, "I could do that." He wrote, "The catch is that short minimalist pieces are hard to write. Rouse succeeds, and writes spiky, even danceable music besides." Truth be told, *Jade Tiger* probably had more to do with hanging out in the early '80s with Barry Harris at the Jazz Cultural Theater on Eighth Avenue than it had to do with the minimalists. Press from Europe and the UK was solid, including *NME* and *Sounds* in London. I was never happy with the way I put the *Story of the Year* record together, but it was what it was and it received good reviews. Rob and I had made a cassette demo of the song "Another World," and the studio version just didn't live up to that original sketch. This was probably when I realized I'd need to make a studio where I could create and capture the initial idea rather than trying to duplicate it. But that dream would be years away. Arthur Russell was also doing a release on the Crepuscule label. I remember trying to help coordinate the release of his record *Instrumentals*. This record had many errors, the most glaring being some of the tracks being pressed at half speed. Arthur had sent the record company a few tapes but failed to put them in one consistent transfer speed, expecting that the company would know what to do. I remember expensive long-distance calls at pay phones trying to help him, and his frustration was palpable. Fortunately, twenty-two years later, Steve Knutson and his excellent Audika Records label would correct the errors.

Under the Door/Sleep 1983 and *Colorado Suite* 1984. The US dollar was strong, so Crepuscule decided to put me in the world-class ICP Recording studios, with the great engineer Jean Trenchant, to record the single "Under the Door," backed with "Sleep." I had programmed a lot of both songs on the Prophet 5 synth I was lugging all over Europe while touring. When I first got to Brussels, my publisher sent me to meet Blaine Reininger of the San Francisco band Tuxedomoon. I got the feeling that they sent all the Americans to Blaine and his wife at the time, JJ La Rue, as they both spoke English and French. Tuxedomoon had all become expats due to Reagan's ascent in the US. I loved Blaine and JJ. They were a feast-or-famine couple, living high on the hog in good times and shivering in their apartment rerolling leftover tobacco in bad times. I would hang out all afternoon at Blaine's place listening to him pontificate on all sorts of topics; he would often go into a changing room and don a new outfit numerous times in one session. Blaine had a miniature studio setup with small Roland drum machines and midi gear. He might have been the catalyst for me knowing I could set up my own studio when I returned to New York. We hung out a lot, often at Plan K and a club called Interferences, both launched by Crepuscule, I believe. It was there I first met Blaine's bandmate Steven Brown, smashed and hoping Tuxedomoon would get back together. I also saw his bandmate Winston Tong play a show.

Blaine joined me for the *Under the Door/Sleep* sessions and contributed violin on "Under the Door." I needed a cover for the single, and Rob, who was living in London, asked me to bring a profile photo of myself. When I got to London, he'd already done a profile watercolor of himself and added me to that. A great cover. Press was good and the B side seemed to capture the imagination, "Sleep" being a waltz-like, electronic, optimistic waltz on domestic tranquility. College radio fanzines like *Rockpool* and *Ward Report* were growing in importance, and all gave the single high marks, calling it "lush and hypnotic."

During this time, Blaine and I talked about collaborating on a project. We met with Marc Hollander from Crammed Discs and I liked him immediately. He wondered about doing a mini-LP that we could release and tour while I was still living in Brussels. That record would be *Colorado Suite,* consisting of four tracks, three instrumentals by me and a funny and dire cowboy song written and sung by Blaine. We recorded at a small but comfortable studio called Kitsch Studio after numerous rehearsals at Blaine's place. Blaine programmed the rhythm parts on his drum-machine based on the charts I gave him. By necessity, the parts were simple and repetitive, more in the minimalist vein than I would have liked. But it made for a quicker rehearsal and recording process. The violin parts I wrote for Blaine had a little more movement and bounce over the more static keyboard and programming, slightly reminiscent of the elongated sax style from *Jade Tiger*. We booked a pretty good tour and played multiple shows in London, including the Roundhouse. We also did shows all over Europe, often playing multiple venues in Amsterdam, Antwerp, and Paris. Reviews were good for both the record and the tour, with John Gill from *Time Out London* musing, "Phil Glass collides with 'Bonanza,' and Aaron Copeland doesn't even come into it."

Quorum 1984 and *A Walk in the Woods* 1985. I think I started doing sketches for the drum-machine composition *Quorum* while I was still living in Brussels. I know I completed the score in 1983 in New York. *Quorum* would go on to have a long life (see "*Quorum* (1984)"). I loved working on the recording at BC Studio in Brooklyn. Martin Bisi was a great engineer and musician, and he was recording everyone in the downtown scene, from Sonic Youth to John Lurie. I think the studio started as a Brian Eno project and somehow morphed into Martin's place. I know he and Bill Laswell did the amazing Herbie Hancock album *Future Shock* there, which included the hit "Rockit."

I was excited to go back there with musicians and expand on the Broken Consort quartet. I had written a suite of pieces for extended ensemble, including strings, woodwinds, and brass, but I wanted a slightly synthetic sound in addition to acoustic instruments. Jim helped me find players and I think I also put out ads for musicians. All the music was fully scored, so I needed musicians that could grab the music quickly. This was a highly contrapuntal album with a veneer of propulsive minimalism, but a harmonic language that was much more complex. As Greg Sandow described it in the *Village Voice*, "Rouse pushes minimalism toward complexity not heard in music since the high noon of serialism; even so, there's a spacious lyricism hidden in the mix, underlined by oboe and violin." Well, somebody had to do it. Anyway, we recorded the record pop style, track by track. I was on a budget even though we'd had a fundraiser, hosted by some wealthy folks and held at the classic Gotham Bar and Grill, where the Broken Consort quartet performed. I did all the keyboard and drum-machine programming first, and then we tracked the strings, woodwinds, and brass. Jim Bergman played both upright and electric bass. Marc Hollander from Crammed Discs was interested in releasing *A Walk in the Woods* on the label's Made to Measure series. I was excited about that, but I also wanted to do my own audiophile pressing, so I carved out the deal to be able to do a limited release on my own Club Soda Music label, which had previously released *Quorum*. I designed the cover for the CSM release, and the artist and designer Tim Steele did the cover drawing for the MTM release. Howie Weinberg mastered both *Quorum* and *A Walk in the Woods* at Masterdisk in New York, and I had to go back for a redo on the latter, as there was a tape speed issue. The trouble was, Howie couldn't hear the issue, so we had to start over.

Even before Broken Consort, I was naming chamber and orchestra pieces like *Bright Star*, *Red 20*, and *American Nova* after war game titles, maybe as a way of pointing out the absurd use of romantic names to disguise intent. I had been involved with the nuclear freeze movement and worked the June 12, 1982, Rally for Nuclear Disarmament in New York. I was a supporter of Helen Caldicott, an Australian physician, author, and antinuclear advocate. While living in Brussels, I also traveled to Germany to attend protests to block the deployment of the dangerous "launch on warning" Pershing II missiles. The title for *A Walk in the Woods* came from a famous 1982 meeting between US delegate Paul Nitze, who had his "walk in the woods" with the Soviet Ambassador, Yuli Kvitsinsky, during which they were able to outline possible concessions that President Ronald Reagan and USSR leader Leonid Brezhnev could discuss later in the year. It was a huge missed opportunity, and it inspired the title track of the album, a complex five-part ricercar of rotating meters that threaten to land and merge but just as quickly disappear, mirroring the missed opportunity. Other tracks include "Hardfall," an homage to Charles Ives's "The Unanswered Question" and a wonderfully knotty and pointillistic piece called "The Eloquent Dissenter," a term used to refer to Clarence Darrow, the dazzling lawyer who defended John Scopes in the 1925 "Monkey Trial."

I was over the moon at the critical response to the record, mostly because I knew I'd kind of hit the nail on the head in moving composition away from wallpaper minimalist offshoots. There were features by Gene Santoro in *The Nation*, Glenn Kenny in *Music and Sound Output*, and John Diliberto in *Downbeat*. Kevin Whitehead, writing for *Cadence*, said, "[Rouse] has assimilated disparate native strains to seed a personal music ingratiatingly in the American grain," and the UK's *Sounds* offered, "Rouse succeeds where many lesser mortals have failed." As a capper to all of this, the *New York Times*'s Jon Pareles listed *A Walk in the Woods* as one of his Top Ten albums of 1985.

Set the Timer/Uptight 1986 and *Social Responsibility* 1986. I had made several 4-track cassette demos for what would eventually be the *Social Responsibility* album. But I'd paid particular attention to the songs "Set the Timer" and "Uptight" and thought releasing them as an advance single would be good, as 12-inch singles were a thing at the time. Seymour Stein of Sire Records took an interest in the single. He'd done Talking Heads, the Ramones, and the Pretenders and would also launch Madonna. He'd creatively found a way to bypass radio and payola by breaking Madonna through the burgeoning club scene, thus saving a ton of money in radio promotion. The trouble was, he then started trying to do that in a cookie-cutter way with everything. We negotiated a typical three- or four-album contract (sometimes at Seymour's hospital bedside, which apparently was "his thing") and got a paltry advance for the single. Seymour would later complain that I took the single advance and made an entire album. Spoiler alert: that's exactly what I did. It's what everyone did. Anyway, he liked the single I did at B.C. Studio with Martin and played it at a meeting with Lenny Waronker, who I believe was the head of Warner Bros. at the time. Lenny wanted to speak with me, and when Seymour called and told me this, I sensed a nervousness in his voice, sort of like, this is a big deal, don't screw it up. They wanted me to work with a DJ named Ivan Ivan (DJs were on the ascent), and I said I was certainly open, but also expressed my opinion that I thought Martin and I could do the dance mix. I'll never know if that was the wrong response, but Martin and I did a remix of "Set the Timer" (one with guitars and one without) backed by "Uptight." The B side was a percussion-forward, mid-tempo track with a noticeably anti-nihilist message: "If everybody gives a little, everybody gets a lot." I struggled to find something more edgy or clever, but that's the line that came out and I knew it was wrong to fight it. The lead vocal had a kind of deadpan delivery backed by a quasi-gospel chorus. I still think it's sublime. Jon Pareles, in the *New York Times*, did a great feature on the single's release in the Pop Life section, acknowledging both the pop and classical sides I was pursuing. I heard the single reached number three in Holland. It got good notices from many dance-zines. Mike Robinson, in *Dance Music Report*, was effusive, writing that "Set the Timer" "is so stunningly beautiful it makes one's heart race or takes your breath away."

As stated previously, we had recorded *Social Responsibility* shortly after the single. I got a deal with Rough Trade, run by now legendary Geoff Travis (I would also work on a release of Arthur Russell's material for Geoff). He loved the record, and around this time, I also got an offer from a new offshoot label of I.R.S. Records called Primitive Man Recording Company. Through I.R.S., PMRC (get it?) had distribution through MCA, which felt at the time like a big deal. Geoff was generous to limit his release to the UK, but in hindsight, I think I made a mistake with not going all in with Rough Trade. Live and learn, except in business, I usually don't. Greg Calbi mastered both the single and the album at Sterling Sound when they were on Broadway in Manhattan. Anyway, the record came out to rave reviews. Jon Pareles wrote an incisive *New York Times* article that connected a few pop and classical composers who have used minimalism in some way to expand pop music. The article focused on aspects of the new album, also exploring similar ground with LL Cool J's "Bigger and Deffer" and Wayne Horvitz's band, The President. Pareles did a deep dive into the complexities on *Social Responsibility*, but unlike most critics who focused on the catchy pop aspects of the record, he examined the more complex tracks, "See My Problem" and "Paper Boy," concluding, "Mr. Rouse has a classical composer's structural skills, but like a pop songwriter, he keeps things concise. *Social Responsibility* shows that his two careers aren't so divergent after all." God bless him.

And this analysis would prove to be a prediction of what was to come, in terms of converging these two approaches. *Melody Maker* in the UK saw the similar thread Arthur Russell and I were attempting, saying, "What we have here is the arcane beauty and tension of a small town claustrophobia in a detached context." I remember Arthur being particularly fond of the track "Spin Your Wheels," and as is typical of his insight, he heard it as a great dance track. Great notices from the *Washington Post, Billboard*, the *Boston Phoenix*, and the *Village Voice* also seemed to "get" the record. Both *Set the Timer/Uptight* and *Social Responsibility* were just Jim Bergman on bass and me on everything else. So now I needed a band to tour the record.

Bill Tesar, who was playing in Broken Consort, introduced me to Mark Lambert, who had come to see us perform at the downtown staple Roulette. Mark would later tell me that he knew that night that he would be playing in Tirez Tirez. Bill's brother Rave Tesar, a great keyboard player, rounded out the new live band, and we hit the road in support of the album. Frontier Booking, part of the I.R.S./Copeland group, paired us with The Bears, Adrian Belew's new band. We did a North American tour that included stops in Canada. Bill was running his studio rental business The Toy Specialists and couldn't do the tour, so we enlisted Davo Bryant, a fantastic drummer.

The Bears couldn't have been a nicer group to tour with. Through Adrian, I met his manager Stan Hertzman, who would valiantly try to shop demos for me in the early '90s.

We did good shows, but the stress of being road manager was above my pay grade. Mark remembers seeing me with wads of cash, trying to pay off light and sound operators from town to town. I have lots of fond memories of the tour and enjoyed trying out new songs that would eventually be on the follow-up album, *Against All Flags*. The tour would end at a big hall in Atlanta, where I would reconnect with my sister Cindy, whom I hadn't seen in ten years. I would also meet my four-year-old niece, Katie, for the first time. Which, in hindsight, might have been the entire purpose of that tour.

A Lincoln Portrait 1988 and *Against All Flags* 1988. The *Social Responsibility* tour had allowed us to test and refine a number of songs for the *Against All Flags* record. So we headed to BC Studio to track the album as a band, a welcome event. I'd loved the freedom that drum machines allowed, but I'd missed making records with a band. Martin set the studio up to comfortably record a five piece with appropriate isolation. Some tunes, like "One Way Down," "When Pilots Came," and "Never

Begin" had intricate, fully scored sections, including some really nice doubled lines between guitar and bass that Mark and Jim nailed. Billy's playing was graceful on the odd time signatures, making off-kilter pop songs sound almost normal. And Rave, lovingly referred to as "the master of time and space," did great keyboard work, both scored and improvised. PMRC was struggling but still wanted to release *Against All Flags,* so I carved out a limited license deal. This would be my go-to approach moving forward. I believed that artists should own the copyrights to both their publishing and sound recordings. Even major labels weren't paying advances that warranted them owning the sound recording. Consequently I own all my sound recordings save for one. I certainly couldn't have predicted the digital distribution future, but I was glad that I could eventually offer my entire catalog on my own label, ExitMusic Recordings.

At any rate, while I was working on *Against All Flags,* I'd been working on the new Broken Consort record, which would be released on Cuneiform Records. I wanted a more aggressive sound for the quartet than heard on *Jade Tiger,* so I decided to follow the drum-machine programming style of *Quorum* and have Billy help me program the drum parts. I've always regretted not doing *A Lincoln Portrait* with Billy on real drums, but the programmed drums with sax, bass, and piano did give the record a very contemporary sound, given the complex interlocking of parts. It was a unique hybrid, something that would become common a decade or so later. Phillip Johnston was unavailable for these sessions, so I needed to find a new sax player. It was my good fortune to find Ellery Eskelin, a terrific sax player and composer. The track "Quick Thrust," using a twelve-tone row, captured the imagination of a number of critics, and signaled a fresh look at what was possible in post-minimalism. The galloping rhythm of "#3," with its angular sax line, continued the exuberant thread of *Jade Tiger,* but with a foot firmly placed in drum-machine–forward rock. James Bergman's fully scored bass solo on the track "#2" reminded me I was going in the right direction. And "High Frontier" is an obsessively metric track, with a dotted eighth- and sixteenth-note–alternating riff that appeared in a number of Broken Consort pieces and would prompt Ellery to once muse during a rehearsal, "Ah yes, the tune that Mikel's mom sung him to sleep to."

Tirez Tirez wasn't touring much after the *Social Responsibility* tour. But Broken Consort was playing shows all over New York, including the Knitting Factory on Houston Street. Also shows in Philly and on the East Coast. A memorable show was at Dance Theater Workshop. We were doing pieces from the *A Lincoln Portrait* album, framed by three allegorical paintings of Lincoln by the artist and designer Tim Steele. The buzz in the room was that Sting was coming, as he was starting a new music label and might be interested in Broken Consort. My understanding is he came with his leather trench-coat entourage and left before the set was completed. Someone overheard a member of his group compare Broken Consort to Dewey Redman, which would have been a compliment if the comparison was remotely accurate. In 2021, I released a live recording of this concert called *LIVE 1987*.

Both records came out at roughly the same time, and both were again mastered by Greg Calbi. *A Lincoln Portrait* was dedicated to Morton Feldman and *Against All Flags* was dedicated to Gil Evans. So there were lots of press outlets focusing on the pop/classical comparison. Released on Flag Day, *Against All Flags* was the *New York Times* Rock Album of the Week on its release, and the band would headline many double bills at the Knitting Factory. We also did short jaunts out of town to support the album. *Vogue* did a "Welcome to the '90s" feature that included a number of up-and-coming artists from all fields (see "*Bars & Restaurants* (1965–2021)") and I was their choice for music. It felt like things were starting to jell. I was particularly pleased at how critics were getting the difference between Broken Consort and other post-minimalist ensembles. But with 1987 came the banking crash, and I knew getting the bands on the road was gonna be tough. Both bands would continue doing steady gigs in the city.

After a couple of years of shows, I think Ellery wanted to move on. I asked Mark if he'd be interested in trying to do the melodic contrapuntal sax lines on electric guitar and he rose to the challenge. He had also started his own ensemble called Vertical Fractures, which included the great musicians Kermit Driscoll, Mark Feldman, and Charles Descarfino. We started doing double bills around town, often at the Knitting Factory. A funny memory from around 1990 or so was that I came home to find a note slipped under my door. The note confirmed that my cable, lovingly installed by artist Cliff Baldwin, had been clipped. Mark called me with the bad news that the Knitting Factory had posted the wrong date for a show that we'd already sent out announcement cards for. He laughed at my response to the crisis: "Fuck that! They cut my cable!"

Another great Mark memory was driving home from a show in Mark's soon-to-be-dead car. The car had gotten so bad that white smoke coming from the engine would fill the entire car and we accepted this as normal. At a stop light, a cabbie pulled up next to us and surveyed the car up and down as white smoke bellowed out of the windows. Nodding with a wink, he said, "I like this car."

Soul Menu 1993 and *Autorequiem* 1994. Times were tough following the 1987 crash. I kept both bands busy with New York shows. I was working on new Broken Consort material and constantly doing 4-track cassette demos of songs. Broken Consort had taken on a more "electric" sound with Mark on guitar, and that was reflected in the direction of the new material. But Mark decided to take a break from the band and suggested a great woodwind player named Dale Kleps. Dale was an early adopter of the EWI, a wind controller capable of a wide variety of synthesized sounds. So this was actually a great fit. We did several concerts in New York and along the East Coast, including a double bill with John Lurie and the Lounge Lizards at Merkin Hall. My mom and sister were in town, and I think this was the first show my mom saw. On the same day, we attended a memorial event for Arthur Russell, who had passed away from AIDS. It was a beautiful remembrance and I felt grateful that my family could join and experience this tribute. I had continued to build my digital studio, and I would sometimes have sequencers and drum machines drive a TEAC 4-track cassette player. I couldn't afford to get either band in the studio, but I got the idea to do a midi-album of the new Broken Consort material. I think the pieces would have been better with the band, but there was something I liked about the all-electronic approach. Ben Neill had introduced me to Renzo Pognant's Italian label New Tone Records. Renzo was interested in the album, so I signed a limited license. My good friend Susan San Giovanni did the cover art, I believe from a shot taken at Café Du Monde in New Orleans. I listed all five musicians who had worked on the music live as a way of acknowledging their contribution. The *St. Petersburg Times* gave it three stars, saying, "If Steve Reich teamed up with Deep Purple, something like *Soul Menu* might be the result," and the *Village Voice* Consumer Guide gave it an "A."

At some point during the prep for this release, I got a call from Tom Lee, Arthur's partner and one of my first friends in New York. Phil

Glass's new label Point Records was interested in doing a compilation of Arthur's music, but Tom was overwhelmed at the thought of someone going through all of Arthur's work, which was kept at their apartment on East Twelfth Street. A number of artists including Allen Ginsberg lived in the same building, which was pretty big, with classic old stairways. I went over to Tom's to have a look. There were reel-to-reel tapes everywhere. Indeed, it seemed overwhelming. I told Tom I'd be willing to help, so I met with Michael Riesman, Phil's musical director, and we agreed on a small fee and an approach. If memory serves, I spent two or three months going to Tom's place five days a week. He'd be going off to work but always had a pot of coffee waiting for me. It was an arduous task and emotionally draining, but I felt like I was helping to preserve Arthur's work while also helping Tom. I think I cataloged and repackaged around 980 tapes. There's a photo of me standing next to the numerous shelves of freshly boxed tapes and it looks like I had aged a few years. As I was finishing up the job, Tom had asked me to try to find a track that Arthur had played him but might only be on cassette. I started going through some of the cassettes and was stunned to find a tape of a song I hadn't heard before. Here was Arthur singing, "It's time to go home now." I remember breaking down, sobbing at this loss.

I had still been writing large chamber pieces with very little hope of performances. I was also sequencing and driving the TEAC 4-track cassette deck, striping the fourth track with a sync tone and recording on the remaining three tracks. I'd been experimenting with a vocal technique I called "counterpoetry," which was basically unpitched spoken text in metric counterpoint (see "*Failing Kansas* (1995)"). So I composed *Autorequiem* with spoken voices, strings, and mallet instruments in mind. Renzo was doing a CD compilation called *Century XXI Electronics USA 1* on his New Tone label, and I was included along with Carl Stone, Ben Neill, and Kyle Gann. I also took a stab at a live performance of *Autorequiem* when composer Henry Gwiazda invited me to Minnesota State University to set the piece with a student orchestra. These were lonely days as I struggled with the new vocal writing technique and wondered how I would stay afloat. Tirez Tirez had done a number of demos to shop and that was going nowhere. Michael Lang (of Woodstock fame) was interested in managing the band, but that, too, failed. In what would be a final attempt at recording a follow-up to *Against All Flags,* we headed to Rave's Studio X in Ridgewood, New Jersey, to record a nine-song album. I think the songs were OK, not great, and we weren't jelling as a band. I had been recording and touring with both Broken Consort and various versions of Tirez Tirez for over a decade and I felt like some kind of unknown potential was missing. I was working on a new kind of material, but how I would perform the spoken-word pieces was still to be discovered. I was working part-time at a gallery and still doing Broken Consort shows, but the Tirez Tirez shows just kinda fell away.

Living Inside Design 1994. So I'm working on sketches for *Failing Kansas* and sweating rent and thinking about transitions. I'm spending a lot of time at the New York Public Library, the main branch on Forty-Second and Fifth Ave, researching the Capote archive (see "*Failing Kansas* (1995)"). And as I'm doing all this, I'm thinking: do sketches for the counterpoetry idea. Don't just focus on *Failing Kansas* but do a number of experiments and variations to make sure you nail *Failing Kansas*. At this point, I felt like I was becoming an expert with drum machines and sequencers and reveled in that. I started a track inspired by a visit to the Egyptian wing of the Met. "Never Forget a Face" was a beatbox counterpoetry piece consisting of drum machine and 3-tracks of vocals. And I loved the results and can proudly say, to this day, no one has used a drum machine in this metric fashion. OK, *Quorum*, but I mean in a kind of quasi-pop context. The other thing that is important to me is lyrics and the, hopefully, perfect marriage of words and music. I loved studying Cole Porter and Ira Gershwin. A few years earlier, Jim Bergman, the bass player and coproducer of both Broken Consort and Tirez Tirez records, told me he thought I was a much better lyricist than composer. Coming from a musician I respected, that could have felt like criticism.

But in a Muhammad Ali "Thrilla in Manila" moment, I realized that he was understanding the merging of words and music that I was striving for. With songs like "(I'm Thinking about You Every Minute that I'm Not) Thinking about Myself" and "I Might Never Give Up," I was reaching a kind of synthesis. When I played these tracks and others to Jim, he asked, "What's going on?" I've never forgotten that question, because my response was, "I can do whatever I want. None of the classical or pop constraints matter. I'm on my own and grateful for that." I also remember Rave Tesar coming over and playing him some tracks and, in his congenial way, he declared, "I hate it!" Even this response somehow helped move me forward.

"Left in My Life" and "Kiss Him Goodbye" are the two longer tracks that kind of anchor the album. After completing about half the record with the 4-track cassette recorder, I got hold of the then new Alesis ADAT system, an 8-track digital tape recorder. In another time, I might have taken those tracks and rerecorded the tape parts in the newer, more professional format. But I liked the finished 4-track mixes and decided to leave them as is. "Left in My Life" took advantage of the new format to multitrack layers of voices, bouncing to stereo tracks to clear more tracks for overdubs. With phrases like "I'm still waiting to become the man that I made" and "There's probably still moments left in my life," I think I was describing both my late '30s as well as this new writing approach. In the third and final section of the piece, voices are layered in competing, rap-like text and chorus and the build feels epic. "Kiss Him Goodbye" is the thematic closer (followed by the coda of "Light from a Trailer"), and I'm still amazed at how big it sounds. All drum machine and synths with three cassette mono tracks of single vocals in counterpoint. The rotating voices sound like memory somehow, ending in a revamped use of the "Hey na na" refrain.

Renzo at New Tone was keen on releasing the CD, and I signed another licensing deal with him. The album is dedicated to my sister and Tom Lee, in memory of Arthur Russell. The album was a break-through, and while it received limited press, it had a larger impact on artists and composers. Kyle Gann gave it an "A PLUS" in the *Village Voice* Consumer Guide, and *Keyboard Magazine* observed, "Rouse's art is all parts that circle and whirl with words underscoring how connected they/we are and, potentially, how amazing it is that the whole thing—his music, our lives—somehow works anyway." The record was out, and I was hearing from different parts of the world from composers who saw the record as an unselfconscious hybrid of classical structure and pop sensibility. I remember meeting Rhys Chatham in his apartment outside of Paris and he praised the record.

Over the years, Broken Consort had played a number of the large, new music festivals that popped up around the city. The composers collective Bang on a Can had booked the ensemble a number of times, and their own ensemble did an accurate but academic reading of the twelve-tone piece "Quick Thrust" at Alice Tully Hall. Now they were offering me another spot on their concert marathon, so I considered doing "Kiss Him Goodbye" as a solo performance, with tracks and voices on tape blending with my live vocal. A fairly common approach for hip-hop artists but not what one might expect at a new music marathon. I remember being surrounded by new music ensembles similar to Broken Consort, and here I was standing there, basically naked, doing this song. I remember seeing the composer William Duckworth and his fiancée, Nora Farrell, a day or so after the performance and confessing I felt totally outside of the new music community. Bill responded in his kind, Southern accent, "But that's why we love you Mikel. You're so different." They even asked me to sing a song from *Living Inside Design* at their wedding. I decided to book some solo shows and came up with some video accompaniment.

Sometimes the video was a live monitor feed and sometimes prerecorded video. I took these rough shows to Rome for a series at three different venues, to Poitiers, France, and to stops in clubs throughout Europe. I remember the strange feeling in Rome of learning Richard Nixon had died. I was full of emotion and couldn't figure out why until it hit me that I had cut my political teeth on this corruption. Its own kind of loss. Eventually, I teamed up with video artist Cliff Baldwin, who would do the film for *Failing Kansas,* for a more complete video. Cliff called his montage of video and words digital films, and it was the perfect complement to the performance, with multiple monitors and screens. I booked shows at the Knitting Factory, the performance space HERE, and larger venues like the Governor's Conference on the Arts (see *"Failing Kansas* (1995)"). I had found an affordable way to tour and stay in the game during an economic downturn. And I was feeling good about this approach with the upcoming premiere of *Failing Kansas.*

Failing Kansas 1995, **Dennis Cleveland** 1996, and *The End of Cinematics* 2005. The vocal experiments I'd done with *Living Inside Design* and *Autorequiem* were helpful as I started the recording for *Failing Kansas.* I'd started the recording process with "The Last to See Them Alive," at the Center for Electronic Music (see *"Failing Kansas* (1995)") and would finish the other eight tracks at my studio. Like *Living Inside*

Design, *Failing Kansas* would straddle the transition from synced 4-track cassette to 16-track digital. "Persons Unknown," like "Never Forget a Face," would be sequenced material driving the cassette deck with 3-tracks of vocal counterpoint. The more layered and dense vocal pieces, like "Answer" and "The Corner," were multitracked and bounced digitally over eight or sixteen tracks. During the mixing process, I was also rehearsing the piece in order to know how to mix the "live" sequence where the voices I would sing and speak live were removed from the mix. Painstaking work, but the freedom to take time and experiment, afforded by my own studio, was a revelation. The record came out on New Tone with cover art by Cliff Baldwin. Reviews were good, but as these more theatrical pieces were touring for long stretches of time, the majority of reviews would address the music in the context of the performance. Dean Suzuki wrote in *Wired*, "Brilliantly paradoxical, *Failing Kansas* is at once alluring and disturbing: synthesized harmonica and cozy harmonies act as homey counterweights to the horrific drama."

Dennis Cleveland would be my first all-digital album, with two ADAT 8-track machines synced to provide sixteen tracks. It was a quirky puzzle, as I was enamored with a lot of new pop records, like Tricky's *Maxinquaye*, and would normally dig into the production sonics. But my research at the live talk shows told me the sound had to be a little "behind the times" in order to be believable. The convention of the talk show format provided lots of clear and obvious moves (see "*Dennis Cleveland* (1996)"), but I also knew I wanted the poetry of ritual and salvation. In describing the dilemma of the talk show host mirroring his flock, this excerpt from *Soul Train* hits the mark:

> *And the power of suggestion, in this moment, on this day*
> *Is the way we make religion, how we make up what to pray*
> *Who'd have thought I'd find a meaning, on the road and all alone?*
> *Think: a group of lonely people, create a King, create a throne*

These lines appear twice in the piece, the first time in a darker tonal setting suggesting uncertainty, and the second time in a brighter, major key mirroring the certainty and hypnotic effect of true belief. It was also exciting to pull meaning out of talk show speech fragments, slice them and dice them through sampling, and alter or enhance banal ideas. It was exhilarating to find my own personal feelings wound together with the guests on the talk shows. The album was dedicated to Robert Ashley and in memory of Ulysses Dove. Most of the reviews of the CD were bound together with the live performance, which made sense because the performance was so compelling. Mark Swed, writing for the *Los Angeles Times* two years before he would see the live performance, said of the release, "I know of nothing that has this combination: the compositional intelligence of the best of New York's downtown avant-garde, the musical means of a rock band, and the ability to transform the sleaziest side of popular culture into near-Wagnerian exultation."

The music for *The End of Cinematics* came fast; I think the record was sequenced and completed by 1998. But there were many hurdles in getting the grand production together (see "*The End of Cinematics* (1998) Parts 1 and 2"), so I didn't release the album until the Krannert Center premiere in 2005. I had purchased a thirty-two-channel analog mixing desk and some various analog boxes and was happy with the warmer sound. I pulled my neighbor and ex-girlfriend Veanne Cox into the tracking sessions, and she provided spoken word and harmonies, along with the singer Lisa Herman. These were tough times following the debt incurred by *Dennis Cleveland,* but I remember being happy in my Hell's Kitchen studio, working away on overdubs and taking breaks at the Studio Coffee Shop in the old Film Center building a block away. Without the sonic constraints of *Dennis Cleveland*, I delved into all sorts of music and production ideas. I also had an old-school editing moment where I chopped up completed songs into smaller fragments so I could move them around in the sequence to create a theme and variation arc. Moving the sections around in my workstation reminded me of the early tape days, when I'd do it all physically with a razor blade and splice block (which I still have). The center attraction of *The End of Cinematics* is "The Treatment." This is a multilayered vocal extravaganza that obliquely references a film treatment but goes off the rails with meditations such as the following:

> *Who says abort imagination? Intel Inside Entire Nation*
> *What's not ahead is usually behind*
> *Pity the mind, the mind that wanders I can't imagine any longer*
> *A single life so singularly refined*

As if to frame the entire arc of the piece, the film pitch is made as the choral voices grow and add depth to the narrator's hapless idea:

> *So, the girl and the guy, they're like . . . um . . .*
> *Overcast—you know, they don't even have a clue.*
> *And when the neighbor gets involved, it's like this triangle . . .*
> *(And explosions, lots of explosions) . . .*
> *So that when everyone wakes up, it's like it was a dream:*
> *And now they can see how hurt they've been—like all those broken*
>   *promises—but nobody meant to do it.*
> *And then . . . he walks into the sunset . . . yeah . . . the sunset . . . that's*
>   *good.*

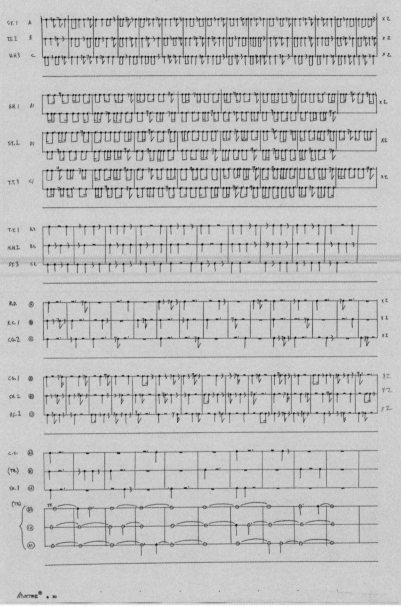

Quorum master patterns.

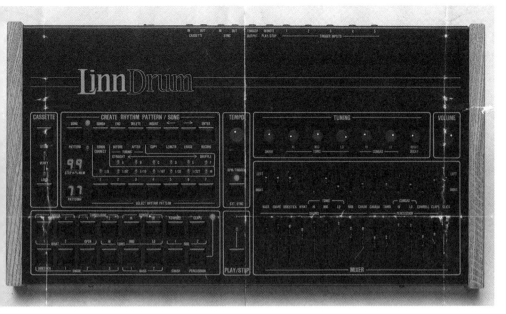

LinnDrum Machine Brochure.

Alvin Ailey Vespers American Dance Theater in Ulysses Dove's
Vespers, 1987.

Quorum (1984)

I'm sitting at the bar of the Baby Doll Lounge, one of the last few remaining strip bars in Manhattan. It's December 1987, and I'm accompanied by Jim Bergman, Ellery Eskelin, and Bill Tesar. Why I'm here with three of the best musicians I've ever had the privilege to know and work with is easily explained. We're killing time after a sound check at the Alternative Museum on Mercer Street. This is one of those gallery kinds of concerts with folding chairs that were pretty common in the 1970s and would hang on until the eventual gutting of Soho and the surrounding area. This is the current lineup of Mikel Rouse Broken Consort, and we're most likely doing stuff from the *Jade Tiger* album and from the new album, *A Lincoln Portrait* (pun intended). It's a reasonably full house and we do a reasonably good performance, and after the set there's the mingling and glad-handing. I'm approached by a woman who, by the glint in her eye, seems fairly enthusiastic about the set. She introduces herself as Sylvia Waters and says, "Do you realize that the Alvin Ailey company is doing your piece right now at City Center?" Of course I didn't realize this, so she fills in the details. At some point I get the idea that she's talking about the music for *Quorum*, the piece I wrote and programmed for the LinnDrum machine at the tender age of twenty-six.

I had come up with the idea of writing a piece for drum machine in 1982, and I think I completed the piece in 1983. After a disastrous studio session with an engineer who owned a LinnDrum but had no idea how to program it, I sought to procure one and attempt the programming myself. This is how I met Bill Tesar, who would go on to play drums in both Broken Consort and a later lineup for Tirez Tirez. Billy owned a new company called Toy Specialists with his wife, Rita. When they were starting out, I think they had just two pieces of equipment: a LinnDrum and a DX7. So he gave me a good deal on a rental, and I took the Linn-Drum to my Hell's Kitchen studio and started messing around with it. As you might imagine, it was all fairly basic stuff and the limitations, in terms of time signatures, were to be expected, based on how these things were being used in pop and hip-hop. You could only program just one basic time signature, like four beats or six beats to a measure.

But the score for *Quorum* was extremely intricate, with multiple meters. The themes for the piece were developed through the synchronization of the three generators 3–5–8, whose complementary factors yield counterthemes. Power series are then applied to produce harmonic contrasts from the original themes. So it dawned on me that maybe I could add up all the combined meters and make the common denominator "a measure," which became a 120-beat measure. It was arduous, but it worked. It's hard to describe how thrilling it was to have this machine just keep playing as I added parts. Prior to this type of programming, most of the work was all done on tape. Play, rewind, fast-forward. But here was a device that just kept looping. It obviously sounds pretty common now, but to me this nonlinear approach was a very different thing that I hadn't experienced, and it stood in stark contrast to all the recording I'd done before.

I programmed all the parts in small sections and decided I wanted a warmer sound than the raw LinnDrum, so Jim Bergman and I went to BC Studio in Brooklyn. I'd known of Martin Bisi from the downtown scene and would go on to do five records with him. We transferred all the individual outputs of the LinnDrum to a 24-track tape machine. Then we would run the sequence and, following the score (with six hands at the ready on the mixing desk), we would pop the various percussion instruments in and out. Once we did one small section, we'd rewind the 24-track and do it again. The final composition was then edited from the various 2-track masters to form the final complete master. Maybe it was the naive hope of youth or blind ambition, but I really thought I was onto something. Consequently, I made a bunch of cassette copies and set out to land a record deal. I have a memory of getting a meeting with Jonathan Rose. Somewhere along the line I'd heard he liked some of the Broken Consort material. I remember sitting in his office at his jazz label, Gramavision, and after some informal chitchat, I handed him the cassette and excitedly waited for his enthusiastic response. After a few minutes, he turned off the machine, looked me straight in the eye, and said, "Why would anyone want to put this out?"

I love this story now, but you can imagine at the time it was a letdown. Several of my earlier records were available through Carla Bley's New Music Distribution Service. I decided I'd make my own pressing of 200 copies and distribute it through NMDS. I remember wanting an audiophile pressing, so I had it mastered by Howie Weinberg (more on Howie later) and pressed it at Europadisk. Jeff Burk, the original bassist of Tirez Tirez, did the stunning black-and-white cover photo. The release was a 12-inch single, with only parts 1 and 2 of the total thirteen parts.

The record got lots of good press in places like the *Village Voice*, *Percussion Magazine*, *Option*, and *Rockpool*. I got postcards from both David Byrne (he had also picked up *Jade Tiger*) and Steve Reich. David thought both were great. Steve couldn't understand why there were no pitched percussion instruments, which I found revealing in that this groundbreaking composer missed that the sonic floor was shifting. To this day, almost forty years later, I still get correspondence from all over the world asking if this is the first techno/electronica record. My answer is always the same: probably not, but how did you get this number? And that was that. Happy with the piece and happy I got it out there.

But now I had to buy a ticket and see what was going on at City Center. It turns out a choreographer named Ulysses Dove had taken this recording and made a ballet called *Vespers*. It featured six amazing female dancers and a breathtaking lighting design by William H. Grant III. Over the years I've had the good fortune of having my music used by several great dance companies. But Ulysses's intuitive understanding of the structure and accents of the music was uncanny. I'm not sure if he read music, but the energy of his choreography with the high-volume drum machine was electric, and the audience responded by constantly jumping to their feet and yelling approval. This was clearly a breakthrough piece. Ulysses was a dancer in both the Merce Cunningham company and a star with the Ailey company back in the day. I have to believe *Vespers* helped fuse his classical structures with the pure emotion that I was always drawn to in music, dance, and film.

I can't remember if we met on that first night, but shortly after we became friends and I had him over to dinner. We also met at his favorite restaurant in Hell's Kitchen, Chez Napoléon. It's still one of my favorite places, and he introduced me to their *cerises jubilée*. *Vespers* was originally commissioned by the Dayton Contemporary Dance Company and premiered in 1986. The Ailey production premiered in 1987. I never brought up that no one had asked me about rights or permissions to use the work. But he did tell me how he discovered *Quorum*. Judith Jamison, a principal dancer and muse to Alvin Ailey, had used *Quorum* in a piece she set for the Houston Ballet. I eventually saw a video of this piece; it was OK but certainly not the breakthrough of *Vespers* (I honestly think Judith kind of held it against me because I knew the difference). Ulysses pleaded with Judith to let him use the music. I later learned that there is a kind of honor system in which choreographers don't lift the music of someone else's dance—at least not from each other. This story was also confirmed by Judith herself when she came over to my apartment in early 1988. I was excited to have her over, and I remember telling the impresario Jim Fouratt (Danceteria, Peppermint Lounge) that she had spent the afternoon with me. His excited response was, "You had all those arms and legs in your apartment?!"

I'm not sure, but I think by that time she might have been co-artistic director of Alvin Ailey American Dance Theater, as Alvin Ailey was in poor health. At any rate, it took years before I figured out what to do about a license, which came to a head with a new production of *Vespers* in 1994. At this point I also met Calvin Hunt, who I believe oversaw touring and production. I truly came to love Calvin. He saw that a couple of wrongs had happened, and he set out to right them. (While Ailey's slight was basically a sin of omission, more blatant was the refusal of Ann Williams, from Dallas Black Dance Theatre, to credit me. In trying to avoid signing my normal license agreement, she left a message on my voicemail, saying, "We don't use that Rouse music." After I sent her a link from their own website clearly showing that they were indeed "using that Rouse music," they paid up.) We came to an agreement on licensing, including past performances, and he made sure that with the new production, I'd have my overdue acknowledgment with Ulysses onstage opening night. Calvin passed away in 2014 and the entire arts community felt the loss. I remember sitting backstage with Ulysses, who had been an accomplished member of the Ailey company. As we sipped champagne, we could hear the faint strains of the gospel score of the Ailey classic *Revelations*, and hilariously Ulysses said, "If I hear that music one more time, I'm gonna puke."

This seems like as good a time as any to speculate on why the music worked so well, beyond Ulysses's vivid choreography. I've always hated canned music in dance performances. It always feels like I've been a bit cheated. But what made *Quorum* so different was that it was composed for a digital and recorded medium. And I feel that, even before the rise of DJ and electronica concerts, the audience somehow intuited this. It was as it should be, not a recording of something that would be more authentic performed live.

Which brings me to the Great Performances airing of the film by David Hinton, *Two by Dove*, in which the Alvin Ailey American Dance Theater and the Royal Swedish Ballet performed two works by Ulysses, *Vespers* and *Dancing on the Front Porch of Heaven*. This was a film experience—not simply a view of a proscenium performance—shot from many angles. I think this was frustrating for Ulysses, but I always thought that David was not only honoring our work, but also bringing along a more inclusive vision for a film realization. Enter Margaret Selby, who was working with Ulysses at the time and, I believe, was a producer on the film. Margaret was a unique and sometimes difficult collaborator, but she was a pit bull for Ulysses, and I both respected that and probably secretly wished I had that kind of support as well. Be careful what you ask for (see "*Dennis Cleveland* (1996) Part 2"). I think Ulysses was lucky to have her, especially since he'd been diagnosed with AIDS and was struggling. The time spent with Ulysses in the sound studio was valuable time. I had already lost many friends to AIDS, including the composer and songwriter Arthur Russell.

Two interesting things happened during those post sessions. The first was that for the film, I wanted the highest quality master possible, so I went back to the original analog master for the editor to use. We made the transfer and they got to work. Days into the process, we were listening to the sync track, and Ulysses thought something was wrong. He thought it sounded "too clean" or too "digital." We went round and round about this until we went back and played what he had been listening to and what Ailey (and numerous dance companies) were using. It turned out that Ulysses had made a cassette from the vinyl release and had gotten so used to the low-fi quality that he couldn't "hear" the actual master. I was pretty upset, but I held it together, thought for a minute or two, and said, "*Quorum* is mine, but *Vespers* is Ulysses's. Use the version he wants." I could see from his face that he was grateful. I'm not sure Margaret understood the sacrifice. The second issue was an editing problem with the film. There needed to be a brief cut in the music to sync with the way the performance footage had been edited. Normally I'd put up a fuss, but after the cassette issue I figured in for a dime, in for a dollar.

To Margaret's credit, she and others worked hard to give Ulysses a fitting tribute before he passed. "For the Love of Dove" was an amazing tribute at New York State Theatre, intended as both a fundraiser for AIDS as well as a retrospective of Ulysses's remarkable legacy. Because I donated the music for the event, I was invited to the $2,000-a-plate dinner. I took as my date the remarkable Jean Vong, a gifted artist and photographer. The next day I went to see my neighbor and fellow Hell's Kitchen artist Mark Lambert. He asked how the event was, and I expressed my dismay at how I couldn't afford the expense of a $2,000-a-plate dinner. He asked why I thought I would have to pay to attend, as I had previously told him that this invite was the result of my fee waiver. I said, "I know. I simply couldn't enjoy it unless I had doled out the money I can't afford." Go figure.

The film was a great success and won two Emmys. The audience hysteria at City Center lasted easily for five years, and the piece has been in repertory with Ailey for over thirty years as well as being regularly performed by numerous other dance companies. It still elicits an excitement and enthusiasm that feels vital all these years later. In 1997 I was invited to a Merce Cunningham benefit at the Brooklyn Academy of Music, where I met my future wife, Lisa Boudreau, who was a Cunningham dancer. When she asked me what I did and I told her I was a composer, she thought, "Sure, you are." When I told her I wrote the music for *Vespers*, she lit up and said, "Oh! You really are a composer!" I was that certain that she would know this seminal work. Having been seen by over a million people, I guess it's not a bad legacy for a record no one would want to put out.

Failing Kansas, New Zealand Festival, 2002.

Failing Kansas (1995)

I'm sitting in La Côte Basque with Kyle Gann, the preeminent critic, scholar, and composer. Why we are here is a testimony to our belief in ghosts and forging your own way into the history of the world. I'm happy to be here. I'm eating Chef's cassoulet Toulousain with white beans and delicate duck sausage. I know this because I'm referencing the very clever feature that Kyle wrote for the *Village Voice*, which was conducted at Côte Basque. I had the idea to do the interview here because the work we're discussing, *Failing Kansas*, was inspired by Truman Capote's true crime novel *In Cold Blood*, and Côte Basque and the gossip he overheard there were ultimately his undoing. I also like the martinis. I've never had the chance to thank Ann Powers, who was the music editor for the *Voice* in 1995, for this meal. Kyle had told me he got $100 for a meal when the interview was for a feature. I had done a deep dive into Capote and read all of his books, so I knew the stories of La Côte Basque and said, "Too bad they can't spring for more. This would be a great place to connect the dots." As I understand it, Kyle went back to Ann, and I guess she was enthusiastic because she upped the figure to $250. It got even better when, a few days later, the *Voice* sent me back with a photographer to shoot the pic for the article; that photo would become a great memento for me after Côte Basque relocated a few months later, ultimately closing in 2004.

Failing Kansas started out as what would be one of many pieces designed to survive a recession. After the Wall Street crash of 1987, I was having a tough time keeping a band on the road. Both Mikel Rouse Broken Consort and Tirez Tirez were limited to local shows, and I felt like I needed to figure out a way to stay in the game. I also wanted to find a way to not only bring in my multimedia interests but also try a more visual performative approach.

I was inspired by Capote's craft, for sure, but I also loved that he developed the idea of the nonfiction novel, kind of building on Joseph Mitchell and others. I wasn't interested in merely telling the *In Cold Blood* story (there was already the faithful film adaptation by Richard Brooks with music by Quincy Jones—who wants to compete with that?). I wondered instead if there was a way to access the source research materials Capote and Harper Lee collected and assemble a non-narrative retelling of the same events (Capote brought Lee to Kansas as both a research assistant and go-between with the locals). I found out that the Capote archives were at the New York Public Library, and after a few hurdles and ID checks, I was able to get access.

This was an exciting time. I never knew I had a hunger for this kind of research. I certainly didn't have it in school. But I found going through court transcripts and newspaper articles to be just the break from my normal routine that I needed. Though I had read *In Cold Blood* several times, I couldn't resist reading it all over again in the *New Yorker*, where it originally appeared serially over four separate issues. The files for *In Cold Blood* take up about two-thirds of the entire Capote archive, so I must have spent almost a year studying and making notes. This change of pace also led me to the idea of experimenting with voices in a way I hoped would be new and parallel to Capote's own innovations.

In 1989 I hadn't yet built my own recording studio, but I had the good fortune of getting a grant of sorts from the Center for Electronic Music, which was run by a great guy named Ron Goldberg. The grant provided studio time for a short project. While I knew I wanted to do something new vocally, I also wanted the feel to be folksy and rural. An acoustic guitar, harmonica kind of thing. I had completed the score for one of the four large sections, "The Last to See Them Alive," so I thought this would be a good way to start experimenting with spoken text and basic instrumentation. This slowly evolved into a more complex layering of multiple meters of unpitched text in spoken counterpoint, a technique I dubbed counterpoetry. I'm sure this was influenced by both hip-hop (which was exploding in New York in the late '70s, when I moved here) and the heady work of artists like Robert Ashley. But this sounded like nothing I had heard before, so much so that I truly didn't like the sound of it. I even found it a little disturbing. But somehow, I think that made me trust it.

Between research, writing, and other projects, *Failing Kansas* took a long time to complete. In the five years I spent working on the piece, I continued to do shows, started building my own studio, and found part-time work at an art gallery. I released a Broken Consort record called *Soul Menu.* I also started work on the quasi-experimental pop record *Living Inside Design,* mostly to continue working and testing the counterpoetry idea. This record came out before *Failing Kansas* and was originally released on the New Tone label out of Italy, receiving great reviews, so I felt good about this new solo approach. *Living Inside Design* also provided an opportunity to test performing solo. The artist and filmmaker Cliff Baldwin and I made a compelling solo show that I performed at a number of venues, including the Governor's Conference on the Arts, which in 1996 held "The Arts, Entertainment and Technology: The Role of the Artist in the Digital Age."

I had known the composer Ben Neill for years. He lived in Soho with his wife, Amy, and we got along. At some point he became music director of The Kitchen in New York. He made the decision to book *Failing Kansas*, and that's where the piece would premiere. Because this needed to be a suitcase show, I had to figure out a way to perform the piece solo, so like *Living Inside Design,* I multitracked the overlapping voices and basically spoke and sang to my prerecorded self. It also made sense to ask Cliff if he'd provide a film to accompany the performance. He used grainy films that he'd done over the years as well as some new footage. I gave him complete freedom to go as abstract as he wanted, provided he have some cuts that landed at precise spots in the score. The entire effect was much greater and more startling than I could have imagined. The consensus for the audience was that the vocal layers and flickering film created a space where you were inside the thoughts of the murderers Perry Smith and Dick Hickock, the murdered Clutter family, the crime investigators, and other characters.

Because of the advance press and radio interviews, the run sold well and had a huge buzz. I was blown away that after the opening night performance, there among the mob of folks waiting to say hello were Robert Ashley and his wife, Mimi Johnson. Bob was so enthusiastic that Ben even mentioned it later. And the pleasant smile on Mimi's face signaled to me that she also realized Bob was genuinely excited. We made a plan to get together soon, and I went to his loft in Soho for cigars and vodka. Bob was an amazing original in the world of so-called new music, and he had come up with a vocal vocabulary that featured vernacular American speech. As we discussed *Failing Kansas*, he gave me the greatest compliment when he asked, "So how did you do it?" I knew exactly what he meant, and when I explained my scoring approach, he kind of looked up to the sky, nodding. He asked what I was currently working on, and I generally told him that I was working on a talk show opera called *Dennis Cleveland*. He thought for a moment and replied, "Good title." I visited Bob a number of times after that and will always remember his kindness and genuine interest in other people and their work.

The suitcase idea worked, and I took *Failing Kansas* around the world for fourteen years, from London to the Sydney Opera House, from the Melbourne International Arts Festival to St. Louis. In Melbourne, when I wasn't rehearsing or doing the show, I parked it at Pellegrini's Espresso Bar, overseen by a prince of a fellow named Sisto Malaspina. Pellegrini's didn't serve booze, but the day we were flying out, he invited Michael Mushalla, my agent, and me for a morning dinner with wine in the kitchen with Mama. It was yet another momentous, on-the-road food experience. In 2018, Sisto was murdered in a stabbing attack and given a state funeral. As a plaque on Bourke Street states, "Sisto loved Melbourne—and Melbourne loved him back."

I remember family members coming from my hometown to the St. Louis show; my grandmother sat with my mom, constantly asking her, "What's he doing now?" I can imagine that the startling contrast of live and prerecorded music and images, along with my choreographed counting, made for a curious spectacle. In Cedar Rapids, Iowa, an audience member was so shaken after the show that I had to hold her hand to calm her down. She loved it, but the experience clearly overcame her. As we spoke, I slowly came to realize that so complete was the spell cast that she thought all the voices were emanating from me. I guess working in the carnival paid off. Other standout moments with

Failing Kansas included *Los Angeles Times* critic Mark Swed making the performances on the West Coast one of his top ten events of 2000. He even went on to write an amazing essay on Sunday, December 3, 2000, "When Telling a Story Just Isn't Enough," in which he argued, "Narrative is only part of an opera, and not necessarily the key to conveying emotional truths."

Gratifying to be sure, but nothing could have prepared me for the aftermath of the performances at the New Zealand Festival in Wellington in 2002. I say aftermath because I actually didn't find out about the scandal *Failing Kansas* created until after the last performance. Some brief background first. We had rolled into Wellington after a big run at the Perth Festival, where I performed *Failing Kansas,* premiered my film *Funding,* created a multilevel sound installation of John Cage's *Roaratorio* in the Perth Bell Tower, and performed Cage's *James Joyce, Marcel Duchamp, Erik Satie: An Alphabet* with Merce Cunningham and John Kelly (see "*Cage/Cunningham* (1997–2013)"). We had a week to kill between the festivals in Perth and Wellington, but the Wellington festival generously offered to put us up in a hotel for a week rather than having us fly halfway round the world only to return a week later. I used that week wisely and, armed with a laptop and external drive, did the first rough cut of *The End of Cinematics*, a film shot in Paris (see "*The End of Cinematics* (1998) Parts 1 and 2"). Traveling with me were my agent Michael Mushalla, his partner, Mary Anne Lewis, and my production manager, Carolyn Cubit. A great memory from the week of editing *Cinematics* was Michael cooking and testing out New Zealand wines. Not wanting to disturb me, each day he would print a menu for that night's dinner and slip it under my door. I even made a running cartoon commentary of our four varied opinions on the numerous wines, which I gave to Michael as a parting gift.

During this week I also did some advance press, including a radio interview with the leading public radio station in New Zealand. Upon our arrival in Wellington, I made an unexpected but rather simple request to Michael and Mary Anne: after collecting the press for the last twenty years or so, I didn't want to do it during performances. I knew I'd eventually have to see it because I would most likely be the one posting and cataloging it. So I was simply asking them to collect it and give it to me later. They both thought this was a reasonable request.

We were performing at the Paramount Theatre, which is a beautiful 1,000-seat movie house that was occasionally used for live performances. By this time the playback of the show had been streamlined to DVD (after going through numerous format changes over the years, the most irksome of which was using a time code DAT machine for audio to sync and drive a lousy VHS tape machine for video). Mel Andringa and F. John Herbert at CSPS in Cedar Rapids were instrumental in helping me finally merge the audio and video into a digital format.

After performing *Failing Kansas* for about seven years, it occurred to me that I didn't have any video of the live performance. Some presenters may have made a one-camera shoot for their archives, but I never saw anything. So I decided to hire a camera operator to shoot the shows. But I couldn't afford what I wanted: a four-camera shoot of a performance. I could afford one camera, so I came up with the idea of having the camera operator shoot four performances from a different angle each night. I also recorded the four nights of audio on DAT from the soundboard. It took me twenty years to see if this idea would work, but I was finally able to edit this show (these shows) in 2020 during the pandemic lockdown. I defy anyone to be able to tell it's not one show. That's how well I knew the piece after seven years.

Carolyn and I started to do preproduction with the local team a couple of days before the premiere. As this was a lean show, I wasn't traveling with my usual production team. The gap between Perth and Wellington and the week of video editing in the hotel left me feeling a little rusty, and I wanted to make sure the performance would be tight, so I did something I'd never done. I decided to skip the festival launch event so I could continue rehearsing. Michael and Mary Anne agreed to go and represent the *Failing Kansas* troupe.

I knew something was up the day after the first performance. Michael called and just suggested there were some rumblings. He tried not to tell me because of my previous request of not seeing the press. But it was clear it had something to do with that. So I asked him if it was good or bad, and with a quizzical sound in his voice, he implied maybe a little of both. The first show was well attended but certainly not sold out. Michael had instructed Carolyn and the crew at the theater not to mention press to me. When I got to the theater the second day for sound check, I said hi to the cameraman I'd hired and, as he shook my hand, he burst out laughing. I then saw Carolyn, and she had the mischievous grin of the Cheshire Cat. That night the audience seemed more animated than before. Also, it was a larger crowd. By the end of the run, we were completely sold out. And the final performance was electric. *Failing Kansas* is a kind of dark piece, not your "whoop and holler" kind of show, but now people were standing and applauding after each of the nine sections of the piece. Obviously, something was going on.

What follows is an account over dinner after the last show from my three companions.

Since I didn't experience it in real time, I must rely on their telling of the story. We sat down and I could tell everyone was just dying to spill their guts, so I asked, "OK, what happened?" And then it just poured out of them. Apparently, a reviewer named Rod Biss had attended opening night for the *Sunday Star-Times*, the national paper, which is located in Auckland. He gave the show a scathing review, which is fine; that's part of the game. But the review ran on the front page above the fold, with a huge photo of me performing, my arms spread out wide. Michael told me Seán Doran, the artistic director of the Perth Festival, was walking out of his hotel and saw a long line of the papers ready for guests of the hotel. Upon seeing my picture on the front page, he supposedly said, "Well, that's gotta be good," I guess meaning there is no "bad" press. Michael and Mary Anne were shopping for groceries and knew a review was coming in the national paper. From the other side of a large supermarket, Michael heard Mary Anne scream, "Oh my god! We're on the cover!"

I think it's important to note that there's a rivalry between Auckland and Wellington. And I think that rivalry contributed to Auckland's view of the Wellington festival. But a lot of the work I saw in Wellington was fairly provincial, so I was expecting *Failing Kansas* to ruffle some feathers. Anyway, the locals weren't happy with how *Failing Kansas* was covered in the national paper, especially when it was learned that Mr. Biss was seen walking out about ten minutes into the show. On the second night, the nice woman with whom I had done the radio interview came and announced to the crowd, "I'm here to support the opposition!" At about this time, a well-known artist hammered a manifesto he had written into the theater lobby wall. The radio interviewer challenged Mr. Biss to come on her show and debate the merits of the piece with the hammer-wielding artist and he accepted, only to be busted on air over having the nerve to place a review on the front page when he'd seen just ten minutes of the show.

Meanwhile, Michael and Mary Anne were fielding phone calls at all hours of the day and night from TV and radio. The festival director, Carla van Zon, was freaking out and calling frantically, trying to limit the damage. A TV reporter went on air and said, "It took Mikel Rouse to knock Osama bin Laden off the front page of the national newspaper." When Michael and Mary Anne attended the opening ceremony for the festival, the mayor told the crowd, "We have Mikel Rouse and company to thank for doing what our publicity department has failed to do in the last five years!" It just kept growing from there. Michael looked at me, almost stunned, and said, "I've never been in the middle of the storm." Michael also represents the Mark Morris Dance Company, and when I was living in Brussels in 1982, I remembered the tumultuous tenure of Mark when he was dance director of the Théâtre Royal de la Monnaie, the Belgian national opera. I asked Michael about that, and he said, "I wasn't repping Mark yet."

The next day we were all heading back to New York on different flights. Mine was later in the day, so I had a leisurely lunch and headed to the airport. I was fortunate in the festival years to mostly fly business class, and I was looking forward to a comfortable trip. When I was checking in, the flight agent looked at my passport, then looked at me smiling and said, "Oh, you're the fellow who caused all the controversy." As I boarded the plane, they were handing out copies of various newspapers. I grabbed the weekly *Star-Times* and settled in. As I thumbed through the paper, there was a second review! The title was "*Failing Kansas,* a New Art Form." I smiled to myself and decided it would be OK to read this notice now.

There was no rule or discipline	or anyone to show me right from wrong	hours of the night to see if I wet the bed

| She would throw back the covers

with a large black leather belt-

& drag me to the bathroom

& turn the cold water on

& the sheets | & furiously beat me
pull me out of bed
by my hair
& throw me in the
tub
& tell me to wash
myself | She would throw back
& furiously
with a large black leather
pull me out of bed
by
& drag me to the
& throw me
& turn the
& tell me to wash

& the sheets |

Every night was a nightmare
                Every night was a nightmare   Every night was a nightmare
Later on she thought
                                        it was very funny
on my penis
                    to put some kind of ointment

| This was almost
unbearable
This was almost
unbearable
This was almost
unbearable |

It burned something
terrible
It burned something
terrible | She was later discharged
from her job. But this
never changed my mind about
her & what I wished I could
have done to her & all the
people who made fun of me. |

| She lifted me, I could
  have been light as a mouse
we went up, up, I could see
the Square below,
  We went up, up,
      men running, yelling,
the sheriff shooting at us
  everybody   everybody
  sore as   sore as
  hell be-   hell be-
  cause I was cause I was
  free   free
I was flying
  I was flying
      I was flying
I was better
  I was better
      I was better | He speaks and the sound of His
  voice
Is so sweet the birds hush their
  singing
And the melody
That he gave to me
Within my heart is ringing

I'd stay in the garden with Him
Tho' the night around me be
  falling
But He bids me go
Thro' the voice of woe
His voice to me is calling

And He walks with me
And He talks with me
And he tells me I am His own |

19

Failing Kansas
Libretto.

Failing Kansas
sketch excerpts.

Cage/Cunningham (1997–2013)

In the debate concerning where to find the best tuna fish sandwich, there can be no doubt that Eisenberg's Sandwich Shop at Twenty-Second and Fifth Ave reigns supreme. After touting this claim to Laura Kuhn, director of the John Cage Trust, we are finally sitting here in 2001, around the corner from the quaint LRP recording studio where we are embarking on a unique sampling project. A year or so before, I approached Laura with the idea of creating a prepared piano sample library of John Cage preparations. I liked the idea of bringing the prepared piano concept into the digital age, offering new sounds to composers and home recording enthusiasts, but I was also excited about the possibility of folks being able to play Cage's prepared piano works if they didn't have access to, or the ability to prepare, a piano. Her response was an enthusiastic "You can do that?" So less than a year later, we're sitting here with tuna on rye while, back at the studio, pianist Nurit Tilles is preparing the piano with the original preparations used by Cage (Laura and Nurit would consult and prepare the piano together as well). After a lot of research and prep work, it was decided that we would use the preparations for Cage's *Sonatas and Interludes*, as this was the most well known of Cage's prepared piano works. The recording would prove to be one of the more challenging projects I've encountered in a recording studio.

Once the piano was prepared with the bits of wood, metal, and rubber preparations, we were ready to begin the methodical process of sampling each note (though only forty-four notes on the piano are altered, we opted, for acoustic reasons, to sample all eighty-eight keys). Each key would be sampled at three dynamic levels (piano, mezzoforte, and fortissimo), and in five articulations (staccato, long notes with natural decay, long notes with sustain pedal for soundboard interaction, long notes with soft pedal, and long notes with soft pedal staccato). I'm reminded from Laura's excellent program notes for the Big Fish Audio Sample Library release that a total of 1,320 samples were created. After tons of research, I came up with an elaborate catalog system that would allow us to keep track of all the sounds that were recorded at both 24- and 16-bit on DAT. The longest samples with the sustain pedal could last longer than a minute (I learned that the longer the sustain was allowed to fade, the greater the possibility of the programmer finding a smooth loop that would be undetectable), but they were sometimes interrupted by occasional footsteps heard from the floor above. Nurit's consistency in performing these samples was uncanny, and our recording engineer, Mike Cyr, provided a much-needed calm and professionalism to the sessions, which ran over a number of days. Larry Larson was brought in and, with Laura, provided a great liaison with the Big Fish Audio folks, Tom Meadows and Matt Haines.

I first met Laura after she attended my solo benefit concert at the Theatre at St. Clement's (see "*Dennis Cleveland* (1996) Part 2"). I think Fran Richards from ASCAP may have invited her. A little while later I was talking with Fran, and she suggested Laura and I meet. We became fast friends and Laura was a supportive ally. We shared many meals and drinks and did quite a bit of traveling in those early days. We enjoyed debating art over steaks at Raoul's in Soho and martinis and fries at Pastis, which was near the Cage Trust in the West Village. Because of my tech knowledge and archiving skills (in 1992, commissioned by Point Records and Philip Glass, I had archived over 980 tapes of my friend Arthur Russell after he passed away), Laura threw a lot of Cage Trust archive projects my way. I digitized many different formats as well as unearthed several recordings thought lost, including rare tape pieces by Morton Feldman and Earl Brown. This was thrilling for me, as I was hugely influenced by Cage, Jasper Johns, Robert Rauschenberg, and Merce Cunningham. Having come from a small rural area, I felt a little behind the curve when I was studying in Kansas City in terms of art and music history. Stephen Sidelinger, a design teacher at the Kansas

City Art Institute, took pity on me and said I should go to the excellent library at KCAI and just start reading books on esthetics. He also told me he didn't think I had a soul, which, in the early nihilistic days of punk, I took as a compliment. That's how I stumbled upon Johns, Rauschenberg, Cunningham, and Cage. Little did I know that this early archive work with the Cage Trust would set the stage for numerous collaborations and memorable moments.

In 2001 the John Cage Trust commissioned me to realize the score for Cage's radio-play-turned-theatrical-production *James Joyce, Marcel Duchamp, Erik Satie: An Alphabet*. I completed the score at Louisiana Tech University during the beginning of my three-year Meet the Composer Residency in Ruston. I was excited to bring a project of this scale to the residency. Ruston is a small town that I'd heard a lot about. One of my best friends, the artist and original drummer for Tirez Tirez Rob Shepperson, hailed from there, and in the early days together in KC, we would compare notes about our small-town roots. I had set up a makeshift recording studio on campus and would record the albums *Test Tones* and *Music for Minorities* over the course of the residency. But the studio also provided a great room to record and sample sounds for the *Alphabet* piece. In a rare departure from the chance operations he's known for, Cage's notes call for a combination of "rational" and "irrational" sounds. The "rational" sounds are cued effects that highlight the text in a literal way. I was fortunate to meet and work with a young instructor named Michael Rasbury. He taught at Tech but also did live sound, so his help both in collecting sounds and becoming our live sound engineer was a score. We included a number of music students to help collect the sounds called for, such as an exotic birdcall from Australia.

As we continued to collect hundreds of sounds, we devised a low-rent way to do a surround-sound score: we mixed a front and rear 5.1 speaker idea and eventually authored a stereo "front" DVD and a stereo "back" DVD. I think Michael was skeptical that this would work, but sure enough, the dual DVDs synced perfectly. I remember David Harrington of the Kronos Quartet being quite impressed as he was soon to be working on a surround score. He assumed we had a very expensive system, and when I told him how we did it he seemed bemused. This performance was at UCLA; as with my own Los Angeles shows, the Cunningham company always stayed at the Hotel Del Capri in Westwood. The hotel had a 1950s-style layout, with wraparound balconies and cottage-style rooms surrounding the pool. On one early trip with the company, we celebrated Merce's birthday and decked out the area around the pool with tiki torches. The company did an impromptu Esther Williams-meets-Cunningham swim ballet, culminating in the dancers removing their bathing suits and laying them at Merce's feet. In addition to stays at the hotel for *Dennis Cleveland,* I remember having Pink's Hot Dogs sent to the *Alphabet* company when we stayed there for performances.

Laura, who was directing the show, wanted me to play the part of James Joyce; Merce Cunningham would play the role of Erik Satie and John Kelly would play the Narrator. But I would also be following the score/script and playing the "rational" sounds as called for by the text. I remember one of the "rational" sounds being roller skating; we found an old-school roller rink in Ruston, and as I circled in skates, Michael followed and captured it all with a boom mic. In addition to the recordings taking place in Louisiana, there were also many New York sessions. One of the most interesting was recording Jasper Johns in the role of Rrose Sélavy, Marcel Duchamp's feminine pseudonym. Laura had asked Jasper if he would read the part with the understanding that it would be a "recorded character" and Jasper agreed, with the stipulation that he'd retain the right of refusal if he didn't like the results. Our engineer for the prepared piano project, Mike Cyr, knew of a studio in Midtown on the East Side. We all decamped there and began the recording of the Cage text, which is delightfully surreal, with topics ranging from mathematics and geometry to easily missed puns. When we finished the takes, Laura, Mike, and I went into the recording room where Jasper was sitting. He asked how it sounded and I said, "It's great! I actually think I almost knew what you were talking about!" This seemed to delight Jasper and he let out a great laugh. Laura walked Jasper to a cab, and Mike and I started doing cleanup work on the recordings. I could tell Laura was nervous when she left, but she came back much calmer. As Jasper got into the cab, she asked him if he thought it would be OK for us to use the recording. Without giving it a second thought, as he shut the door, he said, "Oh, it's fine!"

Michael Mushalla, my agent, decided to help us book the piece and we assembled a great collection of shows. The first stop would be the Edinburgh International Festival. We were booked into the majestic

Royal Lyceum Theatre. This would be Michael Rasbury's first trip outside the US, so I was particularly concerned for him, especially when his luggage was lost and he had to go to Marks & Sparks for some essentials. As usual, I was overly prepared. We did a full reading of the score and sampled sounds in Ruston before we headed to Edinburgh. Our load-in went smoothly, and Michael and I were set up while everyone else was frantically trying to put out fires. The set for the piece was beautiful in its austerity, but it was far from road-worthy and there were lots of build issues. I suggested he and I hit the pub, but he seemed concerned about leaving when there was so much chaos. I reassured him by saying, "We're set up and our systems are working." A day or so later I got extremely ill with what might have been West Nile virus, as the virus had been detected in Louisiana. Whatever it was, I was down for a day or so. I remember loving the sound of the surround score in the theater and marveling at how well the makeshift DVD system worked. The shows were packed and we got good reviews. I'm not sure where we stored the set, but a few weeks later, after returning to New York, we would be heading to the Hebbel Theatre in Berlin.

On September 10, 2001, the *Alphabet* troupe made its way to Newark Airport for the flight to Berlin. I remember arriving at the airport and there was some kind of commotion; maybe a fire, but something felt off. When we arrived in Berlin on September 11, our rooms weren't ready, so we all hung out at the hotel bar as rooms became available. I finally got into my room in the afternoon and, as we were going to meet the local cast and have a read-through that evening, I thought I'd take a nap. As I was turning off the TV, I heard that a plane had hit the World Trade Center, but the impression was of a small plane, and small planes had hit buildings in New York before. I fell asleep pretty quickly only to wake up to Michael Rasbury calling my room to tell me about the plane. I kinda blew him off and said I know, I saw it on TV, and his response, embedded in my mind with his Louisiana accent, was, "Mikel, I don't think you know what's goin' on." I turned on the TV and everything started to come into focus. At about this time, Laura called me from the hotel lobby. She and David Vaughn (the Cunningham archivist who also played Marcel Duchamp in our show) were going to the theater early and wanted to know if I'd like to come. I'm sure I was pretty incoherent, but I frantically tried to convey the news as it was rolling out. I remember saying to her that we needed to reach out to loved ones in New York. I think Laura might have thought I was pulling her leg or being dramatic, but when she responded, "Everyone I love in New York is here," I was overcome with emotion. Then she knew it was serious and told David they needed to go to my room. David asked why, and Laura said it was something on television. In his proper English accent, David replied, "I don't watch television."

In rapid succession, things in Berlin started moving toward a lockdown, with barricades springing up around monuments and sirens howling all around. No one knew if this was an isolated incident or a bigger plan. But we continued with the read-through rehearsal that evening and it's a good thing we did. The local cast, some of whom were important political figures and artists, were in shock. Some expressed disbelief that this could happen to the United States; after all, one actress said, we were viewed as Europe's protector. However misguided that view was, it was clear that we were all experiencing a possible game-changing moment. The next day I was desperate to get news from Lisa and New York. Phones were down in New York, but I discovered I could call Mary Anne Lewis, Michael Mushalla's partner, in Ruston and she could email him. He then emailed Lisa and we had a four-way convo going. Mary Anne's take on our good technology fortune was, "This is kinda cool . . . I mean, if it wasn't under these circumstances." (I later learned that as Lisa was leaving the Cunningham studios at Westbeth, she looked south on Washington Street and saw the first tower go down. I asked her what her thoughts were, and she replied, "I need to go home now.") That evening we all gathered to do a rehearsal on stage. I remember seeing Merce sitting in the wings alone rehearsing his lines, and I went over to see how he was doing. I'll never forget what he said to me: "Aren't we lucky we have this to do?" To my surprise, all the shows were full, and every night after a performance the cast would journey to a bar or restaurant to talk about the latest news. We were headed to the Dublin Fringe Festival after Berlin, which was handy as we couldn't fly back to the States for a couple of weeks.

Somehow or other they managed to get Merce a flight back to New York, so the rest of us arrived in Dublin and wondered what was to come. The festival helped to find accommodations, as we would have to stay longer than originally expected. I don't remember much about

Dublin other than places I'd been to, having done shows there before. I was introduced to two sisters who were somehow related to James Joyce, and they expressed how they enjoyed my performance. I also got my first acting review from a BBC theater program, which was kind of funny. One critic couldn't imagine Joyce being read by an American, and another critic chimed in to defend my interpretation with a "job well done" kind of sentiment. But I mostly remember feeling stuck and anxious to get home. We were scheduled to head directly to the Krannert Center in Urbana, but some of the New Yorkers wanted to stop in the city first. It was surreal and hard to fathom how bad it must have been considering how bad it still was weeks later. I think I only got to stay in the city one or two nights before heading to Urbana. Now it was my turn to lose my luggage, but it somehow didn't seem to matter. We stayed at Jumer's, a mainstay of my many earlier trips to Urbana. Everything was still a fog, but the familiarity of the Krannert Center was helpful. The shows were good. The tour continued with performances at Cal Performances in Berkeley, the Perth International Arts Festival in Western Australia, and the Eclectic Orange Festival in Costa Mesa, California. The Perth shows were intense as I was also performing *Failing Kansas*, screening the film *Funding*, and creating a sound installation of John Cage's *Roaratorio* in the Bell Tower. The tour was truly an experience of art rising above the noise, and for that I did feel lucky that "we had this to do."

One thing Laura and I liked to do was to hang out at the Winners Circle near Times Square. There used to be Off Track Betting outposts everywhere in New York, but as they waned, you either had to go to the track (which we did, to Belmont and Saratoga) or go to the Winners Circle. The place had seen better days, but it was always a gas to go there and sit in a booth having overpriced food and drink and follow the races on the individual table-side screens. Laura seemed to have a knack for gambling, and one favorite memory is a revealing night at Keen's Steakhouse in Midtown. Laura had invited me there for my birthday dinner, and I believe she had just returned from a trip to Las Vegas and had spent some time in a casino there. She took out a large manila envelope full of cash and, still in disbelief, said, "Mikel, I couldn't lose!" I can't remember the total, but I think it was pretty substantial. As if to illustrate her good fortune and surprise, she started throwing money at me, exclaiming, "It's your birthday!" Laura was good this way.

When John Cage passed away, I think it was clear to her that Merce might not extend the effort needed to maintain the kind of social activities that came naturally to Cage. She set about arranging dinner events and other activities, which kept things lively. This was a boon to me, as I became a regular and would often join Merce and Laura for dinner at Merce's kitchen counter. Laura is a great cook and makes a mean steak. Over about a twelve-year period, I spent many holidays and special occasions at Merce's. I met great artists like Charles Atlas and Robert Rauschenberg. It was around this time, at a gathering at Merce's, that Laura let slip she'd been contacted by the MacArthur folks about me. I'm sure she meant to be encouraging, but here I was again, thinking about an award that I wouldn't otherwise care to think about (see "*Dennis Cleveland* (1996) Part 1").

A very memorable evening was when Laura arranged a special birthday dinner for Merce and invited both Bob Rauschenberg and Jasper Johns. It's my understanding that Bob and Jasper hadn't been together socially in many years and, when I arrived, the tension was high as Laura, Bob, and Bob's partner, Darryl Pottorf, waited for Jasper to arrive. When he came in, he placed his hands on Bob's shoulders, as Bob sat in a wheelchair (Bob had had a stroke, maybe two), and the tension disappeared. It was a wonderful dinner to be a fly on the wall, and as I often did, I helped Laura clean up in the kitchen as the three friends finished their drinks. (Darryl was in the kitchen with us, dejected because he thought Jasper was dismissive of him.) As everyone was leaving and Darryl was wheeling Bob out (truly wanting to be clear of the evening), I made them pause and told Bob a story I suspect he'd heard from others many times. In 1996, after the bank-breaking success of *Dennis Cleveland*, I applied for an emergency grant from Bob's organization, Change. To my surprise, one day I received a check for $500 signed by Bob with the iconic signature that I was so familiar with from his paintings. I was in a dilemma: I needed the scratch, but how could I cash this check? I relayed this info to Bob and said I just didn't think I could cash it, and with a mischievous grin he said, "But ya did, didn't you?" And I replied yes, and he exclaimed, "Good for you! Let's have a drink!" Laura poured us both another glass and we sat together and chatted for a while. I felt bad for Darryl, but I simply couldn't let this moment pass.

Around the time that Merce was eighty-five, I remember talking with Laura, who expressed concern that Merce was slowing down and seemed depressed. I had worked with Margaret Selby (see "*Quorum* (1984)" and "*Dennis Cleveland* (1996) Part 2"), who was producing a film for PBS on the animator Chuck Jones, who had created many iconic cartoon characters such as Bugs Bunny and Daffy Duck. Together, we came up with the idea of having Chuck over for dinner with Merce. I know Laura, Margaret, Merce, Chuck, and I were there, but there might have been someone else. At any rate, it was thrilling to see how sharp Chuck Jones's mind and wit were. And as Laura, Margaret, and I had grown up with these cartoon characters, we were peppering Chuck with questions. Merce would chime in and find ways to add to the storyline and basically try to keep up. It was a great evening, but the next day something remarkable happened. I got a call from Laura, who said, "I think we might have saved Merce's life!" I asked what she meant, and she thought that Merce, for once not being the center of attention, fought for acknowledgment and this lit a fire under him. When she said it, I started to remember the evening and agreed.

Somehow our attention to Chuck helped put Merce back in the game. I was happy to have been an unwitting part of this, but I was really happy at how the evening closed. I was in the kitchen cleaning up, and when Laura came in, I asked her if she would show Chuck my sketchbook. I've always carried a book around for forty years, and I just wanted to be able to say Chuck Jones had seen my sketches. A few minutes later, Laura came back and leaned in, quietly saying, "Chuck Jones is making a drawing in your sketchbook." He drew a picture of Bugs Bunny in a tutu with his signature and the caption "Afternoon of a Rabbit." Yet another sublime and remarkable experience of timing and good fortune. And carrying a sketchbook.

New York is home, but Paris was like a second home, and I would happily tag along with the Cunningham company or make a stop there when they were performing. I became friendly with many restaurant owners and would spend days sketching and writing in cafés. I remember taking dancers to out-of-the-way places I'd discovered. There was a funky bar in one of those passages, tucked away so the cigarette smoke could never escape. I remember hosting some of the company members there for late dinner, and barkeep Olivier strumming guitar and singing. I could list maybe thirty to forty favorite old restaurants in Paris, but the one dearest to my heart was Bar de l'X. It was a small hole in the wall that I discovered in the early '90s when I was touring *Living Inside Design*. It was run by Brigette and Alan and had maybe five tables. They had a unique country-style duck confit called Duck Confit Royal, with foie gras added on top. I got to know the family and even shot a number of scenes for *The End of Cinematics* using the family as improvising actors. This place truly became my home away from home. I brought many of the dancers there and we got Brigette and Alan tickets to an outdoor Cunningham performance, and when the dancers, warming up on stage, saw Brigette arrive, they exclaimed, "There's the duck lady!" After this performance, Lisa and I went back with Brigette and Alan to the bar and they made us dinner. We sat outside the restaurant on the street until 3 a.m., drinking and discussing the show. I remember looking at Lisa and her looking at me: how did we get this lucky?

The Alvin Ailey American Dance Theater has had Ulysses Dove's *Vespers* in repertory for over thirty-five years (see "*Quorum* (1984)"). At some point in the late '90s or early 2000s, Lisa, Merce, Laura, and I went to City Center (where the Ailey company does a traditional month-of-December run) to see the piece. Ulysses had danced with Merce, and I think he picked up a unique sense of structure from his time with the Cunningham company. I was nervous, but Merce thought it "marvelous" (admittedly a term he often used) and said to me, "We will work together." This was before *Alphabet*, and if you had told me then that I'd perform on stage with Merce, I would have laughed. But still, I knew my music wasn't a natural fit for Cunningham and, with my relationship to Lisa and Laura, I thought the nepotism factor might be too high, so I filed this comment away and let it go.

In 2001, I got Lisa the first iPod as a Christmas gift. It was a novel device but the audio quality was very compressed early MP3 and I wasn't that interested. Later at the gym, I found the shuffle feature interesting, like a curated radio station with no advertising. But still. Then, around 2005, I was approached by the Cunningham Dance Company to compose a piece of music for iPods. I believe the idea originated from an archival concept of William Knapp (who was the company manager at the time and would later be production manager of *The End of Cinematics, Gravity Radio*, and *One Boy's Day*) and was gently massaged by Laura and administrative folks at the Cunningham Dance Company to include new compositions. I was immediately attracted to the idea of composing for iPods, as so much of my work has been involved with new technologies. The dance piece would be called *eyeSpace*, and my score was called *International Cloud Atlas*.

From the beginning, I knew I wanted *International Cloud Atlas* to employ the "shuffle" characteristic of the iPod as a compositional device, thereby allowing each audience member to have his or her own unique sequence of the score. I also liked the idea that my type of churning rhythms wouldn't disrupt the dancers, who are used to non-rhythmic music and who rehearse in silence, only hearing the score for the first time on opening night of a performance. Indeed, when Lisa learned of the idea, she said, "Great, my husband gets to do a score for the company, and I don't get to hear it." I also wanted to include all the dancers in the recording of the iPod score.

The dancers contributed vocal, instrumental, and spoken-word performances. I am extremely grateful for the creativity and enthusiasm that the dancers brought to these recording sessions. There is also an additional "environmental score" that is performed live in the theater and that represents the cityscape of sounds that music devices attempt to tune out. I think Lisa suggested this idea, as I was losing sleep over this additional component of the score. I am grateful to Stephan Moore for his invaluable contribution to the sound design of this aspect of the piece. As we traveled from city to city, we would collect the city sounds and add them to the vast and growing collection of sounds.

I was aware that some folks might consider the iPod shuffle idea a gimmick, but I considered it a technological homage to the Cage/Cunningham esthetic. Indeed, in his *New York Times* review of the Joyce Theater premiere in 2006, John Rockwell said of *International Cloud Atlas*, "What was thrilling about hearing the music this way was how personal it was. We were all cocooned in our own worlds, hearing something different, just for us. 'All the audience members have their own secret, their own special version,' Mr. Rouse was quoted as saying in *Time Out New York*. It was the purest realization of Mr. Cunningham's chance aesthetic, the ultimate in intimacy." Still, I was aware of some grumbling among the traditional Cunningham composers and some of the politics that surrounded the piece. I've always been pretty good at ignoring this kind of stuff. I knew I wasn't part of this club and that didn't bother me. I knew that some had said Cage would never have approved of a digital realization of the prepared piano. Please.

But there was a humorous complication. In what I assumed was an appeasement to those who weren't happy about me doing a score for Merce, the company decided that two other composers would also make a score for *eyeSpace*. But after the initial reviews in New York, most presenters only wanted the original. Go figure. I remember feeling gratified from city to city as audience members came up after the performance and wondered how we had manipulated their iPods (this was early days for the player, so we traveled with 1,000 iPods, though if you had an iPod, you could download the score). I would happily tell them that they were a collaborator and that their perception was their own. But to be fair, having lots of propulsive prepared pianos possibly guaranteed that beats and dance moves would often coincide. In the end, the image of Merce sitting in the wings watching the dance and listening to the score on an iPod with a smile on his face will stay with me forever.

Eating dinners with Merce on tour was always a treat. He usually brought his own macrobiotic meal but was always happy with a group of people drinking wine. This reminds me of numerous special times. Cunningham was on tour, and we were in Naples, Florida, for a show. Rauschenberg invited the company to Captiva Island, where his home and studio are. It was a big affair, a BBQ of sorts. I met several of his assistants, and it was clear they rarely had a day off. I remember a story of one of his assistants wanting to take a vacation with his family, and Bob was flummoxed. Did he need to pay him more? No, no, the assistant replied. He just needed time with his family. I remember the spotless studio. So clean and different than the typical artist studio. He had paintings on the wall from what he called the "Runt" series. (I believe these would be the last paintings, and they were remarkable for a few reasons. When assistants would go away for anything, he would encourage them to take photos. Because of the ubiquity of a wide variety of digital cameras, some not so high quality, this lent a very "current" look to the pairings. Once again, Bob was ahead of the curve. But the other thing is Bob had lost use of his right hand due to a couple of strokes. So the new left-handed Rauschenberg signature was startling and poignant.)

There were tables of screen images for printing, and the environmental inks he championed were aligned on shelves in a neat order. In the center of the room were objects he'd collected around the island. A bathtub, lots of aged metal things, a ladder he'd constructed. It was a beautiful assemblage of objects that created an effect simply by being in the space. I remember showing Bob my sketchbook of drawings based around transfers, and he seemed happy to see them. He looked at me and said of this approach, "It's fun, isn't it?" The Cunningham company did a glorious drink-inspired performance on the lawn outside of Bob's studio. I watched as Merce and Bob watched from wheelchairs. Lives lived and fading was not lost on me. (I remember Laura telling me a story near the end of Bob's life. He told a caretaker that he thought his time might be nearing completion and he was sad, saying, "I had so much fun." I thought, what a lucky way to feel.) At the end of the day, we were all heading to the tour bus, but Russel, one of Bob's assistants, was stopping each of us as we stumbled down the wide stairs to the bus. He was wrapping a small, long piece of titanium around each person's finger and then snipping it and placing it in a small yellow envelope with each person's name on it. This titanium was used to frame the final Rauschenberg Runt paintings, and now the same material was being fashioned into rings to commemorate our time with Bob and his family of artists and assistants. It's a prized possession that will eventually go to my nephew, the artist Brennan Mikel Ponder. His sister, Katie, will inherit my dad's diamond ring. Katie gets the bling and Brennan gets the King.

We toured *eyeSpace* all over the world for two years. I was in the pit performing the cityscape portion of the show with Stephan whenever I didn't have conflicts with my own shows. One memorable performance was at Théâtre de la Ville in Paris. As we brought the city sounds up and down to various degrees, we would always have a few spots where we got very quiet, so as to not overwhelm the iPod listeners. At a certain point when the city sounds were very low, Stephan leaned over slightly confused and asked, "Do you hear that?" I said yes and wondered what it was. We both quickly realized the sound we were hearing that was filling the sold-out, 1,750-seat theater was the high-pitched, cricket-like leak from the earphones of each iPod. It was a truly remarkable sonic moment and we decided to let it ride. Years later, I would again be on that stage, rolling the dice to determine which score would go first for Merce's piece "Split Sides": Radiohead or Sigur Ros. I should have worked harder on my French.

It bears mentioning that along with the Cunningham Trust, *International Cloud Atlas* was also co-commissioned by Betty Freeman, who was a leading supporter of music and art in the twentieth century. She had learned of my work through Laura, who brought Betty to the Eclectic Orange performances of *Failing Kansas*. Laura confided in me later that she was very nervous at what Betty's response might be and was relieved when Betty leaned over during the performance and whispered, "He's a genius." Sue Devine from ASCAP had once again sent Pink's Hot Dogs, and I remember Betty's delight as she saw Dean and I tearing into those beauties. Betty became a fan and sent me many letters, and anytime I was in Los Angeles I'd love having a drink with her in her powder-pink or -blue matching suits. I heard this irked some composers, as Betty had lost interest in American composers after fifty years of support. When Betty passed away, a month or so later I got a card and it looked similar to the many cards I'd received over the years. Even the writing on the envelope seemed like her handwriting, which was disconcerting. Inside was a card with the David Hockney portrait of her and a note. She had planned in advance that these cards were to be sent after her passing. It was a remarkable and meaningful gesture.

There were memorable *eyeSpace* shows all over. But I have a fond memory of us landing at a hotel in Urbana for the Krannert Center performance. Paul Damski (see "*The End of Cinematics* (1998): Part 2") had cleared my head in the early Urbana days with the best coconut cream pie at his establishment, Carmon's. It had been a year or so since they closed, but knowing we were heading there, I reached out to Valerie Oliveiro, who had served as production manager for many of my shows. She reached out to Paul and told him I'd love to resample his pie, and he responded by saying he hadn't made them in a long while. But he made them for us, and Val and I showed up at his home to retrieve the pies. I took them back to the hotel and invited the Cunningham company to my room to tell them the story of Carmon's and possibly the best coconut cream pie ever. Then I carved those babies up and shared with the company. In return, they all signed an iconic reproduction of an early Jasper Johns poster of a target used as an advertisement for the Cunningham company in the '60s. Val and I took this signed poster to Paul, and I remember him crying in gratitude. The real deal. A funny addendum to this is when, a couple of years later, Jenny Goelz, my stage manager and two-time award-winning pie baker, decided to branch out and try to make a coconut cream pie. She brought it over to Mary Anne Lewis's house, and when Brad Hepburn and I heard a blood-curdling scream, we ran out to see that the container lid carrying the pie had come apart and the pie had landed meringue side down on the sidewalk. Jenny was heartbroken, but I ran inside and got us all forks and said, "This will be great!" And thus was born the Sidewalk Pie. I also relished landing in Venice after my performances with *eyeSpace* ended and losing days at Harry's Bar.

I also remember a non-*eyeSpace* event at New York State Theater. I think the piece was called "Occasion Piece" and teamed Merce and Mikhail Baryshnikov doing a duet of sorts with an amazing sculptural set by Jasper Johns. A set that included dance bars, so Merce had a place to hang onto as he did limited movement. Truly beautiful, and as so many of these types of fundraiser events do, it ended with a plush but mediocre dinner, and I remember going from table to table saying hi to folks. And there was Jasper, hovering over a bowl of ice cream, as if life depended on it. And at one time, it did, and my contention is you never forget. I also remember meeting Lou Reed at another Cunningham fundraiser. He was in tow with Laurie Anderson, and you would see them out and about in New York. He'd be at Blue Ribbon Sushi in Soho drinking a Diet Coke. You know. Anyway, I introduced myself and to my surprise he knew my band Tirez Tirez. But the truly surprising thing was he knew *Quorum* (see "*Quorum* (1984)"), but not from the Ailey and other dance performances. He knew it from the limited pressing record I made on my own label and distributed through Carla Bley's New Music Distribution Service. He compared it to his own "Metal Machine Music." Off the mark structurally, but god did I love that comparison.

All things must pass, and I was at my sister's place in Birmingham, Alabama, when I heard Merce had passed away. A week earlier, Lisa and I had gone to Merce's to say goodbye. Laura had skillfully, painfully, helped set up times for folks to come to say goodbye, as we all knew Merce was fading, but the drop-off seemed to happen quickly. I remember Lisa and I sitting with Merce. He asked for Laura to bring the three of us a glass of wine. Merce said something along the lines that it was good to see both of us, though acknowledging he wished it were under different circumstances. I remember that moment vividly. I didn't have nor ever sought a mentor. But Merce had become a kind sounding board. I remember when I didn't get a big award I was nominated for (so what else is new?), and I'd told Laura I was bummed, but on the other hand, maybe if I'd gotten that particular award, I would no longer be relevant. She relayed this story to Merce and told me later he laughed in recognition and said, "He'll be fine." As thoughts rushed in, I also remembered a dinner at Merce's when Jasper came. Merce had told Laura that things were looking up and they could increase the wine budget. So now they were getting $35 or $40 bottles. As you can imagine, I loved this. Anyway, that night Laura poured Jasper a glass of the upgrade, and he proclaimed it "delightful." Laura asked him, "Oh Jasper, do you know wine?" Jasper took another gulp, and with no hesitation replied, "Not at all." I've never forgotten that moment of clarity and honesty. Here was a guy who could have any wine in the world, but he knew the priorities. Jasper drove both Laura and me home afterwards, and I was surprised that he was listening to Bryan Ferry and asking me, "Do you know about this fellow?" Unexpected worlds meshing.

So there I am with Lisa and Laura and Merce at the end. And I told Merce I would send him an IOU for all the wine I drank at his place over the years. He laughed. A few days later I'm at my sister's place, as she's going to help me clear out a storage space in Ruston that Michael Mushalla (whose idea it was to store stuff there because it was cheap) has made clear is now my problem. I was sleeping in my nephew's bedroom the day before the drive from Birmingham to Ruston, and there was a powerful thunderstorm that woke me up. I felt disturbed and had a feeling that Merce had passed. And sure enough, it happened. My thoughts were with Lisa and Laura, but now I'm on the road to fix a problem. On the drive I got a call from Frank Oteri, a composer and great advocate of new music. He wondered if I would consider writing my memories of Merce, as I had been one of the last composers to work with him. With Frank's help, I managed to write a tribute for NewMusicBox.* I remember Merce's place being locked out, as there were countless art pieces from friends and archival materials worth lots of scratch. In fact, Lisa and I were invited to the auction at Christie's to sell the works and raise money for the Cunningham Trust. It was a wild and distinctive

---

* See my article, "Remembering Merce," NewMusicBox, accessed June 21, 2023, https://newmusicusa.org/nmbx/remembering-merce. I would later write another essay for NewMusicBox; see "The Dangers of Secondhand Music," accessed June 21, 2023, https://newmusicusa.org/nmbx/the-dangers-of-secondhand-music.

experience, being in a private room with great champagne and hors d'oeuvres overlooking the live auction. But my best memory was trying to show moral support for Laura as they cleared out John and Merce's loft. One day, when I arrived, she had a box with four medium-sized cacti, and she wondered if I would take them. These were the "amplified cacti" that Cage used in a performance. On January 1, 1984, twenty-five million viewers tuned in to watch "Good Morning, Mr. Orwell!," a live satellite program created by the Korean-born video artist Nam June Paik. And Cage played these cacti with a feather! I'm happy to report that not only do they continue to thrive, but I have replanted smaller offshoots.

The year 2012 saw the John Cage Prepared Sample library turned into an IOS and Android app, an installation of Cage's *James Joyce, Marcel Duchamp, Erik Satie: An Alphabet* along with a soundtrack CD for Cage's Satie and a film commission from the Cage Trust for the theatrical piece *The City Wears a Slouch Hat*. The app is kinda fun. As part of the Musée d'art contemporain de Lyon's exhibit "Cage's Satie," I was asked to recreate my score for Cage's *James Joyce, Marcel Duchamp, Erik Satie: An Alphabet* as a sound installation. The installation included the surround-sound score I created as well as interactive keyboards for museum participants to experience the sampled sounds from the original realization. I loved being in Lyon and had a good time exploring the city. The exhibit was beautiful, and the museum curators were great to work with. The film for *The City Wears a Slouch Hat* was an enjoyable project. This was basically a "stage film" for a live performance. It was part of a larger series called John Cage: On & Off the Air! *The City Wears a Slouch Hat* (CBS Radio, 1942) is based on a play by Kenneth Patchen. The commissioned film of light and shadows accompanied five onstage readers with music performed by the Canadian-based percussion ensemble NEXUS. It incorporated the use of shadows to simulate characters of a live performance. In this way, the "shadow film" mirrored the live action appearing on stage, as well as becoming a portable set.

I remember going to the Pony Bar in Hell's Kitchen and asking Katie O'Donnell to help me find five young shadows. We found five young guys who were willing to let me film their shadows for free beer. Seemed like a reasonable trade. We went across the street to what used to be a gas station and filmed several different length shadows. I knew I wanted to use the "film/sound triggering" effect I'd employed in *Gravity Radio* (see "*Gravity Radio* (2010)"), but I also knew that the effect of the pre-recorded shadows attached to the live performers onstage would create a wild double take, as what appeared to be the live performer's shadows would often move out of sync. Together with the onstage reading and music triggering the projections, it made for a subtly disorienting set.

Then in February 2013, the New World Symphony presented Making the Right Choices: A John Cage Centennial Celebration, a spectacular three-day festival dedicated to the music and ideas of John Cage. As part of the festival, NWS hosted a new video installation I created and entitled *NWS: 4'33"*, which consisted of video performances contributed by Cage fans via a special YouTube site set I set up. *4'33"* is John Cage's most famous—and controversial—work. Composed in 1952 for any instrument (or combination of instruments), the three-movement score instructs the performer *not* to play the instrument for the entire duration of the piece. The work, commonly referred to as "four minutes and thirty-three seconds of silence," consists only of the sounds of the performance environment. To create the video installation, I worked with programmer Austin Lin, the National Center for Supercomputing Applications (NCSA) at the University of Illinois at Urbana-Champaign, and the Illinois eDream Institute. I was the first visiting research artist of NCSA, an organization that is dedicated to promoting arts that are conceived, created, and conveyed through digital technologies. The public was invited to record and submit their own video and visit the installation during the festival to see their work in the SunTrust Pavilion at the New World Center. These videos were included in an online archive of the event, a lasting tribute to this defining and seminal artist. It was nice to meet Michael Tilson Thomas, who hosted a party at his place in Miami. I also somehow wangled a nice hotel on the beach, close to some of my favorite Cuban haunts. Which brings me back to 2001, sitting at Eisenberg's Sandwich Shop with Laura. Could that tuna fish sandwich on rye be as good as I said it was? In what could be seen as a harbinger of the many adventures Laura and I would have together, she took a bite and said, "That's a damn good tuna salad sandwich."

The End of Cinematics (1998)

I'm sitting at McManus bar with Joe Melillo. He would become the Brooklyn Academy of Music's (BAM) executive producer in 1999. But here in 1997, he's BAM's producing director under President/Executive Producer Harvey Lichtenstein. He's eating a sloppy burger and I'm pretending to not be hungry because I can't afford a sloppy burger. This was the decade I had holes in my shoes and avoided telling dates that I walked to them on the outer edges of the shoes in the rain, avoiding puddles in Soho. Joe had seen *Failing Kansas* and "appreciated the artistry" but didn't think it was for BAM. But seeing *Dennis Cleveland* at The Kitchen premiere changed all that, and Joe invited me to come meet with Harvey. The meeting went well, and Harvey, being a man of few words, basically said, "We want to work with you on your next project." Fortunately, I had the project in mind. As we left the meeting, I could see Joe was smiling and he could see I was stunned. He asked me what I had expected. I said I wasn't sure, but I was happy for the meeting to be so definitive. That's been rare in life. So we're having a quick meeting to talk about first steps moving forward. How to get me in front of some important folks in BAM's circle.

The End of Cinematics started out as a germ of an idea after reading two widely noted late essays by Susan Sontag in which she lamented the end of classical cinema, "The Death of Cinema" and "A Century of Cinema," both written for the *New York Times*. While she received a lot of pushback for these pieces, her nostalgia for a time when movies meant more than just a franchise resonated with me. And thematically, I could make a connection between both *Failing Kansas* and *Dennis Cleveland,* from issues of corporate consumption to ritual experience. I also knew that after the unique staging of *Dennis Cleveland,* I'd want something grand and magical, perhaps a melding of both film and live theater. I'd already started recording the soundtrack, a combination of '60s retro sounds, complex vocal counterpoint, and driving beat box grooves. I remember working on the Beatles-esque track "Drop the Ball" on New Year's Eve (I always liked to record something each NYE). It was about fifteen minutes until 1998, and I took a break to run outside to Times Square to see the ball drop (this was before police barricades and huge tourist crowds). I was underdressed in the freezing cold, and as I ran to Times Square, my lungs filled with cold air and I became lightheaded and thought: I'm running toward my future.

I had asked John Jesurun (see "*Dennis Cleveland* (1996)") about codirecting *Cinematics* and he seemed to like the idea, especially with the interest of BAM. He wrote a script that revolved around the movie business, and we even got so far as doing a staged reading with music at Arts at St. Anne's in Brooklyn in 1999. It was received well, but I wasn't thrilled with the script or John's behind-the-scenes maneuvering. Long story short: after 9/11 (*Cinematics* would ultimately take seven years to mount), Michael Mushalla, my agent, and I were having a hard time finding co-commissioners, and John got frustrated and pulled out of the project, which was for the best. So, Michael and I slowly set about regrouping and thinking about how to move the project forward. All the music had been written and recorded, and by 2000 I was doing a variety of shows that were increasing my profile as well as introducing my work to new presenters. BAM was also inviting me to events, including a benefit for Merce Cunningham where Anthony Creamer (a supporter and on Merce's board) introduced me to my future wife, Lisa Boudreau (this meeting would be immortalized in a cartoon of the two of us with the caption "Dick Hickock meets Holly Golightly").

Then I had an idea about shooting a feature film and incorporating CGI to remove performers from the set locations and replace them with live performers. I had no idea how to achieve this, but with the music component done, this would be the next hurdle. It doesn't sound like much now in these days of HD video on our phones, but I had acquired a semi-pro Sony PD150 DVCAM camera and set about to make films. I shot the film *Funding* (with Veanne Cox, Susana Ribeiro, and Lisa

Boudreau) in various locations and also shot a number of shorts. In November 1999, the Merce Cunningham company would do a two-week run at Théâtre de la Ville in Paris (the same theater we would do my dance score for Merce and iPods [see "*Cage/Cunningham* 1997–2013"] in 2007). I had become friendly with most of the dancers through my wife, Lisa, who was a dancer in the company, so I thought I might have a willing cast. Lisa also graciously participated in filming around Paris in the brief moments she wasn't rehearsing or performing. I remember one amazing sequence where Lisa performed her solo from Merce's *Interscape* on the streets of Paris as merchants and shopkeepers went about their business. We had limited time, but Lisa performed the solo three times so I could capture three different angles. Many people might not know that the Cunningham company always rehearsed in silence, not hearing a new score until the first performance. This meant they developed a very refined internal clock.

This was never more apparent than when I started the rough cut to this sequence on a laptop in Wellington (see "*Failing Kansas* (1995)"). When I lined up the three shots (each about five to six minutes long), I was flabbergasted that Lisa's timing was so precise between shots that it looked like we had actually had three cameras on one performance. I was gratified when I showed the footage to Merce at his kitchen bar, and he said he was happy to let me use it. Merce also attended the BAM performances of *Cinematics*, and those performances were dedicated to him. I shot many scenes with various dancers as well as a party scene. I also shot many scenes of myself, leaving the camera alone on a tripod on the streets of Paris.

I spent a long time cutting this footage into a stand-alone film that would be phase 1 of a complex six-screen edit. After the 2001 performances of *Dennis Cleveland* at the Krannert Center, Mike Ross agreed to be a commissioner on *Cinematics*. Through this commission I was introduced to Donna Cox, Robert Patterson, and Jeff Carpenter, who had started the art think tank eDream at the National Center for Supercomputing Applications in Urbana (starting in 2012, I became the first visiting artist for eDream). With Jeff Carpenter's excellent editing skills, we set about removing people from various scenes using CGI. We also incorporated beautiful abstract images created by Donna, Robert, and contributing designers from eDream. These scenes would provide "location backdrops" for live performers. These "video sets" would be comprised of six rear-projected screens (three at stage level and three above those) behind the performers. The original film would play on a full movie screen in front of the performers. The slick trick was working with the multitalented lighting designer Hideaki Tsutsui on a precise triggering system for the onstage light design that, in effect, turned the light grid into a film editor. When the lights were completely dark, the front screen was opaque like a normal projected film. But with the lights up, the three levels of front projection, performers, and rear projection created a dreamlike setting where an audience member was hard-pressed to know what was real or what was film.

The twelve-foot stage between the front and rear projection screens would appear to expand to forty feet, a powerful optical illusion. I got the idea from the eDream folks showing me HD stereo television. But I couldn't imagine everyone in the audience wearing 3D glasses. When we did tests, I was as surprised as the eDream team that the idea worked so well. They asked how I came up with the approach, and I replied, "You showed me stereo television, but I couldn't afford that."

It's hard now to think back on the long and winding process of getting to the build stage of *Cinematics*. Between 1998 and 2005, I recorded the albums *Return*, *Cameraworld*, *Test Tones*, and *Music for Minorities*. Michael and I had done a pitch session at International Society for the Performing Arts (ISPA) around 2004 and gained the support of Robyn Archer, an Australian singer, writer, stage director, artistic director, and public advocate of the arts. I first met Robyn when she booked *Failing Kansas* for the Melbourne International Arts Festival in 2001. I pulled together a fairly flimsy presentation but managed to project enthusiasm, and after I finished Robyn addressed the gathering thusly: "OK, I'm in. Who else?" Respect for Robyn's history and vision meant many other presenters signed on. Robyn became the artistic director of the Liverpool European Capital of Culture and was keen to bring the opera to Liverpool. Given the Beatles-influenced score, I was excited about this prospect. But the real test would be how and where to build the piece. The Krannert commission would turn out to provide more support than I could have ever hoped for.

After a false start with a designer for the show, Mike Ross suggested an architect-designer named Thomas Kamm. Thomas had worked with Robert Wilson and had a unique perspective on set building. His design became the framework for the rear-screen mounting and was an architectural marvel with a catwalk for performers to get to the upper-level screens. As the designs moved forward, I got the superb news that Krannert would host a one-month build of the piece in August of 2005 before the September 17 premiere at Krannert. Although I had garnered support for previous pieces I had financed, I had never had this kind of support at the initial build stage. The company would come to Urbana in waves, with the set builders first, followed by my camera crew, Jeff Sugg and Richard Connors. We had multiple cameras to capture the performers in front of the CGI-altered rear-projected video. These cameras would take their live feed (directed by Richard) and project the images onto the front screen (switched by Jeff). Jeff was also in charge of syncing the seven DVDs that fed the program material to the seven screens.

WATCHOUT is a multi-display software that has become a standard, but it was new in 2005 and we couldn't afford it. But the parent company Dataton made a more affordable alternative called Trax that could be used to sync multiple machines (like DVD players). So I had to take the final seven films that I edited with Jeff Carpenter back to my studio and author multiple sets of DVDs for the show. It's always hard to know when to save time or when to save money. We got a deal on six high-quality (but very old-technology) projectors for our rear-projection system, which was mounted backstage on a scaffold. We also got a deal on pro (but older) DVD players. Somehow, we mixed tenacity with a crackerjack production team and it all seemed to work.

In addition to the numerous stationary cameras around the stage, we managed to procure a $30K Sony robotic camera that traveled a train track, unseen by the audience, that was placed in front of the lower-stage performers. On tour, this was Richard's nightmare to wrangle, with Jeff's help. But during the build at Krannert, Tom Korder and Ray Dobson would delight in providing much-needed support and even traveled to a couple of dates to make sure everything ran smoothly. One precarious moment in the early stages of the build was when a boom hit Richard in the head, causing quite a gash. We were all concerned, but Richard said he was fine. He took out a cigarette and unrolled it, pressing the tobacco into the fresh wound. He said he learned the maneuver while working in Vietnam. I'll be darned if it didn't do the trick!

Working with Karen Quisenberry, I managed to get two more grad students for *Cinematics*, stage manager Jenny Goelz and sound designer Chris Ericson. I had worked with sound designer and instructor Jon

Schoenoff on the Krannert production of *Dennis Cleveland*, and, to my good fortune, Chris was John's first choice as sound designer for *Cinematics*. Chris and I have continued to work together even as he's gone on to work with major rock and hip-hop acts. I thought that filling Carolyn Cubit-Tsutsui's (stage manager on *Dennis Cleveland* and other solo pieces) shoes would be a challenge, but true to the Krannert grad program's history, Jenny was a perfect candidate for stage manager. She was an indispensable part of the *Cinematics* team during the entire tour and worked with me on many other, smaller shows. I remember a funny moment when the cast arrived, and the set was complete. We were working on blocking of the actors, and I wasn't very good at it. I would sit with Jenny in the theater and, like a kid with a magic box, we would move the actors to various locations while watching the effect on the various screens (often our affable carpenter, Brad Hepburn, would don my coat and fill in for me). At one point we were finally done with a small section that I would have sworn took hours. Seeing how exasperated I was, Jenny patted me on the shoulder and said, "That wasn't so bad for ten minutes of blocking." Jenny was soft-spoken, which could be deceiving when local crews on the tour thought they could take advantage of her. She always had a way of getting the regional teams on her side. Because of her position offstage (we had limited room because of all the backstage technology), she was in the sight lines of a very bright side light, so when calling the show, she took to wearing big sunglasses that reminded me of late-stage Elvis.

We tried to do casting in Urbana, as I've always been a fan of supporting local artists. We did a casting call around campus and town and set up a day or two of auditions. Jenny was there to supervise, and we had a piano player. While we had a couple of good choices, we needed the full cast to either come from Urbana or New York due to logistics. One particularly memorable moment was a young guy who came in with no music. He said he didn't need any accompaniment. He then broke into a thoroughly disjointed rendition of "Seventy-Six Trombones" from *The Music Man*. When he left, the room was completely silent, so surreal was the presentation. Back in New York, I set about to assemble a cast. I grabbed Robert Arthur Altman, who was previously in my piece *Cameraworld*. And I got Penelope Thomas from learning about her through Cunningham. Most fortunately, I met my future music director, Matthew Gandolfo, through Cynthia Enfield, who would also later join

Cinematics for the tour. Christina Pawl and Georgina Corbo rounded out the cast. The idea was to have three females play Lisa's filmed character from different camera angles and three males (including me) to play my role in the film.

With matching costumes and hairstyles, this synchronization of filmed and live characters helped create the otherworldly quality to the piece. The casting was complete, and it was great when they all arrived in Urbana. The cast and crew seemed to meld together in a convivial, shared commitment. When the cast arrived, Rebecca and her partner, Betsy, invited the cast and crew to their cabin-like house for a welcome BBQ. As a gift, I brought her a bottle of Don Julio Añejo, which Jeff, Richard, and I managed to kill. A vivid memory is seeing Jeff make a perfect jackknife into Bec's pool wearing Jenny's tiara crown made of corn (she had been christened Corn Queen by the *Cinematics* team after she wore the tiara to the Corn Festival in Urbana).

Dress rehearsal and opening night proved to be exciting and unique. I had wanted a full concession stand with soda pop, snacks, and a popcorn machine, for both their sensory impact and the consumption aspect, as well as for the shifting of perception this would create. This doesn't sound like anything now that even most Broadway theaters allow for drinks and snacks. But in 2005 this was not the case, and it took some time to convince folks at each and every venue. Another part of changing audience perception was to start the piece with a minimum of fifteen minutes of current "Previews of Coming Attractions." Luckily for me, I was able to rip these from the newly created iTunes video store (and, as if to prove my point about corporate entertainment, during the total *Cinematics* run of three years, there were no less than three different *Batman* movies). The seductive feeling of snacks and trailers truly set the audience up for the totally unexpected 3D film they would experience. For the final section, "WhiteBlackYellowBat," I was looking for a choreography that would heighten the finale. Matt had suggested the idea of using sign language, and Robert knew how to sign. We experimented with signing the closing lyrics (with the cast in pajamas and nighties). I liked the effect so much that we also employed it in other sections of the piece. I was excited to learn that a group of deaf students came to the show and were thrilled at the effect, which also included a visceral feeling due to the earth-shattering sub-bass that Chris had achieved in the sound design. The audience seemed genuinely blown away, and I could tell that Mike and the Krannert staff were pleased. I remember enjoying doing the talk-back with Mike to a packed house in my pajamas. I later learned from Dr. Robert Graves, dean of the College of Fine and Applied Arts, that after the show a theater student threw his program at the front screen, exclaiming, "Mikel Rouse is trying to destroy theater!" I wondered how he knew. But Mike Ross told me that the great opera singer Nathan Gunn had attended the performance and declared the piece "the future of opera!" He later took this opinion to Peter Gelb at the Metropolitan Opera (see "*Dennis Cleveland* (1996) Part 2").

At the end of the run, I was taken down to the lower level, where rehearsal spaces and offices were located. The scene shop had built a makeshift wooden ladder and platform for me to climb. The long hallway wall was the sort of industrial brick common in the 1960s, and to commemorate the *Dennis Cleveland* performances, they had painted one brick and asked me to be the first artist to sign the wall. I think I signed and dated it and drew a cartoon of myself. Soon the entire wall was painted as well, to start a tradition of artist signatures. My sound designer Chris Ericson told me that a year later, choreographer Ralph Lemon signed the wall but dated his stone earlier than mine so he could say he was the first. By the time Chris told me this, the wall was full of hundreds of artists, but hey, to each his own.

Michael Mushalla had rented a large tour bus packed with food and booze to lure many presenters from the Arts Midwest Conference to the Krannert premiere. This proved to be a winning strategy, as we got several commitments, including a generous invite from Joe Melillo to open the BAM Next Wave festival in 2006. Earlier in the build, I had been at a grocery store with Jenny and noticed a hard-to-find, high-end tequila called El Tesoro Paradiso. I hinted to Jenny that the cast would probably want to get me an opening night gift, and the cast took the bait.

When we got to Tod and John's, a nice dive bar for the after-party, it was packed with presenters, cast, and Krannert folks. I wanted to share the Paradiso with everyone, and the bartender generously proffered numerous shot glasses. I remember pouring this fine sipping tequila into many glasses, but the humorous part was that every time I filled Joe Melillo's glass, he downed it like it was a shot of Powers at Rudy's. So, all felt right with the world. Now we just had to figure out how to get this behemoth on the road in a year.

The End of Cinematics, Krannert Center for the Performing Arts, 2005.

The End of Cinematics, Krannert Center for the Performing Arts, 2005.

The End of Cinematics (1998)

Part 2

One of my favorite things to do in Urbana over the years was to go to a diner called Carmon's. It was run by a friendly guy named Paul Damski. He excelled at making possibly the best Coconut Cream pie I've ever tasted. The incarnation of Carmon's that I loved ended in 2007 (see "*Cage/Cunningham* (1997–2013)" for a great Paul Damski story). Around the corner and down a hill was an old-school BBQ joint called Po' Boys. Rebecca McBride knew I loved the historic places, so when a local paper did an article on Po' Boys, I jokingly busted her for not telling me about it.

Anyway, during the build at Krannert, the crew and I went. It was sublime in its decrepitness, and, as often happens with me, I ended up with the owner in the kitchen, trading shots with Jeff Sugg and Chris Ericson. A truly memorable night, but my mind was on how we would tour *The End of Cinematics*. I felt for the first time that I had a "dream team," but I also knew we'd need a production manager. I had met Will Knapp from working on the iPod score for Merce (see "*Cage/Cunningham* (1997–2013)"). Will had recently left his position at Cunningham and my wife, Lisa, had suggested him. It was a stroke of genius and Will slipped into the team perfectly, rounding out a stellar group for touring. From around 2002 to 2006, I was working on a three-year Meet the Composer residency in Ruston, recording and releasing three new albums (*Love at Twenty* from the Joe Goode Performance Group's production of *Grace*; *House of Fans*; and the iPod score for Merce's *eyeSpace*,

International Cloud Atlas). But there were numerous meetings to move the 2006–2007 (and beyond) tour of *Cinematics* forward. We knew we'd be rolling into the BAM Next Wave Festival in fall 2006, and we were hoping for a show or group of shows beforehand to make sure we had all the moving parts still moving. Next stop: Mondavi Center at UC Davis, so close to Swan Oyster Depot in San Francisco I can almost taste it.

We rolled into Davis and thankfully Tom Korder and Ray Dobson joined us to make sure everything still worked according to plan. I seem to remember an oddly cumbersome loading dock bringing in the set. I also remember a long man-made creek with ducks that took up all my free time. Michael had found a supreme wine bar near our hotel, and we made lots of progress there. I remember my mom and sister, along with Laura Kuhn from the Cage Trust, came for the show and I took them all for lunch, which might not sound like much, but I was feeling flush and picked up the tab. As I write this, I realize that part of the reason writing about *Cinematics* feels so vague is that I had a great team, so I wasn't always present for certain aspects of the build the way I was with previous shows. This was never clearer to me than on closing night at Mondavi as I walked back to the hotel and noticed a giant 18-wheeler parked outside of the theater. I wondered what big Broadway show was moving in after *Cinematics*, and someone told me: that's your show. I remember overhearing students outside after the show saying this was the future of cinema. Clearly it wasn't, but I liked the impact this had on them. I remember an after-party in Richard's room. I was both shocked and delighted that every mirror in his room was scribbled in Sharpie with notes and ideas for camerawork after each show (think John Forbes Nash Jr. from *A Beautiful Mind*). Now the show would be shipped for storage until the fall 2006 tour.

Enter Emil Kang, Executive Director for the Arts at the University of North Carolina at Chapel Hill. I remember arriving in Chapel Hill with cast and crew. We would be performing at Memorial Hall, which was a beautiful theater. The local crew was accommodating, and we all meshed together well. The interesting thing was that Chris Ericson, the sound designer we grabbed from the Krannert grad program, would later land a job as sound designer for the theater in Chapel Hill. So, when I came into town a year or so later with the Cunningham company and *eye-Space*, he would know the lay of the land and that made our load-in all the better. He also knew the best place for chicken biscuits. Emil had planned a number of symposiums around the show, and there were a number of high-profile panel discussions, many taking place in conference rooms in our hotel, which was walking distance from the theater. One such discussion involved a number of important university professor types who had done a deep dive into my work. At one point, it took on the feeling of "This Is Your Life," and I remember my agent, Michael Mushalla, and his partner, Mary Anne Lewis, being moved to tears for the recognition they felt I deserved. I was more stunned than anything. What I had presumed would be the traditional dog-and-pony, prerequisite publicity was taking on the air of a career tribute. Again, stunned. I remember chatting with some students after the show, who asked what the show was about. When I replied that it was about ninety minutes, they nodded in approval.

It's hard to imagine now, but there was a moment, racing to be forgotten, when performing at BAM was a sign of arrival. And this would be an even bigger season, as, after a week of shows at BAM, the Cunningham company would premiere *eyeSpace* at the Joyce Theater the following week (see "*Cage/Cunningham* (1997–2013)"). So, there were a lot of things to juggle. The company moved into a hotel near BAM, and it was decided that even though I lived in Manhattan, it might be smarter for me to stay there as well. Strange feeling, but I was happy to stay with the company. The folks at BAM's Harvey Theater (formerly the Majestic and renamed for Harvey Lichtenstein) were incredible. I remember the costume people being particularly inviting, and the show seemed to benefit from the build time in Chapel Hill. The fit of the set and rear projection setup was tight at the Harvey, and a day or so before opening, we realized that the rear projection throw was off, and we'd need lens adapters to accommodate the issue. The trouble was, these were very old projectors and finding the lenses proved difficult. If I remember correctly, we found three in one state, two in another, and still one more in another. These would all have to be FedExed overnight—and also work. I remember feeling a serene sense of calm as opposed to my normal mode, and I attributed this to having the best team available. In a rare moment of clarity, I knew everything would be alright. I had received the Foundation for Contemporary Arts award in 2001, and Stacy Stark, the executive director, had asked me if she could bring a group to see some of the build. The set was a site to behold, and from city to city, presenters loved to show off the build.

I had hired a publicist, hoping that the two weeks I would have in New York would be enough to encourage some advance press. But as the dates quickly approached, we weren't even getting normal listings. Don't get me started on publicists. But one thing luckily happened that may have turned the tide. Steve Smith, the shining classical critic, did a feature in *Time Out New York*, which also placed a pic on the table of contents page as well as a blurb on the cover. Some other small preview pieces trickled in, and suddenly there was buzz mere days before the opening. It was also a shift in importance to a younger generation. They were more clued in to *Time Out* than the *New York Times*. I remember the constant battle for a concession stand, and food and drink in the theater was particularly difficult at BAM. Fortunately, at some point, Joe Melillo relented and said that if I thought it was essential to the show, we could do it. Again, hard to imagine now, but there you go. Opening night was electric, with lots of artists and muckety-mucks cramming into the lobby. I was nervously going back and forth from the dressing rooms to the lobby to get bags of popcorn (I always liked to test it). There was an additional level of stress moving into BAM, as Lisa and I found out we were being audited, because that's who you go after: struggling artists. This would be the first of two audits, both coinciding with runs at BAM (see "*Gravity Radio* (2010)").

I think on opening night, the top stage-left rear projector went out. It hardly mattered. The piece was a hit and something that most folks were hard pressed to describe. Even at the toast backstage, which was packed, Joe Melillo contemplated his kind words. Mike Ross from Krannert was there along with Michael Mushalla, and Joe thanked "the three Mikes" for "whatever it was we just saw." I found this expression marvelous given BAM's reputation for challenging work. Matt Johnston wrote on NYTheatre.com, "When I left Mikel Rouse's revolutionary *The End of Cinematics* at BAM, I felt as if every sense I had, and possibly a sixth, had been completely sucked dry. In the late nineteenth century, there was an artistic movement in Europe led by Richard Wagner for a 'total work of art,' or a 'synthesis of the arts.' Rouse, in *The End of Cinematics,* may have unknowingly stumbled upon an answer to a great many of the questions Wagner and his followers spent years trying to resolve. And he has done it with a uniquely twenty-first-century flavor." And the *Voice* opined, "On the way in, the audience receives a free cup of popcorn and is then treated to a series of actual previews for such upcoming Hollywood blockbusters as *Spider-Man 3* and *The Simpsons Movie*. But what comes next is like no other movie you've ever seen." Even Allan Kozinn from the *Times*, while not fully understanding it, couldn't ignore it: "Maybe proposing a grand concept for a nonlinear work is, by definition, asking for an argument. But the argument shouldn't obscure this work's strength, which is Mr. Rouse's music. Sometimes built on heavy, repetitive beats, and sometimes couched in Beatlesesque psychedelia, the songs are vivid, pleasingly visceral, and often engagingly harmonized, with amusingly off-kilter lyrics. That should be a sufficient draw, bigger themes notwithstanding." Bigger dreams notwithstanding. Just sayin'. But Joseph McCombs in the *Voice* missed a traditional narrative, saying, "Rouse has created a technologically stunning production, with filmed projections on the scrim that are more real than holograms, but his destruction of plot is ultimately isolating." Next stop: Gainesville, Florida.

Michael Blachly had come from UCLA and was now the arts director at Florida State University. He had booked *Cameraworld* in 2002 and had a long running relationship with Michael Mushalla. The cast and crew were there building the show, and my memory is that I was in a few places at once. The Merce tour of *eyeSpace*, the *Grace* shows in San Francisco with the Joe Goode Performance Group, and other travel. It was truly a whirlwind, and I would literally be flying in on the day of the show and flying out the next day. I had remembered loving a 100-year-old burger joint in Gainesville during *Cameraworld* called Louis' Lunch (not to be confused with the classic Louis' Lunch in New Haven, Connecticut, which claims to have invented the hamburger), digging both the decor and the food. But I was informed that due to rehearsal, press, and general time crunch, I wouldn't get to go. Without the atmosphere it wasn't the same, but Jenny brought me a burger from Louis' Lunch and it was still sublime. I was grateful to Michael Blachly for co-commissioning the show and showing support. But because of my schedule at the time, I don't remember much about the show there. Now, Liverpool. That's a different story.

I remember there being all sorts of issues shipping the set, but thankfully, with the passage of time, I can't remember all the particulars. But I do remember the stress. The crew went a week or so before and started the build. I also remember arriving with Lisa (or she might have joined later in the week) and hitting the ground running. Lisa had given me a book of the fifty oldest pubs in Liverpool. So, there was a lot of work to be done. The show was loading in to the Royal Court Theatre. Space was cramped and you could hardly get on or off the stage. The Royal Court had a large, wooden, engraved bar at the back of the house, in full view from the stage, with the smell of alcohol wafting about. It felt so much more real and less stuffy than other spots, and obviously the concession stand issue was moot. It felt like real reverence for the days when high art and popular entertainment weren't so separate. There was also a door offstage that had a big sign saying ASBESTOS. I arrived around the same time as the cast, and, as was custom, the cast and crew met in the hotel lobby for an itinerary briefing. It was clear that many high jinks had already begun. Brad Hepburn, our carpenter, had accidentally managed to spend his entire per diem in one day, possibly confusing the exchange rate. Or the strip bar. Hard to know. Liverpool is a drinking town, and with the buzz of Liverpool as the European Capital of Culture, there was a feeling of fun and camaraderie with the locals and our cast and crew.

I remember going to the Cavern Club (way past its prime and a tourist trap) and being confronted by unruly drunks who hated Americans (blame former president and current portrait painter George W. Bush) and were ready to punch me. Since Lisa is Canadian, I said I was as well and averted a showdown. Lisa and I also toured Strawberry Fields and had cocktails across from the roundabout at Penny Lane. It was a good but odd moment of wandering. We also went to Lennon's favorite bar and saw a painting by Stu Sutcliffe (look it up). The pubs were great and authentic, but everything else was Beatles capitalism and made for a bit of a letdown. Speaking of minor letdowns, Michael and Mary Anne had tried to get Paul McCartney to come to the opening, but word had it that he was in the middle of a divorce and couldn't get a leg up. I truly loved doing *Cinematics* in Liverpool, and it remains a highlight of my life. Sitting in the pubs and our hotel around the corner from the theater. Eating fish and chips. Reveling in the connection of this piece and my childhood fascination with England. The feeling that you can go home again, even if it's not your home. Eating curry late at night with Lisa in our hotel. The feeling that I wouldn't forget this, even though I have misplaced it. Many hotel memories and cast and crew tearing it up but never missing their cues.

The shows were exceptional, and something about being able to see the crowd and the bar through the front scrim made for an exciting event. Lisa had actually worn the Agnès B. houndstooth coat that was the model for the female costumes. Her hairstyle had changed since that long-ago shoot in Paris, but we had a fourth wig in wardrobe just in case. I came up with an idea of a practical joke (this company was constantly pulling jokes on one another), where Lisa would subtly join us onstage. The surreal montage of live performance and film was such that I wondered what the effect would be. I wasn't gonna tell anyone, but my respect for Jenny was so profound that I told her, so as not to blind-side her. So, when the song "Be More Really" started, both Lisa and I entered stage right. Everyone was on stage at this point, but now there were four Lisas instead of three. Lisa moved and lip synced to the song as the rest of us did our routine. I later learned that Mary Anne leaned over to Michael in the audience and said, "That one really does look like Lisa!"

The last show was followed by a long night of partying, starting with the load-out. Michael had gotten a case of beer for the crew, and I remember him sitting at the loading dock. We met up with some cast and crew at a pub that was just down the hill from our hotel. I think Lisa and I retired by 1 a.m. or so, but for some the night was just beginning. Chris was famous for making friends everywhere, and somehow a couple he met ended up in his bathtub until he finally told them at 5 a.m. they had to leave. We had to travel early, and when Lisa and I got to the lobby, it was clear that some folks were still MIA. I remember Michael asking the concierge about some of our crew. He replied in a perfect upper-crust accent, "I do recall a Mr. Hepburn coming down and asking for beer at 5 a.m." Things were getting tight, so Michael sent some of us ahead. Lisa and I were sitting in the airport as cast and crew wearily entered in waves. This slow-motion film played out until everyone eventually arrived, a fitting end to one of the best times. Phillip Key in the *Liverpool Daily Post* said of the show, "*The End of Cinematics* is one of those shows that you are unlikely to forget. Directed, produced, and written by American composer Mikel Rouse, it leaves the jaw dropping, the eyes widening, and the ears filling."

I had been to the new Carnival Center in Miami with the Cunningham company and knew we would be bringing *Cinematics* in a couple of months. It was a giant space and I remember how our set, which usually barely fit into most theaters, looked like a tiny house in a giant airplane hangar. As Chris commented recently, "We thought we were badass until that venue." I don't remember much about the shows. Woody Allen's ragtime band was playing across the street. I think we were there New Year's Eve week. There was an old Cuban sandwich place I knew about from previous shows in Miami, and I took a long cab ride to get there. I also don't remember a lot of specifics about the Eclectic Orange Festival at the Irvine Barclay Theatre in California other than my gratitude to Dean Corey for being the first presenter to have presented all three operas of the trilogy (though the Luminato Festival was in the offing). As was often the case, I was already working on a new piece, and I had a rough mix of the song "Wait for Me" from *Gravity Radio*. I played it for the cast on the drive to the theater one day and they seemed genuinely impressed, especially since Penelope had sung on it. I remember Jenny couldn't make this performance and Valerie Oliveiro, who had done several of my solo shows, would take her place. Val was a great stage manager as well, and since she and Jenny were close, the transition was smooth. I remember continuing the tradition of bringing fifty or 100 Pink's hot dogs that the cast and crew devoured in someone's room. After a load-out, there was usually a party in someone's room, and as the party devolved, we would usually play a game of flipping beer bottle caps across the room. Jenny always hated this game and would reprimand everyone, warning that someone is "gonna shoot an eye out." As luck would have it, this happened, and Chris was struck in the eye and seemed in really bad shape. But as he held his eye, he knew the priorities and pleaded, "Don't tell Jenny."

HOLLY GOLIGHTLY MEETS DICK HICKOCK ...

Food sketches and cartoons.

Bars & Restaurants (1965–2021)

My radar for great places to eat and drink started as a very young child. It's amazing to me how natural my connection has been to chefs and bartenders over the years. Music, performing, filmmaking, and painting have all been rewarding, but always a struggle of hard work. Not so with restaurants; from the earliest days I would find myself invited into kitchens all over the world. I've never known why it came so naturally, but many friends have witnessed and commented on my good fortune regarding the hospitality world, telling me I had "the common touch." I think part of it may have been my early disdain for corporate fast-food chains. I was always drawn to the indigenous, homespun places, and growing up in southeast Missouri provided plenty of options. My small town of Poplar Bluff provided many examples of simple, honest food, from the pancakes at the Frontier Motel to the Beetle Burger at the curbside diner Frosty's. The BBQ and pink lemonade at Hayden Drive-In (forty-five years later I would tour-guide John Clark, who runs Hayden, around New York, and he would return the favor by mailing me ten pounds of ribs and sauce). Playing for fries on the pinball machine with Rick Campbell at the Deer Run restaurant. The best chocolate malt, the malt that I would use to judge all malts for years to come, at Belknap Pharmacy before the Walmarts of the world gutted downtown. And bar life started early with Dad every Saturday morning at Cotton's Lounge or the K.C. Hall, sometimes bored to tears and begging to go home. My good fortune in these places might have started there: a waitress or two who felt sorry for my plight and gave me a free Coke and a quarter for the jukebox.

In 2016 my mom, Martha Sue Rouse, my sister, Cindy Ponder, and I visited my nephew Brennan Mikel Ponder in St. Louis. I was born in the Kirkwood section of St. Louis, and Mom showed us the small apartment building where we first lived. Around the corner is a burger joint called Spencer's Grill that we used to go to. I don't remember it because I think we moved from there when I was two. But it had such a strong pull, and I wouldn't be surprised if the community and authenticity of this little diner somehow stuck with me and helped plot my future. I would visit St. Louis several times while attending the Conservatory of Music and the Art Institute in Kansas City, Missouri. Crown Candy Kitchen was a favorite stop. Established in 1913, it used to be part of a bustling community. The neighborhood became all but empty in the '60s, so it was pretty sketchy to go there in the '70s. But always worth the trip. I never did the five-malt challenge, but I bet I could have done it. One of my best friends in KC, Jim Bourgeois, was originally from St. Louis, and he turned me on to a burger counter called Carl's Drive-In, a treasure. But in 1975 I was going through St. Louis to get to Kansas City. Although as a kid, due to proximity, I spent a fair amount of time in Memphis ("that house there"—meaning Graceland—"is where Elvis lives," I would say), KC was my first big city. I was working on a deficit in terms of book learning, so there was a lot of catch-up to do. But from the very beginning, I would hear about a legendary BBQ place that was the Mecca for aficionados: Arthur Bryant's Barbecue.

There were and are many great BBQ joints in KC. Having cut my teeth on southern BBQ, I was potentially a skeptical snob. A couple of weeks in, I decided to make the pilgrimage. And to say I was underwhelmed would be an understatement. Weird sauce. Focus on beef more than pork. Whatever. But there's one quality I've always liked about myself: I often question what I don't like rather than write it off. This happened with the early stages of *Failing Kansas* and similarly, two weeks after going to Bryant's, I couldn't get it out of my mind. So, I went back and tried it again, and I'll be damned if the clouds didn't open and the angels started singing. It was sublime and like nothing I'd ever experienced. It was original while still being BBQ. And the gravelly, vinegar-based sauce is like nectar. It became my go-to spot and I'd look forward to seeing

Arthur Bryant perched on the stool pouring the Budweisers, flanked by his two Doberman Pinschers.

The sauce used to come in antique glass beakers that would crust around the top so that sometimes only a trickle would come out. A favorite memory is when the Cunningham company and I came to KC almost thirty years later and I took them on a tour (literally, in the Cunningham tour bus) to multiple spots: LaMar's Donuts (which brings a memory of trudging through a snowstorm with Rob Shepperson in 1976 for a box of the glistening lard delights), and Stroud's Chicken ("We choke our own chickens"), where Merce even joined us and watched with curiosity the "family-style" service. I even took them to a crack in the sidewalk on Wyandotte Street, where, in 1977, consumed with fear of mortality and nuclear conflagration, I looked down, saw the crack, and had the epiphany: you won't solve these problems, get on with living. But I was most excited to take them to Bryant's. The food and vibe were exactly the same and as good as I remembered, and I wistfully commented on this. My good friend Jim Bourgeois burst out laughing when my wife, Lisa, with no intended irony added, "And just think, Mikel, most of these dancers weren't even born when you used to come here."

Sanderson's Lunch was a staple on a steep street all the way downtown that usually got interesting around three a.m. Same with Wolf Burgers near the Plaza, where fellow student and painter Mike Stoughton worked for a spell. When I returned decades later with my friends Mark Lambert and John Margolis, Mark would exclaim as we headed for the rental car in the Wolf Burger parking lot, "Does the car look like it's gotten smaller?" Also in the Plaza was Putsch's Cafeteria, a favorite old-school place. Russell Stover chocolates on Linwood Boulevard (Jim's young son twenty years later would say of it, "I want some of that candy in the paper"). Maxine's for soul food placed directly on plastic serving trays. Town Topic for late-night burgers. Dave's Stagecoach Inn in Westport and the Jewel Box Lounge on Main Street (originally on Troost Avenue beginning in 1948) were character-driven spots, the latter being where cross-dresser (or as it was called at that time, "femme mimic") Mr. Mickey Marlowe performed, the show culminating in the flashing of a missing front tooth. Also, Milton's Tap Room, a jazz bar, and the Pink Garter strip bar. Solid gold!

Speaking of Mike Stoughton, we did a road trip to New York in 1978, less than a year before I would move there with the original incarnation of Tirez Tirez (Rob Shepperson and Jeff Burk). I think we stayed the night with fellow KC transplant Tom Rubnitz, who worked with the B-52s and was a video artist. That trip solidified for me that the band had to come here ASAP. Eventually, after the band had driven across the country in Betsy, our VW van, we landed in our dream loft on Fourteenth Street and Sixth Avenue. Down the street was Joe Jr's, where every Monday was pea soup day—and Rob and I never missed a Monday. Tom Verlaine of Television lived right around the corner and would always give a kind, approving nod when picking up his coffee. Mayor Ed "How am I doin'?" Koch was often at the counter. Decades later, I would be standing outside of Joe Jr's with Lisa in deep conversation when a tourist couple interrupted us to ask where Soho was. I pointed south down Sixth avenue, and they asked, "How will we know?" Without missing a beat, I replied, "Big sign." The look on Lisa's face was priceless. Also in my hood was the Coffee Shop across from Union Square Park (which was a needle park at the time; and on the other side of the park was Max's Kansas City, past its moment but we were happy to play shows there). The Coffee Shop became trendy in the '90s, and I'd go there with Mark Lambert and Sônia Braga, whom he was dating at the time.

But it was a truly authentic coffee shop in the early '80s. I have a fond memory of being included in a *Vogue* arts section called "Welcome to the '90s," which included Jonathan Demme, Anselm Kiefer, and Melanie Griffith, to name a few. A great photographer named Andrew Southam took me all over the city, including rooftops, to capture the photo that would accompany the article. It was literally an eight-hour shoot, and the next day he called in the bad news that he hadn't gotten "the shot." Luckily, after the shoot, I had asked if he would mind taking a shot of me through the glass window (for that reason alone probably not usable) of the Coffee Shop. When I asked him about that shot, he took another look and exclaimed, "That's it!"

It's hard now to imagine how vacant and dead it was between Fourteenth and Twenty-Third Streets. Billy's Topless was a great bar at Twenty-Fourth and Sixth Ave. Heading north was the classic Terminal Bar across from Port Authority. There were lots of old Irish bars with steam tables. The Distinguished Wakamba Cocktail Lounge still sits at its Eighth Ave location. The historic Landmark Tavern at Forty-Sixth and Eleventh Ave has possibly the best pour of Guinness outside of Dublin, and owners Michael Younge and Donnchadh O'Sullivan were saints helping the locals in Hell's Kitchen during Covid. The band spent a fair amount of time at the watering hole La Bamba at the intersection of East Twelfth Street and Second Ave. I learned PAC-MAN and Donkey Kong at La Bamba while listening to Lou Reed on the jukebox. In those early days living in our loft, much of the action was below Fourteenth Street. Clubs like Tier 3, CBGB, and the Mudd Club. After a late night we'd head to Dave's Luncheonette at the corner of Broadway and Canal for egg creams and fried onions, though the best egg cream was to be had at Gem Spa, a newspaper and candy stand on St. Mark's and Second Avenue that sadly closed during Covid. Late nights after shows at Sam Wo's on Mott street in Chinatown; the Ukrainian triumvirate of Kiev Restaurant, Odessa, and Veselka. The Cedar Tavern, way past its prime, but soaking up that art history. McSorley's Old Ale House, commemorated by Joseph Mitchell in his essay collection *Up in the Old Hotel*, where the saltine crackers, cheese, raw onions, and hot mustard often constituted my only meal of the day (a bartender there swore me to secrecy when he gave me the recipe). I loved going to the old Automat, with its gleaming chrome-and-glass machines; Forty-Second Street over the years. And I recall being there in 1991 with photographer Susan San Giovanni and seeing someone else taking photos of the place. We knew that was a bad sign, and sure enough, in two weeks it was gone.

Below Forty-Second Street on Ninth Avenue used to have a host of magnificent old Italian places. Supreme Macaroni Co. was a reliable red sauce joint where I learned the simple pleasure of pasta with garlic and oil. You'd walk by a small counter and pass through curtains that transported you to another place in time. Red-and-white checkered tablecloths over rickety tables. A friendly cat roaming around. Just a sublime family experience. Across the street was the excellent Italian grocery store called Manganaro's (I'm reminded of Di Palo's Fine Foods, a favorite shop in Little Italy and an original; the joy in reading Mario Batali sheepishly promoting the new Eataly when asked about comparisons to Di Palo's). Manganaro's was run by a friendly guy named Sal Dell'Orto, who made a superlative espresso. The rice balls in tomato sauce were perfection as were the Italian sandwiches on semolina bread. The place was eventually taken over by his daughter, Seline, whom I adored, but thankfully I never crossed her. Anthony Bourdain wasn't so lucky, and I remember Seline gleefully telling me the story of dressing him down. I was reminded how Bourdain ordered tuna on white toast at Eisenberg's and a fruity cocktail at Keen's Steakhouse (missing the best scotch list in the city), and I thought, "You go, Seline." Right next door was Hero Boy, which was famous for its six-foot hero. It was run by Sal's brother, James, and there was a thirty-year feud over the rights to use the "Manganaro's Hero-Boy" name. This was a local drama that only resolved when the grocery store closed in 2011. Hero Boy hung in until 2021 and was likely defeated by Covid. That's a 100-year history gone but certainly not forgotten.

All these places and more were on the Ninth Avenue strip that comprised the Ninth Avenue Food Fair. Considered one of the longest running food festivals in New York, it uniquely focused on small and family-run businesses in the neighborhood. Meaning it wasn't about gouging folks for money but a way to cheaply introduce people to quality products in the hopes of making new and loyal customers. This worked well until high rents and late-stage capitalism forced most family-run institutions out of the hood. A favorite stop on the midway is the ninety-eight-year-old Poseidon Bakery, now run by Lili Fable and her son, Paul Fable. The family-run business has a long and storied history. This Greek bakery still makes their own filo dough, which is the best use of dough in the world. Their spanakopita (spinach pie) is the best in the city, but the secret to my heart is the cherry cheese strudel, which reminds me of a childhood pie my mom always made.

To say that Poseidon is as essential as breathing would be an understatement. Up the street used to be Bruno Ravioli, an old-school Italian market where I'd buy pasta and sauce. At the food fair, a heaping plate of their ravioli would go for one dollar. Grab a couple of plates and head over to Mark Lambert's railroad apartment and listen to music. It was a sad day when they closed. But like a good family, the Fables at Poseidon helped keep the dream alive by also offering Bruno's ravioli and sauce.

At Twenty-Second and Fifth Ave sits Eisenberg's Sandwich Shop, a depression-era sandwich counter, shuttered now due to Covid. Monus Eisenberg sold it to Steve in the 1980s, I think, with the stipulation that certain items must remain on the menu (especially the classic tuna salad on rye toast) and he couldn't put in a grill; this was a classic sandwich place, not a burger joint. In 2005, Steve sold the business to Josh Konecky, an affable guy who kept the vision alive. I remember counterman Phil Perry who was kind of cantankerous, as a New York waiter should be. His section was known as "The Hawaiian Room," where he worked for thirty years and is still commemorated with a sign he hung himself many years ago. Victor was also a great sandwich maker and never asked me for my order. He knew it would be tuna on rye with a lime rickey. For forty-plus years, I've told friends that when Eisenberg's goes away, so will I. We'll see.* I'm reminded of the great Warren Zevon's advice on life: "Enjoy every sandwich."

Speaking of great things going away, in 2012, after seventy-four years in business, Prime Burger, on Fifty-First Street across from St. Pat's Cathedral, closed. Michael and John DiMiceli ran it during the thirty-five years or so that I would go, charming friends with the honest food and the tight booths with swivel trays reminiscent of school desks. I remember in 2004 both Prime Burger and Esca got the James Beard Award, and I remember thinking: I cover the waterfront. The typical corrupt New York real estate story, but when the building was being sold, Michael and John were told they could stay only to discover they had two weeks to clear out. As news spread, I was inundated with calls from friends whom I had introduced to Prime Burger, begging me to take them. I was there every day for two weeks. In the beginning it was sad, and the crowds were sparse. I particularly remember server Artie Ward, a career waiter there for sixty years, looking downtrodden. But as the week went by, more and more regulars began coming until it was packed, and the sadness gave way to ebullient joy as employees and patrons basked in the honesty and quality of a New York institution.

In 2015, Carnegie Deli was another great loss to the New York landscape. I started going there when I moved to Hell's Kitchen in 1982 and co-owner Leo Steiner was working the crowd. I met Henny Youngman there and gave it my best shot: "My girlfriend lost her job at the orange juice factory. She couldn't concentrate." He smiled and said, "Not bad,

---

* In September 2022, just as I was packing my bags, Eric Finkelstein and Matt Ross, the owners of Court Street Grocers, opened the doors of S&P, a restaurant located in the former home of Eisenberg's. An institution continues and a crisis is averted.

kid." At one time it was a twenty-four-hour spot, and I remember being on a late-night date with the place practically empty except for Jackie Mason going from table to table, saying hello to the lucky few who were there. Leo died on December 31, 1987, and I remember hearing the news while sick in bed. I commemorated his passing with a biographical cartoon. Down the street at Broadway and Forty-Sixth Street was the last of three Howard Johnson restaurants in Times Square. While not a great food spot, they did have a decent happy hour. They also had an odd configuration of booths that got smaller and narrower as they approached the front door entrance, culminating in a single, one-seat booth just in front of the large window facing Broadway. As this was the Macy's Thanksgiving Day parade route, I was virtually guaranteed a front-row seat, as most people would be in families or larger groups.

Some friends thought this was sad, to be alone at Thanksgiving, but they weren't cozy in a front-row seat before heading to Rudy's Bar & Grill for the annual free Thanksgiving festivities. There was also a hidden luncheonette that I loved in the Diamond District that overlooked a trading floor. So many lost Cuban Chinese places in HK, where meals were good and cheap. The blintzes at Ratner's on Delancey and pastrami at Katz's on Houston, two sides of the same coin. Mashed potatoes and martinis at Odeon on West Broadway. On the ground floor of the Brill Building was the venerable Colony Records, whose logo boasted: "I found it! at The Colony." Also, the DJ-hub Rock and Soul near Penn Station and the chain Disc-O-Mat.

There used to be jaunts to Harlem after Tirez Tirez shows in the '80s. Some great underground clubs and speakeasies along with stalwarts like the Lennox Lounge. We would invariably end up at the M&G Diner on 125th Street. The beautiful old signage advertised "Old Fashioned BUT Good" and boy, was it. Some of the best fried chicken and cornbread to be had and the 45-rpm jukebox stocked with classic jazz, blues, soul, and gospel. The cover of their menu stated simply, "Soul Menu," which I used as a title for the fourth Mikel Rouse Broken Consort record, and I used a black-and-white shot of me walking out of M&G for the back cover of the original New Tone release of *Living Inside Design*. That's how strong my love is. And heartbroken when the building was sold in 2008 and the owners never returned from vacation. The last time I was up there getting my haircut (from Claudio, the best Italian barber in the five boroughs), I passed by to see a remnant of the small sign still hanging from a pole in what is now a nondescript shoe store. Just up the street on 145th was The Reliable, the takeout and more affordable alternative to the upscale soul food destination, Copeland's. Devouring black-eyed peas and collard greens from the steam table on a Sunday as folks flocked in after church services is an indelible memory of community and humanity. I consider myself a glazed-donut connoisseur and Georgie's Pastry on 125th Street surpassed them all, even LaMar's in KC. Like the unexpected originality of Bryant's BBQ, Georgie's had taken a classic glazed but added spices and seasonings that elevated the lightly fried dough into a masterpiece.

There were many great old-school places in Brooklyn that I'd visit since I had a lot of friends who lived out there. The island of Coney alone has a treasure trove of spots, including the original Nathan's hot dog stand. And the Shooting Gallery. The Parachute Drop. I would make many of my "shaky films" at Coney. Up on the boardwalk is Ruby's bar, which mixes great piña coladas and showcases historic photos of when Coney Island was the center of the world (before ubiquitous electricity made the reality of Manhattan more fantastic than the fantasy of Coney). Toasting the elephant probably didn't help either. Totonno's Pizza on Neptune Ave is the oldest pizza parlor in the five boroughs existing at the same location, and it's still the best. I was once at the Plaza having a cocktail with Lisa, and we chatted with a wonderful older woman until her husband came and we realized he was the owner of the original Grimaldi's Pizzeria in Brooklyn. We had such a nice chat that he wrote his name on a napkin and added a pizza and a bottle of wine and told us to come by and the meal was on him. We did a month or so later, and he honored the napkin. Patsy's in Harlem and Lombardi's and John's in Manhattan are also great.

Hinsch's in Bay Ridge was a classic ice cream parlor. Balmont's is a 1900s-era red sauce joint and, along with Monte's, constitutes the best in old-school Italian. Two Tom's Chophouse in Gowanus, which had portions as big as a house in a social club atmosphere. Keen's Steakhouse in Manhattan is still my favorite place though; sitting at the bar and remembering an old steak house called Frank's in what was once the Meatpacking District of Manhattan. I somehow learned that Frank's would open at two or three a.m. to make breakfast for the workers down there, and I would stop in after late-night shows. Plowing through the snow to get to Tom's Restaurant in Prospect Heights for burgers and malts and family service. Doing radio interviews at WKCR at Columbia University, on a sugar rush from the malts at the Mill Luncheonette.

Walking in any direction, from Harlem or Soho, I could always manage to find my way to the Lexington Candy Shop on Eighty-Third and Lex (just up the street used to be the Ideal Coffee shop, which was a favorite late-night hang, an old-school New York counter but with a German twist, so the pan-fried potatoes were miles above the afterthought home fries of Greek diners). Always a reminder that the city had hundreds of great coffee shops before Starbucks made burnt coffee fashionable. Chock Full o'Nuts's numerous counters were a much better alternative. Like Hoft's Candy Store, which used to be on Burke Ave in the Bronx and made possibly the best malts and egg creams on the East Coast, Lexington Candy Shop used to make their own candy. The menu was a little pricey for the excellent but simple fare of malts, burgers, and grilled cheese, but I chalked that up to the cost of staying put on the Upper East Side. Countless lunches there, but after Lisa and I were married in a private ceremony, we decided to have a party there as well. We rented the place and just used the regular menu. Cunningham board member and a great supporter of the arts Tony Creamer sent over a couple of cases of amazing champagne, and we were set with the perfect combo: milk shakes and bubbly. It might not have been Capote's Black and White Ball at the Plaza, but it sure felt like it, with beautiful people, noteworthy artists, and friends like Merce (he was a vegetarian, but someone captured a pic of him pretending to bite into a burger), Mirra Bank, and Sônia Braga. The place was packed, and it was maybe the best party I've ever attended. And malts.

I'll be mentioning the famed "staycation" of 2008 (see "Luminato (2008)"), but it bears noting how close I became with Katie O'Donnell (chef de cuisine) and her boyfriend, Mario Juarez, a pasta line cook at Esca. I had taken Katie to the classic red sauce joint Gino's on the Upper East Side and introduced her to Michael, the chef there. It was Katie who let me know they were closing. Lisa and I went and stayed the entire evening of their last day, even collecting their iconic zebra pin as a memento. As Lisa and I continued our summer run at Esca, I would find myself wandering over on off days. Katie would invite me into the kitchen, and I'd learn how to cut fish and see, once again, the inside of life. Sometimes the bartenders, Victor Borg (salt of the earth if ever there was one) or Joey Di Gregorio (wonderfully inappropriate), would send back a something-something for us. It was due to Katie and Mario and Esca that I learned how to approach cooking as I approached art: use fresh ingredients and stay out of the way. Lisa says my cooking epiphany came from seeing Katie struggling to draw a picture at the bar, like how I would struggle with cooking. A eureka moment, for sure. I would often meet Katie and Mario after their shift at Pony Bar down the street from me, the first craft bar in HK and brainchild of Dan McLaughlin. I thought it endearing that they both assumed I could keep up. I think bartenders Ciera, Margo, and Daniel also thought I could keep up. A funny story was sitting with Mario one afternoon at Pony. He was engaged in conversation with an older, downtrodden denizen of HK. She might have been in her sixties, but due to the wages of war in HK, she looked to be in her withered seventies. I was nursing my beer and not paying much attention, and as the woman kept a steady stream of dialog going, Mario glanced at me and said, "Ya know, she's talking to me, but she's looking at you." And scene. When the West Side Pony location closed, a new craft bar called Beer Culture opened. The team of Matt Gebhard and Peter Malfatti kept the lights burning during the worst days of Covid and were inspiring as they plumbed the slings and arrows of the ever-changing regulations. I would sometimes go to help Peter with basic maintenance during the lockdown and was grateful for a few moments outside of my apartment, six feet apart, in a Hell's Kitchen watering hole.

Related to Esca through the B&B group, Becco is where I made many friends at the bar. Angelo Ruggiero was the wine guy there for ten years and was always kind and generous with stories and tastings. He even took me and our friend Stuart on a food tour of "his" Staten Island that included Pizza Giove, where they proffered plastic iced-tea pitchers for us to decant the excellent wine we brought. And chef Billy Gallagher is a generous and talented guy. When my dad passed away and I had booked the flight home for the next day, I meandered in around 10:30 p.m. as Billy was heading out. He stayed, asking if I needed anything to eat. I said no and he poured me a beer and we just chatted. The feeling that you're more than a customer and part of a community is the best part of living in New York. This brings up sitting at the lunch bar with staff on their lunch break, with Tim and Kathy and Seth and Maria and Urtina and Caesar and Alvaro; like our lunch date, when that might never happen. And this reminds me of family meals, which is lunch for the staff that they make for themselves. I'm so grateful for those invites all around the world. I remember getting an Xmas gift of an upscale panettone that I had no idea what to do with. When I had Mario over to my studio to listen to music and asked him what to do with it, he said, "That makes a great French toast. Bring it by tomorrow and we'll add that to family meal at Esca." And it was done and it was good (Genesis 1:21).

There used to be a high-end soul food place on a corner in HK called Jezebel, serving smothered chicken livers and great sides. They also opened a small and cheaper take-out place called Monk's Corner just up the street. Marseille is still on the other corner. I've known many chefs there over the years. At one time there were two servers, Terrace and Jesse; they were falling for each other but there were complications. But as time passed, they decided to throw caution to the wind and moved west together, Jesse going ahead first. I remember going there with Lisa on one of Terrace's last shifts and giving her a wad of cash to make the landing a bit smoother. I'm not on social media, but I heard through the grapevine it all worked out and they've got a family.

Before both Tirez Tirez and Broken Consort hit the road to explore continental cuisine far and wide. Before the operas and solo shows start traveling the world that will be my oyster, there's one final New York story I'd like to tell, and this story takes place in 1997 at the Hourglass Cafe in Hell's Kitchen. I had met Lisa on a few occasions but knew I had to rise to the occasion of a date, and, being poor as a church mouse and deeply in debt from *Dennis Cleveland*, this was fraught with anxiety. The Hourglass was a cute place with a small ground-floor area and small bar reminiscent of places in Paris. They had a quirky little thing with hourglasses over each table that would determine your time there (probably because of the quick turnaround pre-theater), but they never really enforced it. There was also a small upstairs room that had a bar. We sat alone up there. We ordered food and wine, but once they served us the waitstaff kind of disappeared. We were having a grand time and I was going to the bar and getting wine for us like I owned the place. Very brazen. The bill comes and as I'm getting ready to pay, I can see Lisa looking down. She leans over and from under the table she's found a 100-dollar bill. She says, "This just paid for our dinner." And I thought two things. One: crisis averted. And two: this one's a keeper.

Epilogue: Jane and Michael Stern's book *Roadfood* and other offshoots were a constant companion on tours from coast to coast. It should be noted that this appreciation for indigenous culture and cuisine started way before the term "foodies" or the repressive commerce of Yelp. The Sterns share a belief in the local and authentic, and I somehow gained that same chip early on. I could, quite literally, write a whole other book narrating my misadventures around cooks, kitchens, and restaurants. I also obsessively made notes in sketchbooks on the merits of any establishment. Just looking through these notes tells me it would be pointless to list them all. But I was fortunate to become a fixture in all sorts of places, from Paris to New Orleans. From Melbourne to New Jersey. So I'll just resist a long boring list and leave this here: *Roadfood* has a website, and you most likely have a phone. And finally, the secret to a table at Rao's in Harlem might be knowing how to draw.

Luminato Trilogy (2008)

I'm sitting with William Knapp, the production manager for *The End of Cinematics* for the last few years. He is now taking on the role of production manager for the entire opera trilogy, to be mounted in three theaters over two weeks at the Luminato Festival in Toronto. I've already made a few solo trips scouting out venues and such. More on that later, but suffice to say that we've narrowed the field and Will and I are here to meet with the crews at the three theaters. The festival has put us in the fancy Park Hyatt hotel, and at the end of each day, Will and I meet for a cocktail at the iconic Roof Lounge. It's a writers' bar, decorated with photos of writers on the Canadian scene. I loved chatting with the bartender Joe Gomes, who was something of a Toronto legend.

But there were many trips before this, mostly on my own. Janice Price was the CEO of the Luminato Festival, and she knew about *Dennis Cleveland* but couldn't find a way to bring it to Philly when she was at the Kimmel Center. Janice is one of the most exciting people I've had the pleasure to know. And she came all in by booking the trilogy to run in repertory at Luminato.

Artistic Director Chris Lorway was also an enthusiastic supporter and has remained a great friend. To say she had a crackerjack team would be an understatement. Clyde Wagner (now CEO of TO Live) and Mitchell Marcus (now artistic and managing director of The Musical Stage Company) would turn out to be the best producers I ever had. And Janice's assistant, Martha Haldenby, was a joy to work with and remains a close friend and confidante.

I spent a good deal of time with Clyde and Mitchell as we scouted out various theaters for the three separate shows. By this time, Adrienne Clarkson was no longer governor general, and she and John Ralston Saul (whose book *Voltaire's Bastards: The Dictatorship of Reason in the West* was a major inspiration for *Dennis Cleveland*) had moved back to their house in the Annex. They had invited me to stay in their guest room on a couple of my trips. When Lisa and I attended the fiftieth anniversary of the governor general's position at Rideau Hall, we had brought Adrienne and John a gift of a framed drawing from Merce Cunningham. I remember the small Porter flight from New York to Toronto: the flight crew gave us grief for not checking the large picture, with one flight attendant being particularly annoyed in her obvious disagreement with Adrienne's progressive views. I was delighted to see the picture hanging in my guest room. I also remember Mitchell collecting me one snowy morning. John answered the door and as I was leaving, Adrienne yelled from upstairs, asking me if I'd like to join her that night for the symphony at the Sony Centre (now Meridian Hall). I said yes, and as Mitchell and I left, I could see he was a little flummoxed. I asked him what was wrong and he sputtered, "I just saw John Ralston Saul in his pajamas."

A funny thing happened at that concert. Adrienne and I were sitting together, looking at the program, and I realized that a piece that evening was by a member of the orchestra, Raymond Luedeke. Could this be the same Raymond Luedeke whom I studied composition with at the conservatory in Kansas City, Missouri? As he began his long-winded description of his piece from the stage, I realized it was. Unlike my masterly theory instructor Dr. Raymond LeRoy Pogemiller, it always felt like Luedeke was marking time on my dime. When I told Adrienne who he was, she said we simply must go backstage and say hello. I managed to deflect that idea but couldn't help thinking how grateful I was to have my very nontraditional approach to music. A side note: in 2011, I was given the Alumni Award from the Conservatory of Music at the University of Missouri at Kansas City. My mom and sister were there, and seated at my table was LeRoy. I had been to his office earlier in the day, and he proudly displayed an abstract lithograph (which included a sketch of Charles Ives) that I had given him and he had framed. I was moved to have left an impression on such a monumental person, who left such an impression on me. But I digress.

The search for theaters was exhilarating but long. So many possibilities and different requirements. I honestly can't remember all of them, but a couple were instantly good. The Factory Theatre was funky and real and seemed ideal for the solo performance of *Failing Kansas*. Even more intriguing was the Toronto Film School's studio/theater in the CBC (Canadian Broadcast Centre). This was pretty much a full-on television studio with a control room. In other words, the TV talk show opera would be run from a control center like an actual TV talk show. I was hesitant due to how the audience would have to enter, by coming up elevators and not through a typical theater entrance. But I was sold on the possibility of presenting *Dennis Cleveland* as an actual talk show. Finding a theater for *The End of Cinematics* proved a little more challenging, but once we landed on the Bluma Appel Theatre on Front Street, we were set. It was wild trudging through the winter weather in Toronto, with snow drifts five feet tall. I remember always trying to hit the Vesta Lunch Restaurant just around the corner from Lisa's brother, Mark, and his wife, Anita. I loved visiting them and staying with them in their basement house in the Annex. When I was doing the audio mix for *The End of Cinematics*, I would make good use of his 5.1 setup downstairs. I'd also make good use of his wine fridge. Mark was into cooking, and Lisa gave him a cookbook that included a recipe for a seven-layer meat pie that took days to prepare. It did not take days to consume. I commemorated this pie with a cartoon of the entire family, including Lisa and Mark's parents, Roe-Enid and George Boudreau. (When I met Lisa's parents, early in our courtship, at Mark and Anita's wedding in Algonquin Provincial Park, George said, "I've been waiting my whole life to meet you.")

Now that we had secured theaters, it was time to figure out the logistics of mounting three separate shows in three different venues. We decided that we'd take the entire *Cinematics* crew and various members would build a show, and as that show was running, some would peel off to the next theater. We thought two stage managers might be helpful given the seesaw between theaters, so we brought both Jenny Goelz and Valerie Oliveiro. We also thought that if we could utilize the five performers in *Cinematics* in the cast of *Dennis Cleveland*, we'd be a little closer to staying on budget. Fortunately, the *Cinematics* cast fit nicely with some of the New York regulars in *Dennis Cleveland*. We decided it would also be economical to do the trilogy out of order (*Cleveland, Cinematics, Failing Kansas*) so that cast members could leave after their respective shows. Matthew Gandolfo had become my music director during the tour of *Cinematics*, so it was natural that he'd continue that role in *Dennis Cleveland* as well as being a performer in *Cleveland*. Along with Chris Ericson becoming my sound designer for numerous shows, this took away loads of pressure going into rehearsals. The New York *Cleveland* cast would rehearse at a studio in Midtown, and Matt ran those rehearsals.

At some point, I made a few trips to Toronto to start casting the audience parts. I was very fortunate that Luminato supplied an excellent assistant director in Natasha Mytnowych. She was great to work with and kept the local cast moving forward. I was also doing a lot of advance press both in Toronto and in New York. I remember doing a feature interview for the *Toronto Star* at the Cupcake Cafe in Hell's Kitchen and holding up a donut for the feature pic. I also remember going with Adrienne and John to a conversation between Leonard Cohen and Philip Glass, who were doing a collaboration. Adrienne took me backstage to meet Leonard, and I remember Phil looking on in that way some folks do when they think they might be missing something. Over the years I would meet Phil and that vibe was fairly consistent. I recall a chance encounter that he had with a friend of mine, and when my name came up, Phil responded, "He's one of the few who've been able to make a living at this game." I guess perception is everything.

The Toronto *Globe and Mail* christened me the "It Boy" of the Luminato festival (which tickled my nephew, Brennan, to no end) due to my association with six events: *Dennis Cleveland*; *The End of Cinematics*; *Failing Kansas*; "Crossing the Line," which was a free discussion with director Marie Brassard and composer Christos Hatzis held on the *Cleveland* set, moderated by the Barbican Centre's Graham Sheffield (when someone brought up Homer's *The Odyssey* during this symposium, I responded with the Homer Simpson quote, "Less artsy, more fartsy"); the Canadian Songbook; and finally "SeeHearFeelTaste," where *The End of Cinematics* inspired a prix fixe menu at the restaurant Bymark. This private dinner landed after opening night of *Cinematics* and was attended by Luminato luminaries, including Janice along with John Ralston Saul and Adrienne Clarkson. I remember Michael and Lisa were in attendance as well. I also remember the duck leg being very good. I have fond memories of the festival opening party. My entire family was there: my mom, Martha Sue Rouse, my sister, Cindy Ponder, and her partner, Jill Holley, my niece, Katie Ponder, and my nephew, Brennan Mikel Ponder. Lisa was decked out in a lush red Comme des Garçons gown (when a Cunningham dancer leaves the company, they get to choose a costume, sort of like retiring a baseball jersey, and Lisa chose wisely). Cindy had cleverly told my mom that smoking was illegal in Canada, so that started the process of weaning her off cigarettes. The party was packed, and it was great seeing cast members, crew, and family floating about.

The crew had arrived earlier as planned and began getting the Toronto Film School ready while also beginning aspects of the build for *Cinematics* at the Bluma Appel. And since we were starting with *Dennis Cleveland*, everyone descended on the hotel at the same time. Such a large, excited group and a family feel. Ryuji Noda, our harmonica player, had recently had a baby and brought his wife and child along. And Chris's wife, Natalie, was expecting their first child and was radiant.

Michael Mushalla was having a virtual coming-out party, as he had both the Mark Morris Dance Company, the National Theatre of Scotland's *Black Watch*, and my trilogy all headlining the festival. I got to know a few folks in the *Black Watch* cast, and the pub next door to our hotel became a de facto meeting place. I became friends with cast members Henry Pettigrew and Jack Fortune. Two great memories: Lisa had left Cunningham in 2008 and was embarking on a freelance career teaching yoga. I think Michael helped set her up to teach classes to the *Black Watch* company, whose rehearsal process included military-like drills. So Lisa was amused to show up for their first class and find them all stripped down to their underwear. The other amusing thing was my nephew Brennan (eighteen at the time, which was legal age in Canada) drinking with the *Black Watch* cast, soaking up the artistic life that he was just beginning. There were also rumors of a post-show evening at the pub that ended with a lot of destroyed furniture, but I somehow missed that.

I was rushing from theater to theater like a mad man and also continuing to do press, including an interview on the CBC Radio One show

"Q" with Jian Ghomeshi; just leaving that here. Anyway, everything was humming along. As I mentioned, there would also be a concert for the Canadian Songbook at the historic Massey Hall (I guess because three operas weren't already enough). Lots of rock stars and folkies and, apparently, me. Everyone would do the classic stuff: Leonard Cohen, Joni Mitchell, etc. Each artist got two songs, and I chose Neil Young's "Harvest Moon" as my first song. But I think I was the only performer who thought it might be a good idea to do a modern Canadian classic, and my nephew Brennan had turned me on to the band Broken Social Scene. I had fallen in love with the song "Anthems for a Seventeen-Year-Old Girl" from their *You Forgot It in People* album, so I chose that as my second song.

Everyone had limited time, but I remember showing up at a large rehearsal studio to run through the songs with the excellent "house band" that the festival had assembled, along with Penelope, Christina, and Cynthia from the *Cinematics* troupe. The four of us had rehearsed in my hotel suite, and the band had already prepared the two songs in advance of our brief rehearsal. The rehearsal went well, and we were as ready as we could be given the schedule crunch. But first we'd need to do the opening night premiere of *Dennis Cleveland*. And that would prove to be memorable.

As we did the build for *Dennis Cleveland*, with an exciting new set design by James Edward Cameron, my team realized there had been a miscommunication regarding TV monitors. In addition to the two large screens behind the guests, we also hung ten to twenty TV monitors above and throughout the audience, as in a typical talk show. The slight subversion for *Dennis Cleveland* was that a talk show would only have the final feed on all the monitors; in *Cleveland*, we would route individual camera feeds to the monitors, thereby multiplying the surreal TV talk show experience. This felt like a huge problem, as both the festival and my production team were already way past being over budget. Leave it to the blazing Clyde Wagner to come up with the solution. Another artist had a large video installation coming to the festival, but since his opening was after *Cleveland*, Clyde multipurposed the monitors and a crisis was averted.

We had been rehearsing at the Toronto Film Studio and would take the weekend off before the opening. The cameras and new set design were all in place, but when we returned on Monday, without warning they had decided to paint the entire theater in oil-based paint. It was a disaster, and no one knew the paint job was going to happen. Memories of the Perth opening with no air conditioning (see "*Dennis Cleveland* (1996): Part 2") flooded my head. As we did the rehearsal, I remember Levensky Smith almost passing out from the fumes. I later learned that they almost tore down the entire set to finish the painting.

But the show went up with a great audience and lots of paint fumes. I was honored that John and Adrienne came to all three operas. Lisa and I had fallen in love with the show "Slings & Arrows," set at the fictional New Burbage Festival, a Shakespearean festival similar to the real-world Stratford Festival. We loved the leads, Paul Gross and Martha Burns, and I was thrilled that John and Adrienne brought them. I was also happy that many of my new friends from the *Black Watch* company came and seemed to have a grand time. As the *Cleveland* run continued, some of the crew paired off to head over to the Bluma Appel to continue the *Cinematics* build. I have fond memories of going over during the day before a *Cleveland* evening performance and seeing Chris and Brad catching a quick nap in the audience seats. Everyone was going full steam. As we wrapped up *Dennis Cleveland*, the reviews were good. Colin Eatock in the *Globe and Mail* observed, "The glue that holds it all together is Cleveland, performed with conviction by Rouse himself: a charismatic guru who speaks in strange aphorisms about 'the animist watusi' of modern life, and 'the confusion of animals riding other animals.' He's part Maury and part Geraldo, with a dash of Jerry Springer—and his penchant for philosophizing in rhyming couplets gives him a suave Leonard Cohenesque touch. ('And the power of suggestion, in this moment, on this day / Is the way we make religion: how we make up what to pray')." Which reminds me that we'd see Cohen again at an opening of his paintings as he struggled out of debt due to a greedy manager. And Robert Crew of the *Toronto Star* said, "There's despair here, but there's also hope. Possible answers to our lack of spirituality and faith are explored and a strong message sent about instinctive compassion, tolerance, and understanding for other people's ways of life. This is not your ordinary talk show. Nor is it your ordinary opera."

Immediately after the *Cleveland* run, we were heading to Massey Hall for our stint in the Canadian Songbook. It's a beautiful, 3,000-seat theater and you can feel the history just walking in. Showing up at the stage door, I realized how a week of paint fumes had leveled me. I felt slightly high, and my voice was hoarse and gravelly. I remember being backstage with various performers. We made small talk, and I remember some of the younger artists being particularly taken with meeting Ron Sexsmith. When my time came, the three female singers from *Cinematics* and I took the stage. We had the entire audience swaying to "Harvest Moon," and the crowd went wild after "Anthems for a Seventeen-Year-Old Girl." It was a great feeling, and I remember going backstage and everyone I'd met before was now much more animated. I don't think any of them expected a "composer" to make such a strong pop performance. As Martin Knelman said in the *Toronto Star*, "Mikel Rouse, the New Yorker whose trilogy of chamber operas is running in rep all through Luminato, provided one of the high points with an unforgettably wonderful performance of Neil Young's 'Harvest Moon.'" And James Bradshaw of the *Globe and Mail* wrote, "Alex Cuba, Mikel Rouse, Nikki Yanofsky, Karen David, and Ron Sexsmith were all particularly strong."

We now head to the Bluma Appel and begin our run of *Cinematics*. I remember the lobby being decked out in a very convincing movie-house fashion. The shows came off well, with lots of folks in attendance. The buzz was palpable, especially the befuddlement at the fifteen minutes of movie trailers. I think there was yet another *Batman* or *Spider-Man* movie out, and we adapted accordingly. I also remember one enjoyable review that actually combined a review of *Cinematics* with a review of the *Cinematics*-inspired dinner at Bymark. Wrote Karen Hawthorne in the *National Post*, "If only McEwan or McDougall (chef and owner of Bymark) could have gone with me to the show—but they were working—to see how Mikel Rouse, the New York composer and director of *The End of Cinematics*, delivered his take on sophisticated layers." She continued, "The lyrics are fragmented and brilliant when the performers also use sign language or speak in Spanish and French, for layers of dramatic narrative." Otherwise, reviews were mixed, with the *Globe and Mail* saying, "Added to this visually arresting effect were six big screens at the back of the stage, stacked up like Hollywood Squares, each displaying a cornucopia of abstract, fleeting images. And finally, the live action was often simultaneously projected on the big screen. All considered, it was psychedelic and trippy." And Robert Crew of the *Star* noted, "Those actors are filmed in action, and that video is also projected on the scrim.

It's a fascinating, multilayered effect. And the actual music is very listenable, with interesting counterpoint and moments of charm and beauty. But then there are the lyrics. I really can't tell you much more because the words stubbornly refuse to make sense. Okay, so it's a kind of poetry where the sound is as important as the sense." I think the show came off as more of an intriguing curiosity than anything else. There was an internet review by Imelda Ortega Suzara saying, "Whatever one's interpretation, this is a definite MUST-SEE for aspiring multimedia artists who want to combine various creative disciplines, and hopefully Rouse's layered and multiscreened technique will be studied and copied by future artists, until the general public and media understand the complexity of his simplistic messages, and reach an epiphany to match the prolonged clapping for his performance feat in multimedia. Refer to: Definition of Arouse. Refer to Epiphany. Refer to Genius." But that's the internet, Jake, that's the internet. I remember having a lunch in Toronto a year or so later, where John and Adrienne along with Canadian filmmaker Atom Egoyan were in attendance. Atom told me that his film students were particularly enchanted with *The End of Cinematics*.

When the crew loaded out and everyone split, it seemed surreal. We still had *Failing Kansas* to go, but only Chris and Val remained as crew for the solo show. Michael and his partner, Mary Anne Lewis, were there through the end as well. The *Failing Kansas* shows were lightly attended, and I figured that made sense. Toronto had been subjected to a lot of me over the last couple of weeks. Michael and Mary Anne got me a beautiful closing festival gift: an engraved, gold-plated Hohner blues harmonica from Tiffany. I play two different ones in *Failing Kansas*, the key of C and the key of F. This was a C harp, and I debated whether I should play it or just display it. Val thought it better to play it around the world, so I agreed. Little did I know that these would be the last performances. We had planned and built the trilogy at Luminato with our eye on many other festivals, and many presenters had flown in to see everything. We were gonna tour for a year or longer. Then the crash of 2008 hit and it was all over. This made me all the more grateful for the opportunity Luminato provided, but once again, economics beyond my control ended the dream. *Failing Kansas* was well received. Paula Citron of Classical 96.3 FM said, "The sum total of *Failing Kansas* is a poetic stream of consciousness that takes the audience into the disordered minds of the killers with abstract commentary from Rouse. The rhythmic cadence of Rouse's live performance was mesmerizing, and the effect was transportation to another astral plane. Nothing made sense, yet everything did." And Mr. Eatock of the *Globe and Mail* posited, "Despite its gruesome subject matter, *Failing Kansas* is a poised and elegant piece. Rather than choosing to dwell on the gory details, Rouse offers an evocative reflection on the United States in the 1950s—a time when homespun America was fast becoming unspun. Indeed, in all three works in Rouse's trilogy, this composer-writer-actor-director displays a remarkable capacity to effectively rework principles of classical music. Outwardly, his music is unapologetically vernacular in its idiom, with a constant drum beat and short, catchy, syncopated phrases. But it's also sophisticated in ways that set his oeuvre well apart from those pretentious 'rock operas' that are really just a string of overwrought pop songs." And, scene.

Now everyone is gone. Lisa and I are sitting on her brother, Mark's, boat at the Royal Canadian Yacht Club on Toronto Island. I loved walking around Toronto Island over the years; the history and funky houses. I would dream of living there and working on music and films and never leaving. Mark knows wine and we're having great wine and I'm totally exhausted but grateful. And also confused: what just happened? To say Luminato was one of the highlights of my life would be an understatement. Thank you, Janice, Chris, Clyde, Martha, Mitchell, and of course, Michael Mushalla. But to say it also would signal a slow decline was not yet on the radar. So it's a mix of joy, exasperation, gratitude, and excitement for the future.

I made good coin from that run. Not good in the sense of most folks, but certainly good for me. I was feeling flush for the first time, and since Lisa had left the Cunningham company, it was time for a celebration. But since I don't trust flush, I suggested a staycation. Lisa and I hired painters to paint the apartment, and we'd spend most days at the restaurant Esca a couple of blocks from us. As I settle back into New York and contemplate a short break, I run into the great musician Ed Alstrom and his wife, Maxine, also a stellar musician. Ed's passion and uncanny abilities in music (he once subbed for drummer Bill Tesar in Broken Consort, sampling the drum parts and playing with such rhythmic flow and conviction that you would swear it was a live drum kit) are matched by a love of baseball, and around this time he got the dream job as organist of the New York Yankees. He'd heard about the trilogy at Luminato and insisted that Lisa and I be his guests at a game. We got the tour of his organ post, the same organ played by Eddie Layton since 1967. Hearing him play in this context, with clever and subtle references, was thrilling. But at the seventh-inning stretch, Maxine tells us to keep an eye on the Jumbotron. And there it is: "Yankees Welcome Mikel Rouse & Lisa Boudreau." We were touched. I sent a pic of that to my father. He'd never seen a show of mine; it just wasn't in his wheelhouse to get this approach to life. But I heard later he showed that pic to lots of folks. Finally, he had something about my life that he could hang his hat on.

Esca was one of the first upscale places to brave the uncertainty of Hell's Kitchen. Lisa knew about it because the chef Dave Pasternak's wife, Donna, had waitressed with Lisa before her days at Cunningham. I remember Lisa and me both going just before the Esca opening and Dave giving us a tour of the kitchen. I won't forget the way he proudly slapped a large fish he'd caught the day before, and I told Lisa, "This is gonna be huge." We would go to the pool at Manhattan Plaza Health Club (where a spirited older man with one leg would exclaim to Lisa, "You sure are a knockout!") and career over to Esca for lunch. Day after day. Over time we became close to Katie O'Donnell, the chef de cuisine, and her boyfriend, Mario Juarez (a line cook at the time but a great chef in his own right these days). Katie, Mario, and I would have many misadventures (see "Bars & Restaurants (1965–2021)"). Katie learned our tastes, especially Lisa's. We both adored spicy, and Katie would make a plate of various roasted peppers for Lisa. We called it "Russian Roulette": you never knew. Lisa and I always sat at the small bar, attended by Victor Borg (a saint if ever one existed) or Joey Di Gregorio (the most hilariously politically incorrect bartender ever, often with a cauliflower ear due to his love of boxing). Folks wondered why they couldn't find Katie's special peppers on the menu. Because it always was a communal bar, we offered a taste to the curious—at their own risk. I remember a young British waitress took us up on the offer and then disappeared into the kitchen. I was afraid we might have killed her. She finally emerged after rounds of goat milk and said, "My ears have been clogged for six months after a bad flight. No more!"

We also went almost every day for two weeks to mourn and celebrate the closing of Florent on Gansevoort Street, an institution that invented a neighborhood only to be pushed out because of their vision. The times I spent there after gigs munching on French fries and drinking martinis, discussing art and politics. As the weeks progressed, the decadence multiplied: parents brought their children, as if to offer a history lesson. Later in the day, some folks partied naked. Hard to describe the beauty and the memory of an end to a different hedonistic time in New York. But Esca was our 2008 landing. I remember one morning after a typical day, when we most likely ate and drank too much, Lisa rolled over and asked, "Are we OK?" I remember trying to be a comforting sage of wisdom: we weren't imbibing too much; we were celebrating a life we had chosen in the arts. But that attempt at assurance abruptly ended when I noticed the time. 11:50 a.m. Just before Esca opened. I exclaimed, "We gotta go now or miss a seat at the bar!"

Gravity Radio, Brooklyn Academy of Music, 2010.

Gravity Radio, Brooklyn Academy of Music, 2010.

Gravity Radio (2009)

Around 2005 or 2006, I started thinking a lot about growing up with radio in small-town Missouri. Poplar Bluff is in southeast Missouri, commonly known as the "boot heel." We had local stations like KLID and KWOK that played some current hits, and lots of country and western music. But the real magic came from Chicago's WLS, where all the newest pop music could be heard, and seemingly, with hindsight, defied genre description. It wasn't "rock" or "soul" or "R&B": it was everything all mixed. It's what the world, or at least the Western world, was doing all together in popular music. They were all listening to each other, or at least that's how it felt to my eleven-year-old ears. I heard Motown and the latest hits from the British Invasion. But there was also a genuine mystery. Because of all the little local stations' interference, I couldn't get WLS during the day. It would only slowly creep in after 11 p.m. as the small local stations signed off. And in the dark, with very patient dialing, WLS would slowly squeak in with static and fuzz and hope. And at a certain point, maybe around midnight or so, it would be treble-clear, and I'd be there with the transistor radio between my pillow and my head, observing these sounds as if they were coming from outer space. And since I'd never been out of this small area (maybe Memphis, but that could be a little later), for all I knew it could be coming from space. A magic that's hard to remember or recreate. I had also been reading physicist Raymond Chiao and was fascinated by his experiments with superconductors and gravity waves. Hence *Gravity Radio*.

But here I am touring the third opera, *The End of Cinematics*, the solo channel-surfing piece *Music for Minorities*, and gearing up for the Cunningham iPod piece—and, as usual, my mind is elsewhere. I didn't get rid of TV until 2011 (feeling that after talk show operas and channel-surfing pieces, I'd exhausted its potential). I was pleased to visit Robert Rauschenberg's studio in 2005 (see "*Cage/Cunningham* (1997–2013)") and confirm that the stories of a TV being on in his studio, all the time, were true (his assistant Russell told me, "And it's always the same channel"). But before I left TV, I had a renewed curiosity in how news channels were using music to cover stories, obviously orchestrating the audience consumption and response. And of course, the drama in the music was always literal and predictable. I wondered if I could take that idea and subvert it. I landed on the premise of a song cycle that would be interspersed with current news stories from the Associated Press, orchestrated by string quartet, prepared piano samples I had produced with Laura Kuhn and the John Cage Trust (see "*Cage/Cunningham* (1997–2013)"), and singers. The music for each section would be scored but never change. The news stories, however, would range from serious topics of the day to human interest stories to oddities. And since the stories would change for each updated performance, the contrast between news and music would be enhanced. Less dramatic, more reflective; and hopefully questioning the manipulation of hard news.

Like many of these projects, it all started with the recording. In 2006 I started archiving my analog recordings. I had no inkling that in 2010 my archive would go to the New York Public Library for the Performing Arts at Lincoln Center, so the analog archiving was fortuitous. Before this, I either had the time or the money to do this deep dive, but now I briefly had both and it seemed like a good idea to archive. I knew Mark Berger at Dreamhire through Bill Tesar (drummer in both Mikel Rouse Broken Consort and Tirez Tirez), and I hired him to "bake the tapes" and then transfer the analog masters to 96kHz-24-Bit files. I was happy to be doing this and excited to hear some of these older recordings. And I noticed something I'd been missing in the freedom of building my own digital studio: tape compression. But also, just a saturation effect from tubes and analog gear. So before starting the recording *Love at Twenty* (2006), which would be the music for the Joe Goode Performance Group's *Grace*, I went on a deep dive for gear. My goal was to create a hybrid studio with the ease and editability of digital combined with the sound of analog. So much research, but ultimately rewarding. A thing I like about boutique gear is that it's similar to the mom-and-pop food stores in Hell's Kitchen. High-quality stuff made for a select few who "get it." And get it I did, from a new three-way monitoring system (combining Barefoot MM27 monitors with original Yamaha NS10M's and Avantone mixcubes). I picked up some great tube compressors, including an incredibly transparent VT-7 from D.W. Fearn and a Manley Vari-Mu. Dave Hill makes some great gear and I picked up his Avocet monitor controller as well as his very clean Ibis eq and the Hedd A/D converter. And since you're spending money, you might as well pick up a Manley Massive Passive tube eq to enhance your mojo and keep pizza warm. I did a lot of shoot-outs to choose this gear, but never so much as I did grabbing a Telefunken U47. This mic is a great replication of the original Neumann U47, which utilized the M7 capsule that had been developed in 1928 by Georg Neumann. To this capsule was added an amplifier built from military surplus VF14 tubes. I loved my other mics, like a Neumann U87 and various AKG 414s and Shure 57s, but the U47 was the mic for *Gravity Radio*.

Additionally, I bought a portable Grundig world band receiver and began experimenting with frequencies and cross talk that reminded me of the signals struggling to get in from WLS. These recorded signals, along with strings, would provide the "beds" for the spoken AP news text. The text would be interspersed with a song cycle, and, by pulling some lyrics from the songs and adding them into the AP text, I created a sleight of hand that baffled audience members. It left them with the impression that the entire piece, and not just the AP text, was being created on the spot. Once again, my time in the carnival was paying off. I had done a few pieces with the Tony-nominated and OBIE Award–winning actress Veanne Cox. She was in the film *Funding* as well as many workshop films and performances. For the recording, the news stories obviously had to be frozen in the time I was writing from, so I chose stories and oddities that might still be reflective years later.

Think: Blackwater. I sent all the text to Veanne so she could be familiar with it, and then we set up some recording dates. It was an exciting couple of sessions, and I liked directing her to keep her voice low, as it would naturally start to climb a little in tone. She was a total pro, and after some arduous editing, I had my text. I played all the instruments on the recording and brought in Penelope Thomas for additional background vocals and Christina Pawl for some trumpet. When the recording was complete, I readied the CD release and started thinking about pulling together a group of musicians to perform the theatrical song cycle live.

Out of the blue in late 2007, I got a note from Sallie Sanders. She was working with the legendary Hal Willner, who was curating a season at John Zorn's club The Stone. Sallie explained to me that Hal had remembered I'd sent him music fifteen years earlier (true), and that due to some "lost years," he'd never gotten back to me (also true). So now, at her encouragement, he was getting back to me and wondered if I'd do two sets on one of the evenings. The timing couldn't have been better, and Matt Gandolfo, my music director, and I pulled together some strings and hired singers from *The End of Cinematics* and a couple of others. I printed out rough midi parts for the string sections, and Matt went to work arranging, embellishing, and generally improving the parts. I encouraged him to veer as far from my original parts as he desired, and I credit him for outstanding charts. The workshop concert would be the evening before my fiftieth birthday, and I was excited to be doing live music again after all the programmed media pieces. Sallie was great and supportive, and Hal's curation for the month of January was a who's who of downtown New York: Lou Reed, Laurie Anderson, Anthony Coleman, Peter Gordon, David Amram, and Marc Ribot, to name just a few. Hal and Sallie seemed excited that my time at The Stone would be a first public performance of *Gravity Radio* in progress. But Hal also wanted the second set to be different, so Matt and I had to pull together never-before-performed songs from the albums *International Cloud Atlas*, *Love at Twenty*, and *House of Fans*. Meaning, there was a lot of prep and rehearsal. Like so many underfunded first stabs at an idea, the whole concert was slightly ragtag, but the consensus was that this was a very solid idea, and the audience loved it. I knew I was on to something. After the set, we headed downtown to a place Michael Mushalla had arranged to stay open for food and we rung in my fiftieth year. It seemed like a promising start.

After some serious reflection, Matt and I thought to remove the band element and strip the ensemble down to a string quartet, two singers, a news reader, and me on vocal and acoustic and steel guitar, with Matt conducting the singers and strings while cuing the newsreader and the recorded static frequency sounds, and playing prepared piano samples; he would be singing as well. And, hilariously, I thought this wasn't too much to ask of him. He's since forgiven me. Matt was responsible for the excellent updated string arrangements, loosely based on the scores I'd given him.

Through my mastering engineer, Matt Agoglia, I discovered the ACME string quartet. I had originally met Matt when I moved my recording studio to the old Record Plant building on Forty-Fourth Street, around the corner from me. This became a convenient spot to rehearse the string quartet parts. I was excited to learn that after a false start in 2009, the Brooklyn Academy of Music's Next Wave series would be inviting *Gravity Radio* in December 2010. Consequently, the team started working on a tour, and I also wanted to do a performance to coincide with the November 2009 release of the CD. We chose the Galapagos Art Space in Brooklyn. In a rare occurrence, Veanne was available for this record release performance, and Cliff Baldwin, who had done the film for *Failing Kansas* and video for *Living Inside Design* and *Cameraworld*, would pull together some new video to be played over monitors throughout the space. As record release parties go, it was a success with a good house, but we still weren't nailing the essence of the idea or the performance itself. Plus, the acoustics were awful, so we had a hyper sense that we weren't nailing it.

It took a while, but I had an idea of a visual element that would add an even greater sense of "memory" than just the radio history. I wanted to make a film that would front-project on the wall (not a screen) behind the ensemble, and this film would be triggered by the volume of music and speaking onstage. The settings of the trigger had to be very precise so that the loudest passages of sound didn't "blow out" the projection, while the softest passages still revealed memory-like images. It was a beautiful effect enhanced by the vivid lighting design of Hideaki Tsutsui, who had done many of my shows. From *Cinematics*, Hide had figured out how to combine traditional stage lighting with lighting for film/video. Similarly, with *Gravity Radio*, his design combined with the front projection to create an almost holographic environment, a truly stunning achievement for which he was acknowledged in the third edition of *Lighting and the Design Idea*, by Linda Essig and Jennifer Setlow. I shot much of the *Gravity Radio* film in Rio de Janeiro while on tour with the Cunningham company.

I knew that Veanne would not be able to tour the piece, and I was wracking my brain as to whom I could find to capture the role of the newsreader. Not only was the acting and tone important, but we needed someone who was a quick study (as the news travels fast), with the ability to adapt swiftly. I'm good friends with the writer Glenn Kenny and his wife, Claire Kenny. Lisa and I had spent time with them, and I knew Claire was an actress who also worked with Steven Soderbergh. But when Lisa suggested her, I was flabbergasted that I hadn't thought of it. She had the poise and confidence of a newscaster, and like her husband, she is smart and incredibly informed. Up to that point, I had been doing the daily chore of finding the news stories. But with Claire on board, I had a collaborator who would dig into the latest events and oddities. It now almost felt like a newsroom, and I enjoyed this process with her, whereas before it could feel like just one more difficult thing I was responsible for. This was never more exciting than when we played the Walton Arts Center in Fayetteville, Arkansas. The Walton Arts Center was built by the Walton family of Walmart fame. It's a nice hall, and we were happy that it was part of our southern tour as we headed toward the Krannert Center. I remember a news story had surfaced the day of our first show about Walmart laying off 1,200 employees. Claire, Matt, and I were backstage going through the news stories, and we wondered about the politics of including a story that could be interpreted as ungrateful for our invite to the Walton Center. I felt like a pop-art Ben Bradlee, going over the pros and cons. Ultimately, the newsroom determined we had to be objective and follow the story. And we did. Half the crowd loved it and half the crowd didn't. It's times like these that I feel like I'm doing my job.

I think we went from New Orleans (thank you to the talented composer Jay Weigel, director of the Contemporary Arts Center, for all the support) to Fayetteville on the way to Krannert. We got to Krannert with several pickup musicians, who somehow derived from the original ACME string quartet. We still hadn't added the singers, but that was on my mind.

Krannert had always been an amazing place to play, and I was grateful that this show in the Studio Theater would complete my tour of the four theaters at Krannert. It's a great small theater that can be configured in numerous ways. For *Gravity Radio*, it would be set up with tables like a cabaret. But as it was a small setting, there was no backstage, just a curtain that hugged the back wall. This would prove irksome, as a couple of musicians got deathly ill. We lost one string player, so now we would be a string trio along with Matt, Claire, and me. Opening night was going fine, and I remember an enthusiastic Mike Ross, the artistic director of the Krannert Center, encouraging us on. It was a stressful show, but I felt it went off OK given we were one musician short. I remember my sound designer, Chris Ericson (whom I'd been lucky to grab from the University of Illinois grad program five years prior), saying afterwards, "Wild show, huh?" I laughed and said yeah, thinking he was talking about the uneven opening night performance. Little did I know that Claire had also caught the bug that our ill musician was laid up with and was heaving in a bucket just offstage behind the curtain but coming back for each of her cues. She was a true pro! But since she was on the other side of the stage, I had no idea this was going on through the entire show. No wonder Chris was flummoxed when I didn't know the chaos he was referring to.

But now we were heading to BAM. And this is how I met the great impresario and presenter Chad Herzog. He was at Juniata College in Huntingdon, Pennsylvania. He offered two spaces: one that seemed appropriate (beautiful but small), and one that seemed destined for the Harvey at BAM (close to 1,000 seats). I knew we couldn't come close to filling that in Huntingdon, but Chad was all about, how can I help moving you toward BAM? So I embarrassingly said, "Let's go for the larger space." I still have the water bottle he gave me with my name on it. It's a small town, but Chad was dedicated. Not just to the art but to the town. Our load-in and tech were blazing. Jeff Sugg, who worked brilliantly on

Dennis Cleveland and *The End of Cinematics*, joined the group as set and video designer and would move with us to Cleveland and New York. Chad seemed to know that the town mattered, so he took me to great local spots. I remember telling the crew and musicians, "This is a great, generous offer to help us build this piece toward BAM. Please don't be upset if there are only thirty to fifty folks in the audience." On opening night, the house was completely full of the local community and journalists doing interviews. It was a sensation, largely due to Chad stepping up and representing his commitment to both this town and the artists. I was blown away.

Next was Cleveland and a show at some iteration of the Rock & Roll Hall of Fame, which I assumed was the Cleveland Chamber of Commerce. We performed to a full house, but it was a small venue that was kind of an office area, with the backstage being like the space for copy machines (think: the film *Office Space*). It was bizarre but at the same time another great venue to try out the show before New York. There were lots of local artists there, and it was a good performance; on top of the great musicians, we were getting the hang of the triggered projection. I don't want to gloss over all the musicians who contributed to *Gravity Radio*. We ultimately settled on six great artists. The singers Eryn Murman and Sarah Emley were selected from just under 100 singers who auditioned. I credit Matt with really wanting the two singers to meld well. I remember Matt having Eryn over to my studio at the Record Plant building and hearing an aspect of the future in her voice. She had come up in the time of Autotune and her pitch was uncanny. I remember Matt asking her after her audition to try adding a little vibrato. Our excellent string quartet (christened the Low-Rent Quartet as we pulled into BAM) consisted of Kristi Helberg and Nanae Iwata on violins, Kyle Armbrust on viola, and Julia MacLaine on cello. This was the lineup as we moved into New York for the BAM performances. Musicians for The Stone workshop were Ian Smith on bass, Bill Tesar on drums (a happy reunion as we hadn't played together since the Broken Consort days), Cynthia Marcus and Luke Cissell on violins, Liuh-Wen on viola, and Christo Logan on cello. Backup vocals and News Reports were the *Cinematics* singers Christina Pawl, Cynthia Enfield, and Penelope Thomas. The brief tour through the South heading to Krannert consisted of Gillian Rivers and Patrick Doane on violins, Kenny Wang on viola, Isabel

Fairbanks on cello, and Claire as our news reader. The players of ACME were Ben Russell and Yuki Numata on violins, Miranda Sielaff on viola, and Clarice Jensen on cello.

To say my season at BAM coincided with my largest New York season would be an understatement. Steve Smith did a bang-up feature in the *New York Times* about my season culminating in the BAM performances, and it still exhausts me to remember it. As Smith said, "If artists, like illusionists, manufacture their own realities, then the New York composer, performer, and director Mikel Rouse just might be unveiling his magnum opus this week." Smith continued, "But Mr. Rouse's real feat is subtler and more profound. Like most artists, he has been affected during recent seasons by recessionary woes, including canceled engagements. As if in response, he is offering a veritable deluge of creative activity this month, with *Gravity Radio* as its focal point. On Monday an exhibition of Mr. Rouse's notebooks, manuscripts, and video art opened at the Margarete Roeder Gallery in SoHo. On Tuesday he releases two CDs, *Recess* and *Corner Loading* (Volume 1), on his decade-old label, ExitMusic. On Wednesday, 'Passport. 30 Years Drawn on the Road,' another exhibition of Mr. Rouse's sketches and watercolors, opens at the New York Public Library for the Performing Arts, honoring the library's acquisition of his archive. A film retrospective opens at the library on December 15, and the Alvin Ailey American Dance Theater revives Ulysses Dove's *Vespers*, set to Mr. Rouse's *Quorum*." It's hard to imagine now, but this article was one of the first times that films and info could be linked to from the digital edition. A video I had shot and edited on my iPhone (also a very new idea in 2010) of the song "Great Adventure Jail," from the *Corner Loading* album, could be accessed immediately.

The opening reception for the announcement of my archive was quite an event. Jacqueline Davis, executive director of the New York Public Library for the Performing Arts, had brought me into a meeting with Michael Mushalla, and music curators Jonathan Hiam and George Boziwick to inquire about my archive coming to LPA. I was, frankly, stunned. And when Jackie looked me straight in the eye and asked, "What does this feel like?," I knew something big was happening. It would be a "living archive," and over the next ten years, I would make regular deposits. I had borrowed a high-end flatbed scanner from the designer Mark Kingsley. My studio turned into a veritable digitizing factory as I scanned hundreds of scores, sketchbooks, and graphs for the two shows. As part of the Roeder exhibit, I also completed the film installation *False Films*, which incorporated three monitors showing similar footage metrically out of sync. In the middle of all this were rehearsals at the new Carroll Rehearsal Studio (humorously, across the hall was an ensemble rehearsing their quasi-Johnny-come-lately talk show opera) and basically running myself ragged.

Often for big shows, presenters like to have a talk-back after one of the shows. I've been fortunate to do this with many great moderators, including John Schaefer from WNYC's "New Sounds" to Mike Ross at the Krannert Center. My nephew, Brennan Mikel Ponder, had introduced me to the YouTube videos of the Gregory Brothers. At the time, I was particularly impressed with their "Auto-Tune the News #8." When BAM contacted me and offered an impressive list of choices, I thought to send them this link and suggest the Gregory Brothers instead. They wrote back with a "haha, very funny" response, but after I wrote a small essay on why I was serious, they got it and reached out to the group. Andrew Rose Gregory and Evan Gregory agreed to do the talk-back, and we had one of the best events ever. Smart, funny, and well informed. I was honored that in 2017, they asked me to costar as a right-wing uncle to Michael Gregory in the YouTube video "Meet Me in the Middle."

The run at BAM was exhilarating, though the crowds weren't as big as with *The End of Cinematics*. This was happening everywhere, as we had slid into a recession after the 2008 financial crisis and folks just weren't going out as much. Chris Ericson did his usual bang-up job with the sound design, and Hide's light effects, in play with Jeff's video design, were spectacular at the Harvey Theater, with the video melding into the rough-textured wall. Will Knapp kept the machine running smoothly. And while the Thursday night performance followed by the Gregory Brothers talk-back was great, I learned after the show, as we walked to a bar for a celebratory drink, that Lisa and I were being audited again (see "*The End of Cinematics* (1998): Part 2"). The strange coincidence of this happening during two different BAM seasons wasn't lost on anyone. I was pleased with the reviews and happy that Jon Pareles from the *New York Times* came. He noted, "Melding the sinewy stoicism of folk tradition with Mr. Rouse's structural tweaks, [the songs] pondered disappointments and diminishing expectations, personal and political, reaching pensive conclusions in succinct choruses: 'The world got away with me,' concluded the last tune." *Time Out New York* said, "Rouse's singing and songwriting here amount to heady but approachable pop songs, played by his band with a string quartet and a constant din of shortwave radio interference. New-music cognoscenti will relate to the ambitious construction and provocative themes; for pop explorers, think of Rouse as the next step past Mark Everett." On closing night, a few of us wandered to a nondescript bar, which felt less than celebratory. I had an uneasy feeling that things were going to get harder.

In spring of 2011, after fourteen mostly glorious years together, Lisa determined she'd had enough of silly love songs.* We're good friends now and thick as thieves, but this was a jolt. So, devastated and deserving, I found myself heading back to Luminato. It's an outdoor festival-like show, and I traveled with a programmable guitar loaned to me by the fantastic guitarist Jeff McErlain, whom I would work with on the *Hemisphere* retrospective concert at National Sawdust in 2017. This made travel a bit easier, as you could not only program the sounds (acoustic guitar to steel guitar . . . sorta), but also the tuning (from standard tuning to open G or drop D tuning). I think that due to schedule conflicts, we couldn't bring the Low-Rent Quartet. But Matt had refined the parts to a precise degree, and we felt that we could probably make a good local quartet work. At any rate, Luminato provided a great group of musicians in the Annex Quartet, and for singers we traveled with Sarah Emley and Melissa Zimmerman (Eryn wasn't available). Luminato supplied excellent rehearsal facilities, and I remember being calm and composed. I also remember Melissa Madden Gray (who was performing at the festival as her character Meow Meow) coming to a rehearsal and being quite supportive and enthusiastic. Lots of presenters were interested in the idea of a local or celebrity news reader, and in Toronto we were lucky

---

* Song titles include "Lisa, No Pizza Today," "Funky & Free," "Peace Toes," "I'm Not You," "Hippity Hoppity," "Take the Laundry In," and "Stinky Bus."

to get Canadian journalist and commentator Carol Off. She was game and kind and she did a very convincing job, as one might expect. Lisa's brother, Mark, and his wife, Anita, came. It was bittersweet. Afterward, a woman named Anna Kajtár, who worked with the opening act, led us in a strange merry-go-round-like walk to a nice local bar. We all sat and drank and had a pretty good time, but I remember, as I tried to process the last few months, that the absurdity of the final line in *Gravity Radio* hit home: "Chuck Norris wins."

The Demo, Krannert Center for the Performing Arts, 2014.

The Demo, Krannert Center for the Performing Arts, 2014.

The Demo (2015)

Around 2010 or 2011, after we had both had seasons at BAM's Next Wave Festival (my second engagement with *Gravity Radio* after *The End of Cinematics* in 2005), composer Ben Neill (see "*Failing Kansas* (1995)" and "*Dennis Cleveland* (1996): Part 1"), my good friend, approached me with a great idea. I had played a character in a piece of his called *Palladio*, and I remember a location shoot involving a Humvee and lots of disparaging stares. We'd been friends for almost twenty years, and I always marveled at his expansive interest in all things futuristic. I loved going to visit him in his Soho loft when he and his wife, Amy Lipton, lived in the city. He'd built quite a studio there, and he and I always shared an interest in pop music and production. He had worked with a theater company on his BAM debut, an adaptation of *Persephone*. This company had a lot of the usual downtown suspects involved, and I found much of their work had a predictable sameness to it.

Ben had also told me a few of the frustrations he had had with the building of his production. This company also had a relationship with Jeff Sugg, the video designer who has worked with me for years on various productions, including *Dennis Cleveland*, *The End of Cinematics*, and *Gravity Radio*. Jeff had a great collaborative relationship with the director and designer Jim Findlay. I had admired Jim's work for a while, and he was someone I'd hoped to work with one day. So, with all this in mind, Ben approached me with this historic video of a 1968 computer demonstration by Douglas Engelbart and his team from the Stanford Research Institute.

Engelbart's 1968 demo (sometimes referred to as "the mother of all demos") rolled out virtually everything that would define modern computing: videoconferencing, hyperlinks, networked collaboration, digital text editing, and something called a "mouse." When Ben sent me a video link (presented in ten-minute segments) from the SRI website, I must confess that the whole thing looked like one of those elaborate internet hoaxes. And the grainy video had the sort of retro feel that was popular in the early punk days: utilizing 1950s imagery and ironically repurposing it. The more I watched the demonstration, the more I could see how this could be a very cool immersive piece. Ben wanted us to collaborate on the music. I would play Engelbart, and he would sort of play Bill English, Engelbart's assistant. With a mutant trumpet. The mutant trumpet was Ben's invention, and he'd been perfecting this multipurpose instrument for years. It can trigger any number of midi commands, from synths to video. It seemed like a great metaphor, as Bill English was responsible for making many of Engelbart's visions a physical reality.

Having worked on many pieces as a hired gun or collaborator, I realized I enjoy the process of contributing to a piece and not being totally responsible for it. Writing, directing, and performing in a work require a lot of stamina, and if you add in all the other day-to-day tech and admin chores, it can be draining. Working with Merce Cunningham, Ulysses Dove, and Joe Goode were all gratifying experiences, so I thought adding my input to *The Demo* would be a great way to work on a large project and not be totally responsible. I also hoped to make a little coin. So I jumped in with enthusiasm. I had recently been offered the first Artist in Residence position at the eDream Institute, a new digital arts media lab under the umbrella of the National Center for Supercomputing Applications in Urbana. I had a long history with NCSA and had worked closely with Donna Cox, Bob Patterson, and Jeff Carpenter on both *The End of Cinematics* and *Gravity Radio*. I offered to Ben the suggestion of building aspects of the music and concept as part of this residency. I was also excited about this idea because Chris Ericson, the gifted sound designer for many of my pieces, had taken over his mentor Jon Schoenoff's audio director position at the Krannert Center after Jon's untimely passing. The thought of having his expertise at the beginning of the conceptualizing process with eDream seemed prescient. I was not wrong in this thinking. With Chris's guidance, we took over the Studio Theater at Krannert and set up a large computer-based media studio.

Donna and Bob helped with numerous computers and video projection setups. The idea was to run the original Engelbart demonstration and figure out how to orchestrate the scenes while keeping track of the presentation framework. As is uniquely typical of Krannert, Karen Quisenberry, the assistant director of production, suggested Austin Lin as our stage manager and production assistant. He was a great choice, as he was interested in both computer technology and theater. It was a perfect fit. Austin was amazing at troubleshooting any of our connection and sync issues (we were running up to ten computers as well as video and Ben's elaborate music setup. Austin also helped me with the code for the John Cage 4'33" YouTube installation I was working on for the Michael Tilson Thomas/New World Symphony Cage marathon (see "*Cage/Cunningham* (1997–2013)").

Ben and I made steady progress on the music beds. We both loved beats and working with sequencers. Ben was immersed in the language of techno, and I had recently released the techno-heavy album *Boost* as part of a double CD. It seemed clear that Ben could be conceptually linked to Bill English on stage just by doing what he does with his mutant trumpet and various laptops and programs. But as Engelbart, I needed to find a way to emulate the original demo while providing an added layer of content. I wondered how to speak or sing in a way that wouldn't seem corny. I solved this issue with *Dennis Cleveland* by simply utilizing the circus-like performance of the talk show. But I felt at a loss as we composed to the original demo video and watched as Engelbart demonstrated the possible uses of a personal computer. As I watched text being typed, from organizing grocery lists to explaining hyperlinks and displaying complex lines of code, it hit me: the libretto could be made up of code displayed on the screen.

My Engelbart could smoothly vacillate between Engelbart's own speech and singing and speaking the code as it appeared on screen. I was incredibly excited about this idea and by the fact that it had been staring us in the face all along. In fact, Ben and I were both concerned about what we would do with the long, and possibly tedious, sections of text and code on the screen. Problem solved! Around this time, or possibly before, it occurred to me that we might encounter a rights issue in using the full 1968 demo film as our basis. I think Michael Mushalla and I did a deep dive to learn whom we would need to approach at SRI. We finally got permission, but it felt touch and go there for a while.

I think we made three residency trips to Urbana between 2012 and 2013. We got a tour of Blue Waters, a petascale supercomputer at NCSA. We even did some promo shots there, wearing the short-sleeve white shirts and black ties of the original demo, adding that "New Wave" retro thing that was, again, so prevalent in the '80s. During these trips, NCSA also set up a room with three connecting screens for us to experiment with multi-projection ideas and virtual control surfaces. Through all of this, I was thinking about how we were going to make folks aware of the piece and the various ways we would get the word out to presenters. This was one thing I truly hoped would be handled by the theater company, but around this time, Ben's colleague, who ran this company, decided he didn't want our project to be part of the theater company. This set off minor alarm bells, but I shrugged it off and kept working with Ben. With Jeff Carpenter's video editing skills, we simulated the triggering mechanism we would hope to create to manipulate the original video footage. Simple things like having Engelbart sing or repeat phrases from the original demo demonstration in rhythmic variation. These video excerpts would be helpful with grants and promoting the piece. It would be hard to overstate how helpful the Krannert Center, eDream, and NCSA were during these early stages. Also, around this time or maybe earlier, Ben had connected with Bill English. I'm pretty sure Ben was investigating history at the Computer History Museum in Menlo Park. Ben had let someone who worked there know of his interest in the original demo, and to his surprise, this person invited Bill English to join him for a tour of the museum. I remember Ben sending me a picture of him and Bill together. Quite an auspicious turn of events. Bill also sent us a photo of him showing Doug Engelbart our rough promo film. Doug had been battling Alzheimer's disease and he would pass away before our premiere, but it's such a special photo, both men smiling with pride.

The original demo in 1968 introduced several unique hardware interfaces, common now but near-revolutionary at the time. These include the mouse, a keyboard with numbers and letters (instead of inputting information with a punch card), and a chorded keyset, which used chord-like key combinations to send commands. Not only did Engelbart introduce word processing, document sharing, and hyperlinks, he had also integrated text, graphics, and video conferencing. The demo would even foreshadow the internet. By laying thirty miles of cable between San Francisco (where the demonstration happened) and Stanford

Research Institute in Menlo Park, Engelbart and his team simulated the connected future we inhabit today. And through all of this, Engelbart had a humanistic view of using technology to create a more connected and visionary world. In part, he was inspired by a famous 1945 article by Vannevar Bush in *The Atlantic* magazine. The demo's opening statement asked the following question: "If in your office, you, as an intellectual worker, were supplied with a computer display backed up by a computer that was alive for you all day, and was instantly responsive to every action you have, how much value could you derive from that?" This was the aspect that intrigued both Ben and me.

In the original demo, there's a moment in the presentation when Engelbart shows and explains the three interfaces. An over-the-shoulder shot allows the audience to see the three devices as Engelbart explains their function, and, in addition to the many live cameras in the show, Jeff Sugg wanted to capture that shot live as well. That started us thinking about what interfaces I would be using on stage and what those interfaces would be doing. Chris Ericson and I thought it would be great if we could duplicate the keyset and use it as a video trigger. But aside from the original demo video, we didn't know how it functioned. Bill English came to the rescue and sent us a keyset. It wasn't from the original demo, but it was a very similar keyset he had used and developed for Xerox. Chris found a place in Urbana that could both build a look-alike keyset as well as the pin connections to make the keyset function. It's a thing of beauty and it worked well. A special moment was at the premiere in 2015 at Bing Concert Hall, as part of Stanford Live, when Bill English came. The premiere had a week of events and seminars surrounding the performances. I had traveled numerous times to Stanford to work with Wiley Hausam, the executive director of Stanford Live. Bill was one of many speakers and panelists at this seminar, which included Jaron Lanier and Sebastian Thrun. After the first performance, I told Bill I had the original keyset back at my hotel and could bring it to the second show. He thought for a second and then smiled, saying, "Why don't you keep it?"

But it would be a while before we got to any performances of *The Demo*. Krannert, NCSA, and eDream had provided the crucial beginning phase. Now we needed to find another workshop space to continue, and I needed to compose the text and libretto as well as find singers to record the singing that would be doubled live. Ben had floated the idea that we might be able to do some workshop/build at Ramapo College, where he taught. But after months of wrangling and logistics, it just wasn't going to happen. In addition, after fourteen years, I decided it was time to part ways with my agent, Michael Mushalla. So I was on the lookout for a new person, but by 2012, the pickings were slim. Enter Tommy Kriegsmann and his company ArKtype. I can't remember how I connected with Tommy, but we had a light dinner in the Village, and he was immediately interested in working together. I told him about *The Demo*, but I was slightly evasive because I had assumed Ben and his colleague from the theater company would be in charge of this aspect of booking shows. I had already offered my residency to the project, and I was waiting for some reciprocation from this team. At any rate, I later met with Ben and told him I was willing to bring this project to Tommy. Ben and his colleague were both in academia, and they said they would oversee looking for grants and funding. But that never materialized. We did receive a MAP grant for *The Demo*, but only after I pushed to apply, since Ben had told me he thought it was too long a shot to work on. I agreed it was indeed a long shot, but I had received a MAP grant for *The End of Cinematics*, so I pushed for completing the application. As Ben and his colleague had teaching jobs, their attitude was that they didn't need or expect to get paid for *The Demo*. I gently explained that I understood their position, but this is how I made my living. I had shows that toured for ten to fifteen years. Smaller projects, where I was a hired gun, usually garnered two to four years of income through touring and/or royalties. That was my expectation here.

At any rate, I started the vocal writing at my studio in New York. I brought in a number of singers, including Melissa Madden Gray, who worked on *Dennis Cleveland*, to record both scored and improvised material. Mel nailed the recitation of the code and I thought she sounded fantastic. I worked fast and was happy to have a general recorded outline for the text libretto in about four months. This would be just before we'd start a workshop at Jim Findlay's venerable workspace, the Collapsable Hole. Both Jim and Jeff Sugg had used this funky space in Williamsburg, Brooklyn, to build pieces and do performances and happenings. It was also right next to a corner bar called Skinny Dennis that served great frozen bourbon coffee slushes. I was happy to be there but distressed at my financial situation. Somehow, Ben and I had found some financing to rent the Hole. I know Ben kicked in some funds. Tommy and I found a little scratch to help with Jim and Jeff's fees, and Ben and his colleague had made it clear that they were covered by their college teaching positions. All good, but that left me doing a lot of the heavy lifting with no income. This was stressful, and I remember having an episode where I stopped breathing in the middle of the night. I ran to my bathroom window and opened it, hoping that fresh air would help. I saw the building across an empty lot and thought: this is the last thing I'll ever see. I managed to calm down, and when I related this story to the group the next day, someone noted it sounded like a panic attack. I had never had one, but that made sense.

We had a couple of crude midi controllers to approximate triggering video. We tried several approaches, including an excruciating stab at me memorizing the Engelbart text. That fell flat. At one point, Jim raised the question of what the "point" of the piece was. This was helpful, and I remember wishing that Jim would direct *The Demo*, but I'm not sure he would have wanted that responsibility. We settled on the idea that, as Engelbart was demonstrating software and hardware, Ben and I would sort of mirror that with our various controllers. That at least gave him and me a purpose to be onstage. All in all, we made progress at the Hole, and I enjoyed getting to work with Jeff and Ben as well as getting to know Jim and see the amazing two-headed team of Jeff and Jim working together.

I think Tommy got us a short residency at the Park Avenue Armory. It's an amazing performance space with floors of smaller rooms that can house workshops and small residencies. We settled in for a week or two and resumed some of the workshop ideas we were experimenting with at the Hole. Next door, Taylor Mac was rehearsing his *A 24-Decade History of Popular Music*. We brought in about five singers, and I enlisted the help of my longtime music director, Matthew Gandolfo, to block the singers as well as teach the vocal parts. I remember that after the last day at the Armory, I took Matt down the street to Donohue's Steak House, where we downed steak and martinis. A few years prior, a longtime patron of Donohue's left two waitresses $50K in cash when he passed away, as a way of saying thank you. I also revisited the iconic Le Veau d'Or, where Kathy, the manager, always welcomed me. We made steady progress and hoped we had enough strung together to mount a show. Our next stop would be a workshop performance at the Krannert Center.

Tommy had made the connection with Wiley, and Stanford Live was offering a wide range of support. Mike Ross graciously suggested we think of the Krannert performance as a workshop performance rather than the premiere. Mike was always about protecting the art first and foremost. We needed a lighting designer and I offered to speak with my longtime designer, Hideaki Tsutsui. Hide was excited to help. We also needed a stage manager, and I suggested Valerie Oliveiro or Jenny Goelz. I had also introduced Jenny to Tommy; he hired her but had her bogged down with his business in New York, so Valerie agreed to join us. So now, with Matt, Chris, Jeff, Hide, and Val, we basically had my longtime crew (with the addition of Jim, of course). Not to put too fine a point on it, but everything that was happening, from the bookings to the agent to the team, was coming from my end. This was not what I had signed on for, but these things take on a life of their own. I remember a particularly frustrating moment walking through Central Park while I was talking on the phone with Jeff, who shared his own frustrations. Jeff stated, with a wry smile I could almost see over the phone, "We always just kinda work around him." I had my answer. Armed with this insight, we headed to Krannert. We started our build in the Colwell Playhouse, where I had premiered *The End of Cinematics* in 2005. Chris procured some great retro-looking metal furniture that gave our set a cool, sleek vibe. In keeping with the original demo's look, we wanted the front projection screen to resemble the screen from that presentation. In addition, Jim and Jeff created a beautiful rear-projection system that abstractly represented the action of Engelbart's team thirty miles away in Menlo Park. The "look" was coming together. Hide's light design was beautiful and meshed with the video projections almost seamlessly. It was also during this build that I suggested the idea of the performance continuing through the ten-minute intermission, so as not to break from the original demo timeline. I liked the way this helped the "installation feeling" flow. At the end of each day, we'd sit together for notes. I remember that after one particularly grueling session, Val came back to my dressing room and said, "I'm so, so sorry." I asked her what she meant, and she said she thought I might be exaggerating the issues I was dealing with. Now she realized I wasn't and said she'd never sat through such an unprofessional approach. Tell me about it. At any rate, we soldiered on and did a sold-out workshop performance. I still thought the piece had legs.

After we returned to New York, the entire team agreed that Ben's colleague had to go. Ben tried to explain our reasons to him, but he took the legal approach and the team agreed to let him keep his director title, and in return, he would stay away. But for the most part, Bing was an enjoyable build. The concert hall is huge, with wraparound sails that we utilized as projection screens. The hall's acoustics are great for non-amplified music. Chris took this ball and ran with it, designing a sound system of many smaller speaker arrays that allowed us to get volume without annoying acoustic reflections. Hide decided to light the ceiling of the venue as well, so the entire theater was an immersive installation. Fitting for a demonstration in the tech hub of Silicon Valley.

Wiley had hired a great publicist firm in New York called 21CC. I started working closely with them several months before the premiere. They weren't getting a lot of traction, but I had an ace up my sleeve. Ben and I had met for drinks with John Markoff, a journalist best known for covering technology for the *New York Times*. He also wrote the book *What the Dormouse Said: How the Sixties Counterculture Shaped the Personal Computer Industry*. This was a fascinating book and offered a lot of insight into Engelbart, SRI, and the heady early years of tech. John seemed interested in our project, so I asked him if he would be interested in doing a piece on it. He seemed intrigued and said that he had written something for every section of the *Times* except Arts & Leisure. Our premiere at Stanford Live would be Wednesday, April 1, 2015. John's article came out a week before and placed us on the cover of the Arts & Leisure section. In addition, through following many leads, at the last minute I placed an article in *Wired* magazine, the premiere popular journal of all things tech. I think Ben was particularly excited about this.

Then a wild thing occurred. Following the *Times* and *Wired* placements, the monthslong effort by 21CC got supercharged and suddenly, we were getting both domestic and international features. Everywhere, from London and France (Shaun Tandon did a very large piece for Agence France-Presse) to Bangkok, Australia, and Kuwait. Everyone, from ABC and NBC News to *Le Soir* and the *Times of India*. We were poised for just the kind of success I needed to justify all the hassle. Then, in the middle of all the radio and TV interviews, I heard from Tommy that he wasn't coming to the premiere. He had recently had a child, but I thought he could have at least given me a heads-up. He apologized and said he had been trying for a month to make it work. So no one to help take all that press and turn it into solid bookings. I was crestfallen.

We sold out both nights, and the opening was quite a success. The show looked good, and the local singers did a great job under Matt's direction. One of the singers, Claire Karoly, was particularly great, and we've remained friends and collaborators. She sang on the Metronome record *Take Down* as well as the recording *Hemisphere*. One doesn't often think of drugs and psychedelics when thinking of computer nerds, but apparently the mood during the 1960s had an influence on the early days of computing. We didn't emphasize this aspect, but looking back at video of the Bing performances, one gets a trippy vibe. Stanford Live had hired a great camera crew to shoot both shows. I'm happy to have the documentation, but it was a lot of work to coordinate all the crew's camera needs in addition to *The Demo*'s tech needs. Together we must have laid miles of cable. There's no way to know if all this tech led to the second night's performance's near disaster. About five or ten minutes into the show, we began having connection issues to the main program screen. Val wisely called for a stop. Ben and I rose to leave and got generous applause as we exited the stage. Backstage, we were very nervous, and as time passed, things felt even heavier. At the half-hour mark, I was sweating bullets. At around forty-five minutes, Wiley, who had been with us backstage, wondered at what point would we call the show. We were going to give it five more minutes and miraculously, through all that cable, they found the issue. We took the stage and, starting from the beginning, completed the show.

Every performer's biggest fear had just landed on us, and we survived. My mother and sister had come to the show along with my artist nephew, Brennan. As we all sat together after the show, everyone was quiet. I looked at Brennan and smiled, saying, "You sure you wanna get into this racket?" I stuck around after the final show to help with load-out. It was a huge undertaking. We went to a bar to let off steam, and afterward Claire offered to drive me back to my hotel. We ended up listening to Sparks on her car radio and talking about the show. That evening will forever be remembered as "dead battery night," as her car battery drained due to letting the car idle and listening to music. A suitable end to a wild run.

The next day, my family rented a van to head to San Francisco to spend a few days. I remember circling the campus on our way out and feeling so relieved to be leaving. Brennan and I hooked up with Ben and a friend of his, and I could tell he was pleased. I was happy for him but knew our goals were different. Those few days in San Francisco were just what I needed. My family was game, and we hit all my favorite spots: Sam's Grill (where we dined in one of the charming old rooms), Swan Oyster Depot (where I introduced Brennan to oysters), and the Buena Vista, where Brennan and I downed too many of their famous Irish coffees (but not before walking from Swan and meeting the bon vivant Ivan, who was standing in his garage next to his Italian motorcycle. On a previous production trip, Jim Findlay and a small group had passed by and spied Ivan in his garage wearing an ascot. Jim mentioned he could imagine me wearing an ascot, so I surprised him by wearing one at the opening night reception. When Brennan and I walked by, I spotted the bike and told him the story. Brennan was bold and called out. At first Ivan was leery but invited us in and fed us wine and cheese. Brennan said he'd been in an artistic rut, and I think that afternoon with Ivan, who told his amazing life stories, helped). We ended up at the historic Vesuvio Cafe, where Brennan quickly made friends with some street folks while Mom and Cindy and I mellowed out, until Brennan appeared with his shirtless body pressed against the window. Mom still loves remembering herding the cats back to the hotel.

Ben and I had always discussed the possibility of a "club mix" of *The Demo*, a suitcase show that wouldn't require the overhead of the full performance. So I asked Jeff to record both performances of the program screen. I would take the files back to New York and merge them with the soundtrack so that Ben and I could do a scaled-down version. We got exactly one show at the Lied Center in Lawrence, Kansas. Jackie Davis, the executive director of the New York Public Library for the Performing Arts at Lincoln Center, introduced me to Derek Kwan, the director of the Lied Center. He was enthusiastic about bringing the "club mix" to Lied, and his crew was top notch.

But it was clear to me that this wasn't going to go any further. *The Demo* had some thrilling elements, but I never felt that it achieved the effect of feeling "inevitable" the way my favorite pieces did. That was always my goal. Engelbart, in the end, lived in a society that never fully grasped his innovation and goals. He once said, "The rate at which a person can mature is directly proportional to the embarrassment he can tolerate. I have tolerated a lot." And . . . scene.

Recordings (1980–2020)

Return 1999 and *Funding* 2001. In 1986 I completed *Book 1*, a collection of nine string quartets. I got connected with the Laurentian String Quartet and we did a reading. The music was complicated, so Mark Lambert came on board to conduct and help with rehearsals. We premiered *Book 1* at the Knitting Factory in 1989. At the same time, we did a taping of four or five of the quartets at WNYC for John Schaefer's *New Sounds*. Through the '80s and early '90s, I did dozens of shows with John, from Mikel Rouse Broken Consort performances in the studio to interviews and CD premieres. John even devoted an entire show to my music on my fortieth birthday. He was and is a tireless supporter of new music. At any rate, I had recorded the music for *The End of Cinematics*, and the complexities of mounting that show meant it would be a while before that music was released. In the meantime, I was itching to make another record, so I landed on the idea of sampling some of the string quartets and repurposing them in a collection of off-kilter pop songs. After mixing and matching the quartet samples, I then composed woodwind and brass parts to enhance the lush effect. I was working with Dale Kleps, who played EWI and sax in Broken Consort, and he multitracked flute and sax. Tim Ouimette added trumpet on a few tracks, including my favorite, "Tennessee Gold," which achieved a kind of soaring, '60s, "Wichita Lineman" feel.

Return and a couple of other recordings during this time fall into a kind of no-man's land, in that I was starting to release things on my own label, ExitMusic Recordings, and the mechanism for distribution wasn't yet in place. It would be another ten years or so before digital releases were possible. Consequently, there was very little critical response upon its release. It happens. Kyle Gann, writing in the *Village Voice*, said of *Return*, "Stockhausen himself would envy the number of lines and textures Rouse can seduce you into listening to all at once, and the success of that depends on Rouse's amazing ability as a recording producer to locate all these levels in a virtual audio space deep and transparent enough that they don't get in each other's way."

After working with video artist and filmmaker Cliff Baldwin on *Living Inside Design* and *Failing Kansas*, I was itching to get back into making films. I'd studied film at the Kansas City Art Institute with Larry Hope and had the good fortune to be there when Stan Brakhage, one of the most important filmmakers in twentieth-century experimental film, taught for a semester. I learned about the Bates Method for better eyesight from Stan, and his approach would shape several of my ideas. All through school I was shooting 8- and 16-millimeter film and checking out video tape recorders from KCAI. I completed the film *Roundtable*, starring James Gleespen, while in school and continued making shorts when I got to New York. But in the mid- to late '90s, prosumer video was starting to catch on as a legit way to make films, and I quickly scooped up a Sony PD150 DVCAM camera and editing deck. For the film *Funding*, I enlisted numerous actors including Veanne Cox, Susana Ribeiro, and Lisa Boudreau, and filmed them in various locations, some real (like a chiropractic session) and some created (like a fire escape in Beirut). I then wrote narration and had the actors and myself dub dialog, including an English-to-French translation by David Lancourt. The four narrative films are underscored with strings and woodwinds and surrounded by four large abstract films with additional choral parts. Once again, I brought in Dale Kleps for the woodwinds and Mary Rowell, of ETHEL fame, to overdub violins and viola.

The film played at several large festivals, including the Perth Festival in Australia and the Eclectic Orange Festival in California. There were also a few museum installations of the film. Mark Swed, writing for the *Los Angeles Times*, said, "As Kerouac did through his prose, as Godard has done through his visual technique, as Ashley has done through his sung poetry, Rouse finds a musical style that makes these shadowy figures mesmerizing. They don't sing to us but talk over catchy musical lines. There is much in *Funding*, particularly the interaction between video and music (Rouse directed and edited the film himself) that seems new. And Rouse's music, the overlapping rhythmic patterns in strings and winds and electronic keyboards are pure sonic encouragement, lifting us all to a higher plane."

Cameraworld 2001 and *Test Tones* 2005. The world is filled with great ideas that fizzle before they find their place in time. Such is the delight of both the album and the performance of *Cameraworld*. Imagine this scenario: five performers in '60s-style suits moving with Temptations-like choreography to aggressive hip-hop beats and Cliff Baldwin's abstract video accompaniment. What could go wrong? I was doing a deep dive into sampling and creating beats. In fact, I created a number of beats and grooves and used them as a basis for a number of workshops, including one in San Francisco for *The End of Cinematics*. I took these beats to Paris during a Cunningham tour and sat in brasseries and composed complex lyrics to the grooves. I remember it as one of my favorite creative times. Writing the lyrics for the album during the day, seeing Cunningham at night. Pinch me. And everything was coming together. I'm a fan of fashion designer Agnès B. and have mostly worn her clothing for thirty-five years; they even had a poster of *Dennis Cleveland* in their Soho dressing room. We wrangled a great discount on five matching suits for me and cast members Eric Smith, Robert Arthur Altman, David Masenheimer, and Kameko Hebron. I remember cast members fawning over the choices we had.

And to top off the look, I bought matching watches as an opening night gift: a replica of the original Hamilton PSR digital watch from 1970. I also got this opening night gift for my agent, Michael Mushalla, and our lighting designer, Hideaki Tsutsui, who's a watch collector and claims this is his favorite watch. But I digress. Cliff's film is a gorgeous montage of everything that ubiquitous video over-saturates. He's truly a genius. Which was the hope. So, after a year or so of beat creation, I settled into my studio to multitrack the voices that would comprise the recording as well as the parts for the show. It was a glorious time as I remember, riffing and combining vocal tracks over the sparse rhythm tracks. I switched out my analog mixer for a Panasonic Ramsa WR-DA7 digital mixer, and the workflow was smooth.

Tech snags always cropped up, what with sync issues and so many digital devices talking to each other. As Rave Tesar once said, as he and I struggled over midi protocols in the '80s, "I'm amazed at how often it works!" Sometimes great things happen, and you're propped up in a magical belief that you matter. Celebrities come to your shows and folks you respect chime in, and all is good with the world. *Cameraworld* has only one moment like that, but it's memorable. The five of us were rehearsing at Carol Music Studios on Forty-First Street, just off Ninth Ave in my hood. We had playback in the rehearsal studio, but we were also rehearsing the choreography by Robert, which would be part of the performance. Suddenly, there's a knock on our studio door. We open it to meet the immortal Harry Belafonte, who had been waiting in the downstairs office for his own rehearsal. The rooms all had individual cameras and live closed-circuit feeds to the main office where he was waiting. He noticed something curious yet familiar, and he wanted to come up and ask what we were up to. A great way to meet an idol and, again, maybe the entire reason this piece existed.

I remember taking the early mixes from *Cameraworld*, like "When You Turn Your Face On" and "Bounce to Disc," to use as the opening warm-up music for *Dennis Cleveland* on the West Coast. Levensky Smith, an original cast member of *Cleveland*, was particularly impressed with these new tracks. Mark Kingsley did the cover photo and design for the CD, and I would release the album on my label ExitMusic Recordings. We headed to Florida State University where Director of Performing Arts Michael Blachly had landed. He came from UCLA and would become a presenter and co-commissioner of *The End of Cinematics*. The idea was that this would be the first build toward a long tour. But this would be the one and only performance of *Cameraworld*, as interest in touring *Dennis Cleveland* started to take priority. It's a sadly familiar but still strange occurrence that so much work can go into a piece but it just fizzles. After storing the wardrobe for several years (at one point, I had storage spaces in three states holding sets and archival materials), I gave cast members the suits and kept one for myself. Twenty years later, the suit still fits.

From around 2001 to 2003 or so, I was traveling between New York and Ruston for a three-year Meet the Composer residency. I realized a few large works there, including the realization of the John Cage radio play *James Joyce, Marcel Duchamp, Erik Satie: An Alphabet*. I had set up a makeshift studio in an office on the Louisiana Tech campus and furnished it with a basic monitoring system and a Yamaha AW4416 digital recorder—basically a self-contained studio in a box that included preamps, eq, and effects. It was an unwieldy box to learn, but the small footprint and interconnectivity made it a good choice for this studio. I had also brought a couple of AKG 414 mics for the *Alphabet* project, and these would be used on *Test Tones* as well. I set up the studio in spring 2001, I think. It was strange being in this small town, alone after hours on campus. I'd never been remotely involved in academia save for some lectures and master classes over the years. In hindsight, I remember one reason I took on this residency was so I could keep my agent, Michael Mushalla, on board. Sometimes, you gotta pay to play. I remember recording the first song that would be on *Test Tones*, a dark, loping track called "America's Belief." It somehow poured out as I sat in this dystopian setting:

> *And the sleepy town, what goes up goes down*
> *Who's the prophet, who's the thief?*
> *And the falling stars and the whiskey bars*
> *Of America's belief*

I'd set up the studio and was conflicted and heading back to NYC. But I felt like I had to get something recorded just to save my sanity, so I recorded and mixed "America's Belief" in one late-night session. We had also gotten an eighty-eight-key weighted keyboard sampler for cueing the "rational sounds" for the stage performance of *Alphabet* (see "*Cage/Cunningham* (1997–2013)"), and I would repurpose many of those sampled sounds on *Test Tones* and *Music for Minorities*. I continued to work on the record even as we rehearsed for the *Alphabet* tour, which would premiere at the Edinburgh Festival in August. But after performing in Berlin just after 9/11 and being stuck in Dublin for a while, the record took on a darker tone. A disturbing but beautiful choral piece called "Poor God" had voices fading in and out with a spiraling refrain:

> *Look what you have done*
> *I have to start all over*
> *Poor God Poor God*
> *Now I have to start all over again*
> *Poor God Poor God*

As the song "This is the Best" surmised, "This is the best, the best we can do." I also remember playing the title track for Caleb Nelson, my residency director's son. It's a dark, brooding meditation on small-town, lost America, and when I asked Caleb what he thought, he replied, "It's accurate." *Test Tones* would be a companion CD to the next record, *Music for Minorities*, and this would be reflected in the design variations by Mark Kingsley for the CD packages. *Test Tones* was dedicated to Steve Reich and Brian Wilson.

Music for Minorities 2005. We were gearing up for a number of big shows, but I always felt I needed to keep making "suitcase shows" to be able to keep working. And it was starting to be increasingly clear that my mid-'90s strategy of having multimedia shows as a way for the music to be heard was the only way to go. I never sold many records to begin with, and I didn't anticipate the general collapse of CD revenue, which reversed the traditional equation, which had always proposed touring to promote sales of the record rather than performances as the main source of income.

But that's where things were heading, and I was grateful I had that "aha" moment in the early '90s. I was still juggling several shows when I started recording *Music for Minorities*. I had acquired a Manley mic preamp for *Test Tones* and liked the sound of it and wanted to update my mic selection, so I scored a Neumann U87, which had a warmer sound suitable for the material. Through the residency, I had met Po' Henry and Tookie, the stage names for the interracial blues duo of Henry Dorsey and Wayne Collom. They play traditional Delta blues and would invite me to play along at their rehearsal space where Wayne worked, which was basically the small front office of a warehouse that stored voting machines. I learned a lot from these sessions, including hanging on for dear life. Henry would sometimes tune his guitar down to E-flat, and Wayne, on harmonica, didn't miss a beat. We also played a show together where I debuted *Music for Minorities* and they did their normal set. The times playing with Henry and Tookie had a decided effect on the feel of the new record. Acoustic and slide guitars provided a blues feel while being combined with subtle electronic percussion and synths. I remember trying out some of my rotating guitar riffs while jamming with Henry and his surprise and delight at the effect.

The opening track, "That's My Universe," summed up the feeling of the record lyrically:

I made my own religion
I made up my own verse
I gave myself permission
And that's my universe

In addition to the recording of the album, I was making a full-length performance film that would also be included as a DVD with the CD. I did interviews with lots of the locals and combined that with other locations, including New York. By far, my favorite interview subject was Sarah Albritton, a multidisciplined artist at food preparation, restaurant decor, yard art, Christmas decorations, autobiographical prose, poetry, and painting. I met Sarah through my residency director, Mary Anne Lewis. For decades, Sarah had owned and operated her restaurant, Sarah's Kitchen, out of her house. It was known far and wide, and Mary Anne knew of my love for these iconic places. The problem was that Sarah, while still painting and doing cooking demonstrations, had closed Sarah's Kitchen. Mary Anne took me over for a visit, and Sarah was busy preparing food that she would take with her the next day, traveling out of town for a food exhibit. Somehow, I raised the topic of peach cobbler from my childhood, and she looked at me and asked, "You want some peach cobbler? Come back tomorrow morning." I tried to beg off, knowing she was busy, but she insisted. As we left, I told Mary Anne something was off. It's not in my karma to miss out on this kind of place. When we returned the next morning, Sarah had made an entire meal of rib tips, collards, potatoes, and cornbread followed by the aforementioned peach cobbler. As I dug in, Mary Anne stared at me as if she'd seen a ghost. She couldn't believe I'd gotten exactly what I referred to the day before and added, "You can't imagine how many people would give anything to be you right now."

I stayed close to Sarah throughout the residency, and toward the end, I wanted to buy one of her smaller paintings of angels. Her paintings were becoming profitable, and I could only afford a small one. As I chose the small painting in her studio, I was admiring much of the work and noticed a larger painting of the outside of Sarah's Kitchen and reminded her of how special that meal had been. We left and I headed to the studio, but later, on returning to Mary Anne's house, she again looked at me stunned and said, "You had a visitor." Sarah had stopped by to give me the Sarah's Kitchen painting. I was overcome with joy but called to ask if she was sure she wanted to part with this special painting. She replied, "Honey, I don't do nothing unless I want to."

I continued churning out tracks while also filming in rural neighborhoods, Walmarts, and dive bars. I filmed the Tech choral group in robes in the Louisiana woods. I also repurposed videos from *Test Tones*, set to new tracks from *Music for Minorities*. I was happy with the sentiment and offhand approach to lyrics. In an unexpected Leonard Cohen vein, I cobbled together these lyrics for the song, "Change for My Baby":

> *I don't know nothin' and something else*
> *But the world keeps moving all by itself*
> *And I'd probably save her if I only could*
> *Change for my baby make me feel so good*
>
> *Well I guarantee nothing, I know what's right*
> *I got priority seating on the earth tonight*
> *And I even got sanctions in the neighborhood*
> *Change for my baby make me feel so good*

The local residency portion was always having trouble matching the Meet the Composer funds, so I was traveling with all my own video gear and anything else needed to work there. I'm proud of the work I did with the locals, and my goal was to bring attention to an underserved community, bringing artists and musicians in on a regular basis. But the experience was draining, and as I prepped the CD/DVD release, I was looking forward to trying this solo show on the road. The record was dedicated to Kate Sullivan, who graced many of the *Dennis Cleveland* performances. Both *Test Tones* and *Music for Minorities* were mastered by Adam Ayan at Gateway Mastering. The masters came back with lots of digital artifacts, and I spent most of my time finding those instead of focusing on the sound of the mastering, which was annoying and time-consuming. This led me to master several of my own recordings moving forward, until I found someone who I thought actually gave a damn. I would find this person in Matt Agoglia at Masterdisk, who would later start his own mastering suite, The Ranch Mastering.

The first stab at doing this show would be in Seattle at On the Boards, a performing art space directed by Lane Czaplinski. We rolled in and I had a lunch date to meet Valerie Oliveiro for the first time. She would be the production manager for the show. I liked her instantly and we both knew we had to hit the ground running, as we had little time to set lights (once again, the lighting design was by Hide Tsutsui) and such. There was a lot of press stuff to do, as well as radio, and, timing not working in my favor, I got sick as a dog and totally lost my voice. I tried to beg off the radio interviews to save my voice, but my agent was having none of it, so I soldiered on. Anyway, the show, though largely forgotten, went well and set the stage for many big and small shows.

We took the show to many large and small venues, including a week at the Sydney Opera House (followed by a week of *Failing Kansas* performances), the Cork Opera House, and the Galway Festival, hosted by the great Paul Fahy. Sydney was a great two-week run. Wendy Martin was the head of theater and dance at the opera house, and I loved getting to know her. After seeing *Music for Minorities*, she asked me to lunch and inquired if I was a Buddhist. I wasn't, but I liked the impression the piece left on her. I normally resist artist housing, but we were put in a gloriously funky hotel for artists. I was on the top floor and could roll out of bed and walk a few stairs to the roof, where an espresso machine allowed me to perfect a flat white. Val and Chris took the days off learning to surf and meeting an excited German, who would happily declare, "I stands on ze surf!" Chris and I loved our walk to the opera house, where we would stop at the iconic pie cart Harry's Cafe de Wheels. I remember Melissa Madden Gray coming over and clearing magazines off the lobby coffee table to teach Chris and me dance moves.

Writing in *SX News*, Katrina Fox said, "On split screens, moving stories are told in fragments as Mikel Rouse plays guitar and sings songs inspired by '60s pop and Delta blues in the first of his two works, *Music for Minorities*. Accompanied by a soundscape of percussion and multiple guitars, Rouse weaves stories and interacts with synchronized video cut from interviews with a range of personalities from his hometown of New York. He refers to the work as 'romantic channel surfing,' in which he explores the troubled, darker aspects of middle America and offers a voice to the 'Silent Minorities' of the media age." But of all the great press, a favorite memory was an email from a person named Andrew, who wrote, "Whilst a limited exposure to the contemporary performing arts is one possible reason we were so overcome by what we encountered, I prefer to think that the artistry and insight we saw displayed through the music, the images and the poetry, all performed with humility and a palpable depth of emotion, may have had something to do with it. We went out to dinner afterwards, raved about the performance amongst ourselves, discussed the many and varied nuances of meaning and emotion experienced, laughed and drank. It was a wonderful evening. Thanks so much for the huge part you played in it." I've often thought of this kind note and am still grateful to have received it.

We also had stellar shows at UCLA in the Macgowan Little Theater. I believe David Sefton, who had been a co-commissioner of *The End of Cinematics*, brought the show to UCLA. At the time, David and his wife lived in a sort of tree house in Los Angeles. A priceless memory is having lunch there with the legendary Van Dyke Parks. Alan Rich in *LA Weekly* wrote, "Mikel Rouse is not so much a man of the theater; he is the theater. A few years back, alone on another local stage with harmonica and guitar, he turned himself into a pair of Kansas murderers, their victims, and their retribution. This time, in the Macgowan Little Theater, he and his tunes became the interlocking of small points of view into which you and I and everyone we know somehow fit." In the *Los Angeles Times*, Mark Swed's article, "A Composer in Search of America: Mikel Rouse Takes a Clear-Eyed Look at a Crazy-Quilt Country in *Music for Minorities*," wrote, "The life is messy. The songs are not. They attempt to connect the dots, as stories of others merge into Rouse's own stories. The dots can't, of course, be connected. We are all minorities, at least to ourselves, and we can make only partial sense of our stories. Rouse, on the other hand, takes clichés and dangles them in front of us without ever letting them settle into sentiment. The overworked harmonies in his songs don't gel. Stories come in fragments. Two voices speak at once, and you decide what to listen to. Lyrics are elusive comments, more general than specific. Rouse rarely raises his voice. A sense of humor, as slippery as everything else in his work, runs through *Music for Minorities*. Parody and tragedy aren't far apart. *Music for Minorities* is deceptively simple and straightforward Americana. You take from it as much or as little as you want. No one can really say what it is to be an American these days. But this is a meaningful piece of the puzzle." I remember being depressed after the shows, wondering what I was accomplishing, if anything. Michael Mushalla called Val and me to his room in the swank Weston Hotel (sadly, the Del Capri was no more). They had free popcorn in the room, and he handed Val and me a bag and read Mark Swed's review. It felt good, in that moment, to contribute to the conversation.

International Cloud Atlas 2006, *Love at Twenty* 2006, and *House of Fans* 2006. These records all came out around the same time, but *Love at Twenty* came first, followed by *International Cloud Atlas* and then *House of Fans.* I had met the choreographer Joe Goode through my agent, Michael, and his friend David Lieberman, who booked the Joe Goode Performance Group. I think we met at a Meet the Composer conference in San Francisco, and after some meetings, we decided to work together on his new piece *Grace.* I had already done some sketches with percussive prepared piano and acoustic guitar, and Joe liked what he heard. A small commission fee was agreed upon that would allow me to come to San Francisco for six weeks as we built the piece to premiere at the Yerba Buena Center for the Arts. By the time I arrived for rehearsals in Berkeley, I had several songs completed and played some of them for the dance group. I remember someone in the company being amused by the sentiment in the song "Housewife." Along with Joe, who also performs in his works, I believe the company at the time of these rehearsals included Marit Brook-Kothlow, Elizabeth Burritt, Rachel Lincoln, Marc Morozumi, Felipe Barrueto-Cabello, and Benjamin Levy. They were an eclectic bunch of artists and I enjoyed getting to know them.

As has happened before, Joe had seen video of me in my own pieces and wanted me to perform onstage with the company. I've always been grateful that my performances in my own pieces offered me opportunities that just wouldn't otherwise happen. So I agreed and was given some basic moves, a duet of sorts with Marit, and played some guitar and sang. The rehearsal schedule was dense, but I still had plenty of time to traverse the hills of sunny San Francisco.

I discovered that sun helps with depression, as Lisa pointed out a couple of weeks in. It always amazes me that I turn the locals on to their own hidden gems and classic historic bars and restaurants. From Sears Fine Foods to Swan Oyster Depot and Sam's Grill. From Tommy's Joynt to the Buena Vista. I remember coming home from a tour in 2000 and discovering a happy phone message from some of the Sancimino brothers—Steve, Tom, Vince, Phillip, John, and Jimmy—from Swan, in

New York celebrating their James Beard Award and wanting to party. And I loved seeing Guy Spinale, who worked the Swan counter but also fronted the band the Rattlecans, singing his heart out. Over the years, I somehow got to know Donny, the chef at Sam's Grill, who would invite me back in the kitchen as he prepped. When waiter Stefano Crivello brought his family to New York, I got his daughter some serious Backstreet Boys swag. A favorite waiter was Walter Taylor, who schooled me on why he sometimes brought three glasses to a two-top: "Sometimes folks like to buy me a drink." From then on, I always asked him to bring an extra glass anytime I was there. I was thrilled when Walter brought his wife to the show. It was gratifying introducing the company to these and many other spots.

We had a successful run, and the piece was received well. I think the music was nominated for a Bay Area award, but I can't remember the name. Rachel Howard wrote in *The Chronical*, "Then came 2004's *Grace*, a collaboration with composer Mikel Rouse. This music was unlike any heard at a Goode performance before: richly textured, overwhelmingly lovely, awash in pretty chord changes and lush layers." Anne Murphy wrote in *DanceViewTimes*, "A striking note is [*Grace*'s] watery, sweet use of song and sound, by composer Mikel Rouse, who has sampled John Cage's beautifully austere experiments in prepared piano from the '50's and interjected and overlaid them with acoustic guitar." We toured the piece and did performances three seasons in a row in San Francisco, the third season at the historic Grace Cathedral. The album was mostly recorded, but sometime after the first season, Marit came to New York and recorded her vocal parts. The cover photo is from a promo photo shoot for *Grace* by RJ Muna, and the CD booklet layout is by Marit (as are the other two CD booklets, *International Cloud Atlas* and *House of Fans*). The CD is dedicated to Julieta Ribeiro Lampariello, Mark Lambert's and Susana Ribeiro's new daughter. Which reminds me of one of my favorite recording sessions for *International Cloud Atlas*.

There were numerous guest appearances on *International Cloud Atlas* (see "*Cage/Cunningham* (1997–2013)"), including Cunningham dancers, Marit Brook-Kothlow from the Joe Goode troupe, and Mark and Susana, who not only sang on the record but helped with the English-to-Portuguese translations of my lyrics. They were in town with newborn Julieta and would take turns strolling her on the street as the other was recording. At a certain point, Susana came back to the studio and said she thought Julieta might fall asleep if we turned all the lights out. So there we were, recording these translations in the dark while new life slept nearby. A truly special session. Songs like "America's Secrets" (from a George Bush quote exclaiming, "We must protect America's secrets") and "Gaza Strip Mall (Get Happy)" spoke to the political dystopia enveloping the country, while the tracks "When This Side Is Empty," "My Love's Gone Remix" (a new arrangement of the song from *Love at Twenty*), and "Clarion Hotel" meditate on lost love in a tangled time. The use of the prepared piano samples, emphasizing the programmed sequencing, gave the tracks a Conlon Nancarrow–like motor quality momentum. I was fortunate to spend some time with Nancarrow, having been introduced to him by Kyle Gann. I was pleased with the release but even happier with the live performance use of the shuffle characteristic of iPods, seeing full houses all having their own private yet public experience. There was also an unexpected vulnerability to the approach: folks just aren't usually asked to be in a public performance with their sense of hearing private. The approach added an extra layer of tension that felt new. And with over two years of touring, digital sales were brisk.

But with three simultaneous releases, one was bound to fall off the map, and that's what generally happened with *House of Fans*. The title came from a fan store in San Francisco, and the entire record reflected on the consistent trips to San Francisco over the three years I worked with Joe Goode's company. Some tracks were reworked songs that I'd demoed before, like "Where the Lights Are On" and "I Changed My Mind." "All Around the World," a vocal and acoustic guitar piece, would become the encore to the *Music for Minorities* shows. Cunningham dancers came over to answer a *Playboy* Centerfold Questionnaire, which would provide the lyrics for "A Girl Named Jesus." "All That Time" and "Top This Ride" have circular chord changes that add an unsettling feel to the record. I think Matt and I also arranged some of the songs for the second set of the *Gravity Radio* workshop at The Stone in New York.

Gravity Radio 2009, *Corner Loading* (Volume 1) 2010, and *Recess* 2010. The CD release of *Gravity Radio* coincided with a record release party and performance at Galapagos Art space in Brooklyn (see "*Gravity Radio* (2009)"). Press was good for the release, but the larger response would come with the tour starting in late 2009. The *St. Petersburg Times* said of the release, "Rouse does it all, singing (in excellent soulful style) and playing almost all the instruments in a control-freak studio tour de force reminiscent of John Fogerty's one-man show, *The Blue Ridge Rangers*. There's a wash of psychedelic Beatlemania to the sound texture that is remarkable." *Time Out New York* reported, "*Gravity Radio*, a beguiling, melancholy new song cycle newly issued on disc by Rouse's ExitMusic label. New-music cognoscenti will relate to the ambitious construction and provocative themes; for pop explorers, think of Rouse as the next step past Mark Everett." Jay Batzner quoted lyrics in the music journal *Sequenza*: "'For those who lunch alone, welcome to radio'; 'Love comes to those who wait. Those who wait for me.'" He continued: "Who is Mikel Rouse? I think the best answer would be Mikel Rouse is today's Schubert with better operas. The sound quality on the disc is amazing. What sounds effortless is actually some of the most nuanced and intricately orchestrated music I've encountered recently. Not only is he Schubert, he rivals Wagner in *Gesamtkunstwerk*." The 2010 BAM performances of *Gravity Radio* coincided with a multitude of events around the city (see "*Gravity Radio* (2009)"), including the release of both *Corner Loading* (Volume 1) and *Recess*.

Corner Loading (Volume 1) (the working title of the record was *Mono Map*, as I was doing a deep dive into mono recording) is a solo vocal/guitar recording that attempts to blend a polymetric style of writing with country blues techniques. The title comes from an early method of recording a singer-guitarist facing a corner to naturally "roll off" the high and low end of the recording. Taking up where the blues left off after the so-called British Invasion, I thought about what might have happened if the blues hadn't become absorbed in a traditional twelve-bar band constraint. Many artists in the 1930s were dealing intuitively with micro-tonality and shifting rhythmic motifs. I used modern tempo canons and cross-rhythms between the voice and guitar to create a recording that is both old and new at the same time. I also wanted to play and sing the songs in one take, so there was a lot of rehearsal to learn how to play and sing the polyrhythms simultaneously. Similarly, I wanted to take a humanist approach to the lyrics to contrast and highlight the uneasy relationship between faith and belief and the often-contradictory messages in early blues (commonly referred to as "the Devil's Music").

The songs "Busy Humanist" and "Made Up, Oh Lord" are good examples of this.

There are also handclapping songs, again using the voice against claps in a nonbinary fashion. One of those songs, "Great Adventure Jail," comes from a humorous story by bartender Joey Di Gregorio from Esca. When he was a kid, he did something crazy at the Great Adventure amusement park, and after being detained, said with a smile, "I was in Great Adventure jail." When I played him the song, his perfect reaction was "I always like to hear my name in song." Valerie Oliveiro did the photography for the album, which includes photos from Merce Cunningham's empty loft. Oliver di Place, in his "Musings on Music," wrote, "Mikel Rouse shows, on his album *Corner Loading* (Volume 1), that he knows his history, and that he has the skill to apply it in his own work. And here we learn that Mikel Rouse is a great guitar player. He creates intricate patterns and plays in a rhythmic style that frees him from the need of a band. The rhythmic experimentation of the early blues artists is here, and so is the insistent power found in John Lee Hooker's music. This is an album that Rouse could not have made when he was younger. His voice used to be high and smooth, and that would not have worked. But now, Rouse's voice has deepened somewhat, and it now has a gravelly quality, and that is what this album needs. Rouse sings these songs in his weathered voice, but with great emotion." Doug Simpson wrote in *Audiophile Audition*, "The last thing someone might expect from composer, performance artist, and multimedia exploiter Mikel Rouse is an acoustic blues release, but that is what he has created for his newest venture, *Corner Loading* (Volume 1), a thirty-six-minute, thirteen-track album of country blues. In typical Rouse style, there is more than meets the ear here. Rouse's version of Southern blues examines early microtonality, shifting polyrhythms and off-the-beat cadences instead of the constraints of twelve-bar blues. But listen closely and Rouse's technical inventiveness comes to the fore. 'Active Denial' is one example. Rouse sings his opening line in harmony with a six-string blues motif. Then, as he repeats the guitar riff, he vocally adds a beat pause between his lyrical phrases, which slightly puts his voice out of sync with his guitar. Rouse then elongates his melodic line by another beat, so everything comes back into the same time signature when he reaches the chorus. On this and other songs, Rouse's earnest and unassuming voice echoes the personalized political and social discourse championed by early Bob Dylan,

Phil Ochs, or Woody Guthrie. Rouse's character studies are equally compelling." And Steve Smith in the *New York Times* declared, "Both his new CDs—the dizzying *Recess*, on which Mr. Rouse incorporates sounds of the outside world into the music's structure, and the spare, bluesy *Corner Loading* (Volume 1), in which his voice and guitar shift in and out of phase almost imperceptibly—were recorded entirely in his one-room studio.

Inspired one evening to make a video for 'Great Adventure Jail' (a track on *Corner Loading*), Mr. Rouse shot in stark black-and-white from five angles, edited the clip, and uploaded it to YouTube in roughly five hours—entirely with his iPhone."

In the fall of 2008, I moved my studio around the corner to the building on Forty-Fourth that used to house the historic Record Plant. Scott Hull ran his mastering studio in this suite, but when he acquired Masterdisk, he had the space to rent. Howie Weinberg decided he wanted to be in the Forty-Fourth Street location, away from Masterdisk's main location. I grabbed one of the first available spaces. Producer Kyle Kelso took the back room, and Grammy-winning mixer and producer Dave O'Donnell moved across the hall. Guitarist Jeff McErlain moved down the hall, and there were a couple of different smaller rooms that Scott would struggle to rent. Matt Agoglia was assisting Howie and getting his mastering skills together, and he'd eventually start his own mastering business. We always kept a pot of coffee going, and it was a great experience to have breaks with a talented bunch of folks. I learned a lot just from listening and observing. I upgraded a bunch of gear, and I remember everyone being curious to hear the new Barefoot MM27 monitors I'd added. At one point, I think Howie was having marital problems, so he was living in his studio, which would be a challenge. It was also great to share work and get tips from each other. I have a fond memory of recording "Great Adventure Jail," the handclapping song, with a gruff vocal. I asked Dave if he could hear a "digital distortion" on the vocal track. I was trying to describe the sound and I said, "You know, it's like a distortion on the vocal. What do you call it?' And Dave, listening to the vocal, kindly responded, "I call it a gift from God!"

Recorded between October 2008 and November 2009, *Recess* was a lyrical reflection on the state of the world economy and the "reset" taking place before our eyes and ears. Inspired by my piece with Merce Cunningham and iPods (see "*Cage/Cunningham* (1997–2013)"), I collected field recordings and then orchestrated those sounds with multiple voices and instruments. The field recordings reflect every imaginable sound, from a couple's quarrel in a New York park to cicadas from Missouri. Recordings of random conversations are vocally doubled and harmonized to enhance and heighten their meaning. While most people use mobile music players to tune out their environment, my hope was to take the mobile device to a truly collaborative level. The experience of listening to *Recess* on a portable device while walking through a city environment is a new kind of mobile listening experience. I even included a caution on the release: "WARNING: Extreme caution should be used while listening to this music in a public environment or while driving." "Dolls & Dreams" starts with the rhythm of a bank machine dispensing cash, and "Cutting Class" is a multisectional composition with enough twists and turns to make the massive culminating chorus a relief. The refrain from "Designing Women" reads like a condolence card to corporate culture:

> *Designing women that never listen*
> *That never crawl out of bed*
> *And here's a lesson: what's more is less than*
> *Less than waking up dead*
>
> *Designing women that keep on giving*
> *And give a bad name to luck*
> *They're on a mission in every kitchen*
> *In every nip and tuck*
> *Designing women that never listen*
> *Designing women to love*

But perhaps the melancholy of the album is summed up by the song "Plug Nickel":

> *I'm not sorry*
> *I don't wonder anymore*
> *Got no answers and bad credit like before*
> *America under focus PBS*
> *Super cable and Anderson Vanderbilt*
> *I'm not bitter I'm just tired of the fight*
> *Drink to forget drink to regret drink all night*
> *I'm a lucky guy I don't even try*
> *I will live and die never knowing why*
> *Time to say goodbye to this plug nickel life*

I would rejoice when receiving a text from Katie O'Donnell, heading into the city on the Staten Island Ferry to a fourteen-hour shift at Esca, stating: "I'm a lucky gal. Here's the reason why. This plug nickel life." As mentioned before, the releases of *Recess* and *Corner Loading* coincided with the *Gravity Radio* tour, so notices were often folded together. Jon Pareles of the *New York Times* gave a glowing review of *Gravity Radio* at BAM that included this appraisal of the new releases: "His 2009 album, *Gravity Radio*, and two he has just released, *Recess* and *Corner Loading*, Vol. 1 (all on ExitMusic), are collections of verse-and-chorus songs featuring his voice and guitar picking: songs about the state of America, love, aging, and uncertainty. Within the songs and connecting them are the patterns and metrical structures Mr. Rouse has always enjoyed." And Doug Simpson in *Audiophile Audition* wrote, "Media manipulator, post-millennial composer, pop imaginer, and audio technician: there really is no single role artist Mikel Rouse fits into. The modernist uses whatever he can find to reexamine the obsessions, nightmares, and promises of humanity and mirror them back to us in his divergent viewpoint."

Boost | False Doors 2012. *Boost | False Doors* was my first double album. It didn't exactly start that way, but after massaging the tracks, it made sense. I always wanted to make a double album, but I liked the idea of trying to make two records, each a companion piece for the other but starkly different as well. *False Doors* was recorded and mixed from April to June in 2010. In hindsight, a lot of the coming turmoil, from relationship loss to the real effects of the economic crash, are evident. It's a funny record, in that I wanted to record very naturally and without a click track. But after tracking much of the album, I decided to bring in original Tirez Tirez drummer Rob Shepperson to play drums and percussion. Rob always had a wonderfully unique take, and I thought he would add to the overall vibe. And add he did. But it was a bit unfair to him because playing to tracks that weren't intended to be "locked in" made the groove frustrating. I ended up loving the results because the tension is palpable, like how producer Tom Wilson added electric guitar, bass, and drums to the Simon & Garfunkel song "The Sound of Silence."

I also had Rob just play and create beats the way his mind seems to work, and those tracks, like "Words Are Missing" and "The Next World," flow in a more natural way. Both of those songs are just vocals, handclaps, and drums. I always thought "Words Are Missing," with lines like "Once the United States ran for president," would make a great theme song for an HBO vehicle. Dream on. Songs like "Thumb Skills" and "Blow Dried Bodies" use acoustic guitars in simple but satisfying counterpoint and reflect on mortality, both in relationships and life. "Make Her Won" also reflects on the political-economic scene, with lyrics like:

> Economy, it's all we talk about, it's what's for dinner, what we wanna eat
> The Miranda Rights in tiny bites, what the country wants to be
> And the pros and cons of the new fight songs and the body block
> Of freedom just can't see that it's overtime, we've begun decline
> In fact, we're where we ought to be

And "Prosperity Gospel" ponders the trend toward bigger and better church scams:

> When I turn the tide I'll be
> Paying down my misery
> Four out of five jobs agree
> Sinking into history . . .

I borrowed a bass guitar from Dave O'Donnell and liked the combination of bass, mellotron, and prepared piano. This added an airy mystery to tracks like "Sky Sprites":

> Well-endowed and lining pockets
> Homeless striking poses for the frozen few
> Nearsighted, blurry, takes the edge off
> Makes the picture feel more "real" to you

Perhaps the closing song, "Come from Money," sums up the overall mood of the moment: "It doesn't hurt to come from money." *Boost* was recorded and mixed from March to May of 2011, just as my relationship with Lisa was ending. It's a flat-out techno assault, with National Steel guitar and lyrics that merge hedge-fund terms with personal loss. It seemed to make sense at the time. The first song, "Hurdle Rate," exemplifies the seeming futility of it all:

> Observation: looking deep into each other
> To find the possible thread.

Or if I try hard enough, I'll see you
Or find a way to love you

So in other words, I want this so bad
That if you'll sit in front of me long enough
I'll create it

"Professional Smile" is a phrase borrowed from writer David Foster Wallace and is a dizzying track: drum-machine and hurricane-like choral and guitar work. And "Orson Elvis" anticipates my evacuation from all social media (because democracy) in 2016:

Every hit online takes its toll in time
Time you don't get back, running with the pack
Miracles agree: what we really need
Takes us off the grid, back to where we live

"The Movie We're In" hopes to capture the despair of lost love—"Cemetery of hope, cemetery of hope"—while also reminding us that film hacks will most likely rule: "This is the music that tells us what part of the movie we are in now." Valerie Oliveiro did photos and the *False Doors* covers. I did the *Boost* cover, for what I'd hoped would be a citywide photo project of removing ads and replacing them with more interesting images. The *Boost* cover is from Times Square, a few blocks from me. But my favorite part of this record was getting to know Matt Agoglia at the studio. He was mastering stuff on his own using Howie's classic rig. I had him do the *Boost* record, and even though I'd done a good pre-master of *False Doors*, I decided to have him do that as well. He's been my go-to mastering engineer ever since. The double album was in memory of Merce Cunningham and Johnny Dirt. I somehow think they would both like that. *False Doors* was for Anthony Creamer (for his unending support of the arts) and my nephew, Brennan Mikel Ponder, for staying in the game. *Boost* was for Ron and Russel Mael, the Sparks brothers. There were a number of feature articles around the release, including interviews with Seth Colter Walls in *Capital New York* and James Beaudreau for the Masterdisk Record. *Bandcamp* made it a staff pic, saying, "I seriously don't know what to tap my foot to, but I dig it." And John Fleming in the *Tampa Bay Times* gave it an "A" rating, writing, "This is a consummate headphone listening experience; a lot goes on in Rouse's music, and the lyrics are hilarious." Lizzie Simon did a great piece in the *Wall Street Journal* called "Decades of Fun for a Downtown Booster." It included a graphic with lots of figures, including the number of official album releases and deposits to the Mikel Rouse Archive at NYPL. Still, after three decades in the saddle, I was starting to feel like interest in my recordings was waning.

Fortunately, I was wrong.

Metronome–*Take Down* 2016 and ***Hemisphere*** 2017. The *Take Down* album went under the moniker of Metronome, a band name that I'd wanted to use for decades. It was recorded between 2011 and 2015, a long stretch, but I was buried in a large theatrical piece (see "*The Demo* (2015)"). I was pretty much off the road now and funds were tight, so I moved my studio back to my apartment. While I truly loved the years at the shared studio space and getting to know Dave, Jeff, Kyle, and Matt, I discovered I really do like working from home. And the beat influence of working on the music for *The Demo* was seeping into *Take Down*. The record fuses influences as diverse as Abdel Halim Hafez, FKA Twigs, and Delta blues. It feels like a Kafkaesque soundtrack to America's future, and the lyrics cover topics from dead love to water shortages, from mortality to Mayan ruins, from toddlers to allergies.

Another reason I wanted to do the record under a band name was enlisting Claire Karoly, who was in the chorus of *The Demo* premiere, to sing on the record. I remember tracking phrases for "Habit" and "Growing Pains" at my studio. After some editing and moving parts around, and liking her vibe, I wanted to do more with Claire, but she was back home in San Francisco.

Working with Ben in California during *The Demo* rehearsals, I'd stumbled on the idea of recording vocals singing directly into a laptop. With enough production and plug-ins, I figured it would be similar to the 4-track cassette idea from years ago. So I sent Claire some guide tracks and basically told her to have at it. The result would be the epic ten-minute track "Habibi Lossless," which clicks in at exactly the same time as David Bowie's "Station to Station." I can't remember if that was intentional, but I was listening to that track together with tracks of singer Abdel Halim Hafez, and "Habibi Lossless" was the result.

In 2014 I stumbled onto the World Cup and decided to start the Mikel Rouse Sports Blog. Not knowing anything about sports in general and soccer in particular, I thought this seemed like a good idea. After all, everyone else gets to write about things they know nothing about, so why not me? I took a James Joyce approach: covering each game in real time, I would add historical commentary related to the teams' countries of origin. I'd then post these on social media. And in 2015, for almost two years, I posted a daily four-panel cartoon strip called *The Underemployed*, which presented me in various job interview situations. These cartoons would eventually be exhibited at the CSPS Art Gallery in Cedar Rapids, Iowa. But then, not being a huge user, I left social media in 2016. The number of folks who preemptively judged me because they thought I was judging them was remarkable. To each his own. OK, maybe a little judging. Anyway, it's pertinent to this story because on the day of the release, I got a text from Claire asking if I'd seen the *Pitchfork* (*au courant* online music site) missive on "Habibi Lossless." Seth Colter Walls had chimed in, "Downtown NYC legend Mikel Rouse reemerges with 'Habibi Lossless.' Slippery like Radiohead's 'Daydreaming'—and as chaotically clattering as work by Oneohtrix Point Never—it reestablishes Rouse's brilliance." So short but so sweet, as it referenced everything I was listening to at the time (but after the record was finished). Anyway, a kind of happy moment as I walked through Central Park; actually, I was happy for Claire. She deserved a notice in Pitchfork.

Anyway, that was followed by several tweets, most notably from Joseph Stannard from the UK's *The Wire*, who was excited and curious about this track. Seth followed up with a full review of the album in *Pitchfork*, noting the still-fresh wound of unraveling love: "Longing for an affection that may already be lost is not novel subject matter. But Rouse's musical evocation of this psychology is ingenious. The vocals take care of the present-tense melancholy, while the madly cavorting instrumental activity represents all the mental what-ifs and counterarguments that rebel against a discouraging romantic prognosis." Joseph followed up by having writer Clive Bell do a full-page feature in *The Wire*, which reads like an impressive, comprehensive CV. About the new record he wrote, "With *Take Down* Rouse has hit the jackpot. *Take Down*'s opener, 'Habibi Lossless,' [is] a ten-minute tour de force inspired by great Arabic singers like Abdel Halim Hafez and Farid Al Attrach. A casual listen would suggest that here's a cool song, pretty narcotic—especially when Rouse breaks the beat down and jumps into a 'Tomorrow

Never Knows' chamber of Lennon-echo. A minute later he's stood on a windswept beach for a Van Dyke Parks major key, a swooning dash of nostalgic hymn: 'Yes we make love/In your American Dream.'" With lines like "I live like I'm rich when I'm poor," from "Lift Your Hands," and "Even when it's good news, it's bad news," from "Side Myself," to pondering Moby out of water in California, I'd captured a unique approach to my coming milestone of age sixty.

In 2016 and 2017, I was spending time with my mom in Gulf Shores, Alabama (commonly referred to as the "redneck Riviera"), and working on tracks in a makeshift studio I created there. I embarked on two short films, *Yes We Kant* and *Gulf Course*, that utilized computer character–driven voices from dialog I wrote. I orchestrated these two films with several of my past recordings and the effect is both startling and surreal.

I wanted to continue working with Claire in this long-distance manner, so I sent her music and guide tracks to what would be "Inside the Waste of Time," the final song on *Hemisphere*. It kinda started as a sketch to see about the direction I wanted, but I liked the results enough to flesh it out. I followed with an even more complex track, "The Uncanny Valley," which furthered my "harmonic rhythm" approach, where rotating metric structures create their own kind of harmonic cadence. The convergence of lines at the end of the song is a great example of this technique.

The title song, "Hemisphere," was written as a gift to friends following the horrific 2016 election:

> You can hang out, you can hang out
> At my place, at my place
> We can eavesdrop, we can smoke pot
> At my place, at my place
>
> You're not alone, we'll touch and we'll roam
> At my place, at my place
> Do not despair, We're here and we're there
> At my place, at my place

I had attended many protests following the shooting of Michael Brown in Ferguson, Missouri. I recorded the crowd and myself repeating the slogan "hands up, don't shoot" and created a digital phase piece, "Resolver," that updated both the phasing technique and commemorated this moment in time. While working on the recording of *Hemisphere*, I started making a forty-five-minute film to accompany the release. As luck would have it, Kathy Valentine and Steven Weisburd commissioned the video as a silent installation video for his new Austin, Texas, venue The Townsend. I met Kathy at the Louisiana Film Prize in Shreveport, run by a great guy named Gregory Kallenberg. Jay Weigel, a composer who had also presented me at the CAC in New Orleans, suggested to Greg that I might be a good film and music judge for his short-film festival. Kathy would be there as a music judge. This meeting eventually developed into a long-distance relationship that would have a huge effect on a few upcoming projects. I met some colorful people on these trips to Austin. I remember meeting the sensational guitarist Denny Freeman, who was trying his hand at pedal steel guitar. He said he had been dismissive of what he called "hillbilly music" but had now learned that "it's all part of the deal." These words and this view stuck with me.

Through Kathy, I also met John Sebastian and had dinner with him and his wife at the classic Village red-sauce joint Gene's. He told me a great story about having to rerecord the vocal part to "Darling Be Home Soon" because of an engineering error. But for now, I was shooting all over the city in HD on my iPhone and loving the freedom. Filming weddings in Central Park, upside-down train tracks on the way to JFK, and 24-frame travel shots through Europe, while taking meetings for the music/installation piece *One Boy's Day*. In addition to the album and video installation in Austin, I also repurposed this film for a retrospective concert with guitarist Jeff McErlain at National Sawdust in April 2017, using the sound/film triggering technique used in *Gravity Radio* (see "*Gravity Radio* (2009)"). So I got a lot of mileage out of this film. Matt mastered both records at his new mastering suite The Ranch Mastering, and *Hemisphere* was dedicated to the memory of Chuck Berry. Shaun Tandon, who had written a feature on *The Demo* for Agence France-Presse (which was distributed to publications worldwide), did a feature for AFP that was picked up by multiple publications, including *The Guardian*. Said Tandon, "Like much of Rouse's music, *Hemisphere* defies easy genre classification. It breaks away from expected beats, yet the songs—intricately produced and interspersed with Arabic singing—are quickly accessible." I was happy with the response to both *Take Down* and *Hemisphere*, but that nagging question of relevance was still there. Unfortunately the next four record releases would prove challenging.

Swingers Castle 2019. For two summers in a row, in 2017 and 2018, I had the good fortune of spending a week or so in a 1920s-era mansion in the Hollywood Hills. I was invited by Kathy Valentine, who was both vacationing and doing shows with the Go-Go's. The mansion was overseen by a great guy named Bill Miltenberger and came with a pool, tennis court, and outdoor BBQ area. It also had a Steinway grand piano. I hadn't played piano in years and practically glued myself to the thing when I wasn't roaming Los Angeles by myself on foot. Without planning, I started writing music on the piano and then got the idea to set up my laptop and start recording, once again through the laptop's internal mic. I believe there were two sketches that went nowhere. But then I started the song "Hollywood & Sons" (from the Hollywood sign nearby and the "Sons" of Steinway & Sons on the piano) and found myself thinking about Los Angeles and the strange land that it is. So, unexpectedly, I had a theme of sorts and just started writing and recording as quickly as I could. I think the week to ten days that I was there in 2017, I wrote six or seven of the twelve songs for the album. I usually recorded five or more passes of piano tracks so I'd have choices when I returned to the studio in New York. That first summer was mostly a vacation for Kathy and her daughter, Audrey, and each day they'd come back to find me at the piano with a new recording.

In Los Angeles, like most cities around the world, I manage to find spots that resonate with my wanderlust. Hanging with actor and bartender Graham Miller at Musso & Frank Grill, where he made the best Brandy Alexander I've ever tasted (I had my first one at the Troubadour, where Harry Nilsson famously got a Beatle drunk and then proceeded to heckle the Smothers Brothers comedy team). And right next door to the Troubadour is Dan Tana's, probably my favorite watering hole and red-sauce joint in Los Angeles. I loved sitting at the bar and soaking up the local color with bartender Mike Gotovac (who passed away from Covid-19 at seventy-six) and regular Paul Cavallero. I was also in Los Angeles for meetings about the thirteen-hour music/installation piece (see "*One Boy's Day* (2014–?)"), and I would traverse the city and land at favorite spots. Opened in 1924, the Original Pantry Cafe downtown is still the best breakfast around. Since 1908, Philippe the Original, also downtown, has been dishing out the best French-dip sandwiches anywhere. There was something about this time that made for a kind of creative awakening. All I could think about was this record.

Once I was back to New York, I got to work on fleshing out the songs in the studio. I created an imaginary band that would aid in the ensemble feel of the record. As with other records, I played most everything, and I asked Kathy to add backing vocals to "Hollywood & Sons," which added to the melancholy feeling.

> *Where I'm going no one's knowing how to rescue me*
> *Palm trees crying as I'm dying let the battered be*
> *Hollywood & Sons take this soul and set it free*
> *What I'll never be, lonesome guarantee, patent eulogy*
> *What a world to see: Wonders that agree, Hollywood and me*

I kept working on the tracks from the first summer, not knowing that there would be a second summer. I also completed the film *Monument*, culled from footage from Los Angeles, Paris, and London. The film was for a potential commission that never materialized. After completing the film, I was back to overdubs and mixing for *Swingers*. "And Now We Are Not" has a nice "bop" to it and explores the passing nonconsensual dating rituals of the Hollywood elite.

> *In the bedroom, can it be a one-man show?*
> *Bounce against the headboard, both sides letting go?*
> *And now we are not as the angels fall, as the boundaries call*
> *You can be right after all*

"Court Packing" and "Actors with Guns (Sleepwalk through the Mantra)" take on the political and social structures that bug me to no end. So I guess I'm working on the record for a year while working on *One Boy's Day* when I get the unexpected news that I could go back to the mansion. At this point, I'm thinking of the mansion as a swingers castle, so, of course, I'm sold on that as the title for the record. Once there, I squeeze out another four or five songs on the piano and even record vocals in the shower (great tile reverb) for the song "Share the World." We had a couple of parties at the mansion, one that let me reconnect with friends Jim Bourgeois and Peter Keenan, and one ostensibly for the upcoming Go-Go's show at the Hollywood Bowl. And again, unexpectedly, I covered the 2018 World Cup with my sports blog, hunting down bars and hotels to watch the games. "The Edges of Entertainment" provided a glimpse into a world that fascinates and frightens:

> *Trendsetting megachurch, white as white and mega-merch*
> *Walk in daddy's footsteps, make that money, so proud of you*
> *Saving souls and romcom honey, Hillsong Zoe Vous:*
> *Humanistic fuck you*
> *Falwell et al., Robertson, welcome to Adult Swim*
> *On the edge of entertainment and derangement*
> *Freedom elected me a president*

"LA Continental" viewed the homeless in tent cities, much like the song "See the Living" from *Against All Flags*, reminding me that things move around but don't change much. When I got back to New York, I worked quickly to finish the album and had the horrific thought that this might be the best record I'd ever made. So rather than immediately release it, I shopped it to several labels. I had low expectations, but I guess I didn't want to wonder "what if?" Matt mastered the record and I did the digital booklet. The cover is a pic of me clueless, by whom, I don't know, from the *Etudes* sessions at Downtown Sound in 1980. I had reread David Foster Wallace's *Infinite Jest*, and I thought it would be interesting to provide both humorous and factual footnotes to the lyrics. It remains humorous and factual to me. I also did videos for "Hollywood & Sons," "The Edges of Entertainment," "The Pop Machine," and "Share the World."

At sixty-one, with a number of high-end successes and failures, I thought myself fairly seasoned in the realm of disappointment. But the near silence around *Swingers Castle* was deafening. The kind of feeling that makes one question their reality. Joseph Stannard at *The Wire* "got" the record, for which I'm grateful. He assigned Brian Morton to review, and Morton offered, "It's a record to listen to after reading Raymond Chandler or Joan Didion, or coming home from a screening of *Once Upon a Time in Hollywood*. Its literariness is as evident as its imagistic clarity, even if the images don't quite make sense. It's *The Waste Land* done with pop rather than jazz materials, fragments of a dream, drily humorous, sleepwalking but also fizzily alert and utterly compelling." And Kathy, asked by *Goldmine*, the music collectors' magazine, to rate her top ten all-time albums, included *Swingers Castle* among the *White*

Album, *Ziggy Stardust*, *Kind of Blue*, *Exile on Main Street*, and *Never Mind the Bollocks, Here's the Sex Pistols*. She wrote, "Seems like no matter what the state of things are, a true artist always finds a way and a place to keep making art. I watched this artist take inspiration where he found it and before my eyes, a house in the Hollywood Hills and a Steinway transformed into a stunning record. It made me want to create something of my own, outside a band, and led to the soundtrack to my memoir." This was a kind and meaningful gesture and made me glad I'd dedicated the record to "KV and all the Swingers."

Epilogue: My good friend Steven Weisburd, who also happens to be Kathy's ex, got a new place just off Sunset Boulevard, near the castle. I was in town sometime in 2019 for meetings and stayed with him. I learned from Bill that he was selling the place, and he invited me over for a last party. The place was mostly emptied out, and I walked through the space, soaking it in. Swingers Castle was gone, never to return. It's hard to describe what that two-year creative jolt did for my soul. But I was reminded, yet again, that it's all fleeting.

Metronome–*Community Spread* 2020 and *~/Library/Mouth/Congress/* 2020. Enter the pandemic and the merits of solitude. In the early days, my Hell's Kitchen neighborhood cleared out; at its peak, I saw up to two or three moving vans a day on my block alone. I moved to this hood from Fourteenth Street in 1982, and it was pretty rough. But with gentrification and the rebirth of Broadway/Disney, things cleaned up. And there's nothing like those tourist dollars to keep the cops on the beat. But when that all shut down, the cops disappeared, and at the same time, hotels were repurposed to house and spread out the homeless to reduce infection rates. Businesses closed, drugs came back, and there was new gunplay to contend with. Folks were understandably scared, and life was limited to going to the store for basic provisions and walking for exercise. And as dicey as the hood became, there was the promise of a better environment, as all traffic disappeared. People missed their lives of friends and parties and restaurants and shows. But I, not being the most social person around, felt as though I had been rehearsing for this moment my entire life. So I got to work. I used the time to archive numerous videos of full, live performances. And after twenty years, I finally edited the only known performance footage of *Failing Kansas* from the scandal in New Zealand (see "*Failing Kansas* (1995)"). With all this going on, I also tried to stay in touch with people through Zoom.

Bryan Gibson, a data scientist, instructor at Columbia, and all-around good egg (he did the fly-through demonstration video for the set of *One Boy's Day*), set up a Zoom chat for about ten to fifteen old and new friends. It became a lifeline for many, and it became a new piece for me. I asked for everyone's permission for Bryan to record some of our chats. He eventually sent me hours of footage, and I combed through it until I had a usable thirty minutes or so. This would be the beginning of the *Community Spread* video and album. After the video was edited, I extracted the audio of the conversations and began orchestrating and manipulating the voices to create a kind of video song cycle. I borrowed a music track from *One Boy's Day* and added instruments and singing. I also brought in Claire Karoly to add vocalizations, so it seemed appropriate to make this a new Metronome album. Perhaps my favorite section is the "Don't ever change little girl" line, where the voices and mood combine in an unintentional but wonderful Buffalo Springfield "Expecting to Fly"–like way. In addition to Claire and me, the piece included video and vocals from Katie Israel, Brennan Ponder, Bryan Gibson, Veanne Cox, Allison Keller, Sherry Burrell, Katie O'Donnell, Pat O'Donnell, Jean-Marc Dupon, Cindy Ponder, Suzan Bellincampi, Crista Miller, Michael Adelson, Kathy Valentine, Lisa Boudreau, and Peter Malfatti, as well as the screen debut of Hudson Israel. To end the record, I added the song "See You," recorded before the pandemic and featuring my niece, Katie Ponder Israel.

Sometime in 2019, Jeff Burk had sent me a link to a beta version of a project called Citizen DJ. I filed this info away, but now it seemed like a good time to investigate. Citizen DJ is the brainchild of Brian Foo in collaboration with the Library of Congress. To put it simply, he created a royalty-free user interface that provided samples from the Library of Congress's archive, combined with sampled beats from a variety of drum machines including the Roland 808, the Akai MPC, and the LinnDrum. When I dug into the interface, it was still in beta and sometimes features would work and then sort of stop. So I developed a system where I would hit "record" and just scroll through samples and drum loops and sort of perform twenty minutes on the fly. Then I'd put the track into my NLE and start chopping and sequencing until I had a good base to work from. This approach provided snippets of barely understandable words that I could then riff off to build lyrics. *Community Spread* would reflect the isolation inherent in the lockdown, and *~/Library/Mouth/Congress/* would embrace that isolation, with guests sending files that could be flown into the mix. In fact, rather than send guide tracks or scores, I would simply send lyric fragments and ask the contributors to speak or sing or do whatever they wanted into the voice memo on their phone. I'd then use some of the same vocal plug-ins used on *Community Spread* to alter or reharmonize the vocals. Every record presents its own trials and tribulations, and the thing about *~/Library/Mouth/Congress/* that I remember most was that it was a blast to make. I also consciously went for the political jugular and refused to self-edit. By this time, you could sit outdoors at bars or restaurants, and I would take these samples and beats and sit with a notebook writing long lyric passages. It was reminiscent of my time in Paris with beats, working on the lyrics for *Cameraworld*. Sitting outside the Landmark Tavern, looking at the Car Wash sign missing the "W": "Car ash, car ash, burn all cars and car crash." Just an unexpected and creative time amid the crumbling. And the confusion of politics and human behavior, as this lyric from "Spokecard" illustrates:

> *Party people please be careful*
> *Party people please be fearful*
> *Party people please go home*
> *And don't forget to leave me alone*

Among the amazing contributions from friends and artists like Allison Keller, Cindy Ponder, Lisa Boudreau, and Kathy Valentine, perhaps my favorite was Audrey Weisburd's contributions to "Random Forests," "Reverend," and "Pick It Up Audrey": a sense of hope and innocence amid the chaos. I also made videos of the songs "I Broke" (which featured cartoons from *The Underemployed* comic strip, "Spokecard" (which surveyed my bleak hood), "Snowball Earth," and "Why!" Maybe "To Serve Man" summed up a lockdown moment by appropriating a classic line and adjusting it for the moment: "Day drinking and I'm thinking of you." *Swingers Castle* might be my best record, but at least for now, *~/Library/Mouth/Congress/* is my favorite, a choice of hope over despair and comedy over tragedy. The cover is of red, painted hand impressions on the sidewalk on the way to Landmark Tavern. In my mind, impressions of folks representing. In the *New York Times*, Seth Colter Walls acknowledged the record as "the latest independent effort by Mikel Rouse," writing, "Another American composer with a penchant for samples, Rouse assembles his fieriest collection in recent years, and it turns on politically pointed (or exhausted) opuses like 'Spokecard.'" Grateful to Seth for this, but the silence surrounding these two records brought me to paraphrase Lou Reed: "Can you imagine working for a fucking year, and you get a B+ from the *Village Voice*?" Anyway, both records pretty much died, but I was reminded of my ongoing philosophy during the pandemic, which I shared with anyone frustrated with people's behavior or even their own behavior: everyone gets a Covid "pass."

One Boy's Day (*Electronic Beds*) 2021. Here's where we end this section, with fifteen-plus hours of music that passes for a dream. You can read all about it (see "*One Boy's Day* (2014–?)"), including the compositional aspect relating to thematic choices. But suffice to say that when the thirteen-hour and thirty-three-minute premiere was waylaid by the pandemic, I thought I should do something to commemorate the premiere date as well as acknowledge all the hard work so many people shared. And, as many artists were releasing sketches and unfinished tracks during isolation, I thought maybe I should release the electronic beds that were to form the skeletal foundation for live musicians, text, and atmosphere. I had listened to these development beds over several years as I crisscrossed the globe in search of support for this project. I would test text and timings to the tracks in order to adjust for particulars of the performance, including the "live classroom" component so essential to the piece. So I guess I started to get used to the tracks as stand-alone entities. I particularly enjoy playing the tracks in association with their "set time" during the day. Some tracks with morning coffee, some with lunch, and some with dinner. And while each track corresponded with a particular observer that would each last thirty minutes (and then switch to the next track/observer), hearing them as singular separate pieces has its own reward.

I used lots of beat making and sequencing software on this. And as with the previous two lockdown records, I had fired up my old NS10M monitors. I missed them and their naked honesty. I don't know which came first, the riffing on ~/*Library/Mouth/Congress/* or *One Boy's Day*, but I spent a lot of time using a mouse to click through various alternative rhythms and kinda stuck with what seemed right. I guess with both records, the composing happened after the improvisation. But other tracks started out as thoroughly composed. And as the tracks and themes progressed, those tracks got processed through a more complex theme and variation approach that superimposed key sets and rhythm sets, adding to the growing organic complexity. In a funny way, I surmised that the added convolution mirrored the grinding days of the observers.

Most likely I was projecting. But I imagined the people—the eight observers—as the eight themes developed. And it somehow made sense to me: like a lot of my work, a subtle, gradual complexity that some might not hear but others would. And either way, whether you heard it or not, it didn't get in the way of the overall thrust. This record release is exclusive to *Bandcamp*, as no other digital music platform can support the weight. I'm not convinced that *One Boy's Day* is finished, but after seven years and a pandemic, a world-weariness needs to be addressed. So, for now, this release presents a concrete outline of a big idea. And big ideas have a way of coming back around.

One Boy's Day, Classroom Sketch, Stage Design, 2019.

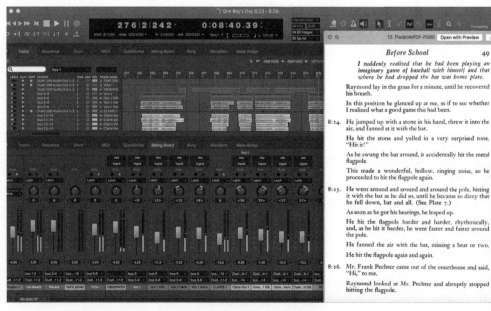

One Boy's Day, Music Sequence, Stage Design, 2019.

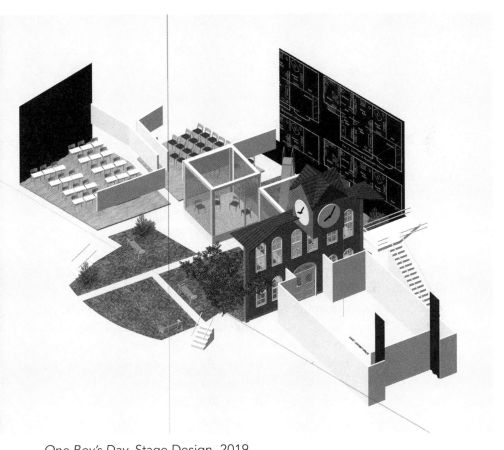

One Boy's Day, Stage Design, 2019.

One Boy's Day (2014–?)

In 2014, amid recording the Metronome–*Take Down* album and juggling the personalities of *The Demo*, I stumbled on an article in *Harper's Magazine*, extracted from a book, on a behavioral research study. On April 26, 1949, eight observers, led by social scientists Roger Barker and Herbert Wright from the Midwest Psychological Field Station, painstakingly documented every word and movement of Raymond Birch, a seven-year-old boy from rural Kansas. Heralded as a sociological milestone, their 435-page report aimed to describe "how children actually behave in real-life situations" and offer insight into what makes an "ideal" American community. Divided into seven parts and structured as scenes from a play, the study is a meticulously timed, minute-by-minute transcription of Raymond's every activity, from getting up and eating breakfast to playing with his friends, from studying English and participating in music class to eating dinner and going to bed. Harper & Row published the report in 1951 as *One Boy's Day*. In writing about *One Boy's Day*, the *New York Times* enthusiastically reported how Barker and his colleagues "brought child psychology out of the laboratory to study children in their natural habitat, much as a botanist goes into the fields to study flowers." The citizens of Oskaloosa, Kansas, gave the researchers nearly unlimited access to their lives. Barker writes in the preface to *One Boy's Day* that the book "marks a milestone in the degree of participation of a whole community in a scientific undertaking."

The book contains many references to the theater. The town is described as "a stage upon which Raymond Birch (all names in the record are fictitious) played his roles." The parts of Raymond's day are listed as "scenes," and the family, neighbors, and friends are itemized as if in a playbill program. In addition, in Barker's introduction, he suggests that along with social scientists, "artists and laymen who are interested in the contemporary scene also may find [the record] of value." I was sold! I worked for several months trying to figure out how to turn this study into an evening-length theatrical work. This was frustrating and difficult slogging until I realized the solution was staring me in the face (or on the page) all along. One of the fascinating aspects of the book is that the record of the observers is marked in one-minute increments, lending itself to modern time-code–based technologies. The entire record lasts for thirteen hours and thirty-three minutes. The horror hit me: it wouldn't be an evening-length work, but a music/theater/installation piece running the length of the original study. Not the wisest approach coming out of the 2008 financial fiasco, but an exciting idea nonetheless.

Aspects of One Boy's Day *must have resonated with me, growing up in a similar rural community. But the late '40s weren't the late '60s, and I compared and contrasted my experience with Raymond's. I have a feeling, at the age of seven, Raymond's first job probably wasn't digging graves for vault-maker Dalton Clark, who referred to the work as "planting people." My dad was a state trooper and heavy drinker. I was born in St. Louis, and after a brief time in Rolla, Missouri, my family ended up in the southeastern boot-heel town of Poplar Bluff, Missouri, named for the bluffs and poplar trees overlooking the Black River. Before the ravages of Walmart and chain stores, the downtown was a quaint reminder of the past, but when I was a teenager, the town took on an edge that would rapidly engulf middle America. At one point in the '70s, after receiving the Gerald Ford boondoggle of "All American City," PBMO had the largest per-capita quota of drugs and prostitution of any American city. I had to wonder what might be missing from the original study and hoped to reflect on that in my approach.*

But first things first: if I was gonna embark on an idea like this, I thought I'd better get permissions in line, as I had done for *The Demo*. After months of internet searches and calls, I found Jonathan Barker, Roger Barker's son, and told him my idea. (The original idea was of an installation with four full-length films shot in four different schools, both urban and rural, to reflect on the social changes from 1949 to now. This plan would change.) He seemed intrigued and was also kind and helpful in connecting me with Herbert Wright's family, and shortly thereafter, I had permission to use the text in my piece. At some point, I abandoned the four-film idea in favor of an actual performance installation. The activity on stage would be that of actual classrooms with teacher and students, orchestrated by music, light, and sound: a beautiful tableau contrasting the original text with the culturally diverse and inclusive classrooms of today. Not to dismiss a school recital or play, but on view here would be students in their actual daily setting. In this way students and teachers would become coauthors and take artistic ownership over a large-scale theatrical work, and, as in watching a movie, the audience might appreciate the simple but profound experience of a child's, maybe their child's, day.

Anything is possible, I thought, as I lost myself in records. My dad had a connection with a drinking buddy at Marvel Music, a place that stocked jukeboxes around the city. He'd go there to drink and play cards and I could rummage through used singles for twenty-five cents apiece. Paul Revere and the Raiders, a Stones or Beatles occasionally. Strapped into headphones, I'd draw and paint and generally lose the world. I was afraid of my father, and except during forty days of Lent when, as a Catholic, he'd refrain from drinking, there was consistent stress. My mom did the best she could, and my sister tried to keep up appearances, but there were chaotic scenes.

My mom was a talented artist, singer, and dancer, and her brother was a musician who at one time ran a music store where I got my first guitar. She did a calligraphy sampler in college that to this day still fascinates me. It didn't help that I was caught up in all the late '60s causes of civil rights and the counterculture movement. I vividly remember the assassinations of Martin Luther King Jr. and Bobby Kennedy. And I was obsessed with Sam Ervin and the PBS daily recap of the Watergate hearings. In the early '70s, PBMO got a head shop, and I would spend any free time there, perusing Rolling Stone *magazine (the newspaper version with the "Fear and Loathing" pieces by Hunter S. Thompson and the radical quill-and-ink drawings of Ralph Steadman). And the music I loved, no matter how diverse, all seemed to reflect the changing times.*

As an update to the 1949 documenting techniques used by Roger Barker and his associates (writing board, watch, sound recorders), my team (consisting of Chris Ericson, Jeff Sugg, Jim Findlay, and Will Knapp) would deploy robotic cameras and videographers to capture the activities of participants onstage in real time. This footage would be combined with prerecorded images of contemporary life and projected onto two video cubes, creating a (hopefully) profound tableau of humanity orchestrated by music and light. The video cubes would also function as staging areas for the live musicians, their silhouettes just barely visible through the scrim. I also got the idea that each of the eight observers would have their own musical theme, and since the observers replaced one another out of sequence, this seemed like a great way to develop the music in an expanded theme and variation style, becoming more complex as the day progressed. The text from the book would be read by performers as well as being projected on the screen, depending on how lively the various classes on stage were. I was also excited about using auto-translation software to translate text as needed. Mike Ross, the artistic director of Krannert Center for the Performing Arts, became enthralled with the idea, especially as it related to community outreach in the Urbana, Illinois, school system. Mike and Krannert have been enthusiastic supporters of my work for twenty years, but I also think Mike was seeing the legacy potential of the piece. I made numerous trips to Krannert and met with the entire Krannert team, many of whom I'd known and worked with for years. I became particularly close with Emily Laugesen and Sam Smith, who worked closely with the school system to bring artists into the classroom and bring classes to see performances and exhibits at the center. A year or two in on the project, Mike also introduced me to Wayne Ashley and Xander Seren, who run a production company called FuturePerfect. After numerous meetings, we decided to work together and began to strategize on presenter and funding possibilities.

I got my own stereo for Christmas in 1970. My sister got one of the first cassette decks. Hers came with a Mamas and Papas cassette, and I somehow got Led Zeppelin II *and John Lennon's* Imagine. *Soon I was picking up records by their covers: Lou Reed's* Transformer, *Bowie's* Ziggy Stardust and the Spiders from Mars. *And sifting through records at Jay's*

Music, I stumbled on the first New York Dolls record. What on earth could be happening outside of this little town? I stumbled onto Miles Davis, and an older guy named Rick Stout turned me on to Thelonious Monk. He would also help me in scoring a composition that I wrote for the high school marching band, as a final project for a music theory course I managed to bluff my way into. I landed a job singing and playing piano at a bar near the high school, and though I was underage, no one seemed to care. Let's face it: as I would learn later in life, it's who you know. I had introduced the manager to the teacher I was dating; the manager would bring me screwdrivers because they looked like plain orange juice. God bless him.

The scramble for producers and commissioners was on. Or, as my friend, the painter Sarah Albritton, would say, "money hunting." I traveled for multiple meetings in Paris, London, and Dublin. I found interested folks in LA and Austin. My friend Valda Witt and her husband, Jay Hatfield, whom I met through guitarist Jeff McErlain, even hosted a big fundraiser at their place on the Upper West Side in New York. All the while, I was grinding away at the music and creating elaborate folders of the individual stems for my sound engineer, Chris Ericson. It's a score of shifting rhythms and ambient electronics that accompanies the live musicians' environment while a voice-over recites the entire 1949 study. Depending on which of the "observer themes" is happening, there are three live musician possibilities: fully scored, note-specific improvisation, and free improv. This would continue my interest in working with local musicians regardless of their sight-reading abilities or musical strengths. Over a three-year period, I made many trips to Urbana-Champaign, with visits to Dr. Williams and Wiley Elementary Schools to work closely with teachers, students, and parents to develop a curriculum, devise activities, produce video, and rehearse sequences that would eventually make their way into the final production. We even set up classes in a school gymnasium to try out aspects of orchestrating the classes. I remember fondly watching musician Jason Finkelman improvise on his laptop as his sight line follows a volleyball sailing over his head. With an English class on one side of the gym and a math class on the other, it was thrilling to get a sense of how this idea might actually work.

Chasing trains bareback on horses or riding to the Black River to skinny-dip. Swimming in a cousin's flooded basement, with oil and gas cans floating around us. Reading Abbie Hoffman's Steal This Book *and trying out the soda pop scam at the local gas station. Traveling with the carnival and learning the sleight-of-hand tricks of the trade. Buying my own upright piano to put in my bedroom. Shoplifting. Art instructors Raona Hentz, Van Vance, and Leo Smith looking the other way in support. Ray even commissioned a mural on a wall in her house and only sold the place thirty years later with the proviso that the mural had to stay. Van helping my mom sneak out my art from a greedy instructor to help us pull together a portfolio for the only college I applied to. In 1986, Leo wept when I came back and brought him my recent album to thank him for being there. Miraculously avoiding the pitfalls of a few friends. Dumb luck.*

I needed a fly-through animation that would give presenters some idea of what the staging would look like. I approached several companies with connections to friends of mine, but even with the friendship discount, it was too expensive. Through Katie O'Donnell, I had met the data scientist and instructor Bryan Gibson. I was having a beer with him one afternoon and was complaining of this dilemma, and he mentioned he used to do stuff like that. He wanted to give it a shot, for which I am eternally grateful. Working with FuturePerfect, we then took that animation and combined it with interviews of Mike Ross and myself shot at Wiley Elementary school to create a six-minute promo film describing elements of the production. Then it was suggested that the piece could use its own website, so I managed to pull that together, even though I loathe the lost hours I'll never get back from doing website maintenance for the last thirty years. And all the while, I was still grinding away at the sound score, which I managed to complete in 2018. On one of the trips to Urbana, I handed off a drive of all the files to Chris. In the meantime, Jim Findlay had started drawings for the set design. He had moved his performance space, The Collapsable Hole, to Westbeth, which was a fond reminder of the years I'd spent there at the Cunningham studio. Terri Ciofalo at Krannert had the great idea of enlisting student videographer Anja Hose, who would help shoot and edit the video we collected over a couple of years: classroom video, playground video, you name it. We were trying to follow the original timeline and cover each section.

"Give it up in the age of reason." Dad was a character. After defying him at thirteen and buying an aquarium from my next-door neighbor, he could have flattened me. I had traded comic books for a small bull catfish, and when he told me it would eat the tropical fish, I contested his theory. Again, he could have flattened me. Instead, I found out years later that he would get up early and, one by one, flush the fish down the toilet to prove his point. Kind of brilliant when you think about it. Struggling with debt after the Dennis Cleveland *premiere in New York, I would introduce a small goldfish bowl into my apartment in a "feng shui" attempt at hope. The fish kept dying, and as I explained the debilitating effect of flushing them down the toilet, Kyle Gann, knowing the backstory, exclaimed, "Well, Mikel, I guess you just had to flush them down for yourself." Brilliant! Dad also had the idea to breed one of his hunting dogs, a purebred English setter named Princess, with a stud from town. After the attempt, Princess made a bee-line for the twelve-year-old collie next door and went at it. Watching Dad eight weeks later at the miracle of birth was a sight. The first eight pups: collie. The last one: looked like an English setter. Another scheme bit the dust. When I was seven or so, I couldn't find my Sunday-school shoes and he went ballistic and left for Catholic Mass on his own. I would remind my sister that due to my shoe incident, we escaped Catholic church and all that indoctrination!*

At a certain point, it became clear to Wayne and me that we weren't getting anywhere.

FuturePerfect brought incredible enthusiasm and ideas to the piece, but ultimately, I needed producers who could raise funds. As great as their ideas were, I kinda had that area covered. We walked away with no hard feelings, though I think we both felt we'd each lost a good chunk of time. It's impossible to overstate the amount of time we spent trying to move this forward, and I remain grateful for Wayne's and Xander's efforts. But still, another scene bites the dust. So now, back to square one. Will Knapp, the production manager, and I began to find a work-able, scaled-down set that would enable us to do a workshop in May of 2020. We adapted Jim's elaborate design into a more compact set for the workshop. I narrowed it down to two musical sections, one scored and one improv, and sent the materials to Matt so he could start pull-ing together the performance scores. I had numerous meetings over a six-month period with Will as we moved closer to realizing the workshop in May 2020, and Krannert had confirmed that they would premiere the piece in April 2021. As difficult as the struggle had been, it felt like it was finally coming together. I've had so many pieces that I thought were crystal clear—a talk show opera or a live 3D film—but I'd learned the hard way that for the most part, folks must see it to comprehend it. And now they would.

How do you leave a small town? A town that made you while you hated it? Maybe not hate it but hoped for something more. Only recently my mom reminded me she drove me to Kansas City. Of course she did, as she did my sister a year earlier to Columbia, Missouri. I'm sure the car was packed. As in 1998 (see "The End of Cinematics (1998) Part 1"), I was running toward my future and not thinking about the person taking me there. Kids. Anyway, my dad arranged a small loan that would take me ten years to pay off. I got a scholarship, which was great, but I still worked three jobs to put myself through school. I didn't care. I was happy to be there. Happy to discover the conservatory next door to the art institute and eventually create a double major–type program. And perhaps most grateful to meet Rob Shepperson, because everything he touched was art, and Jeff Burk, a great photographer: the core that would journey to New York and start a life.

The last meeting I had with Will was in my hood. It was early March of 2020, and he was mildly wondering if his next gig in China might be postponed due to this new virus. A few days later, on March 12, 2020, I settled at the bar at Marseille in my hood. They had introduced a frisée salad and duck confit lunch that I loved (I live like I'm rich when I'm poor). I then learned that the Broadway theaters would close, due to Covid-19, at 5 p.m. And sure enough, folks from the theater world streamed in, stunned but assured for no reason that this would be a two-week bump. I wasn't so sure. I guess I felt something was coming. Long overdue? A penance for our sins? Not sure, but I somehow felt something bigger was in the offing. I went home and thought about all my friends and family. *One Boy's Day* was about all of them. I decided to hold tight, keep going, and hope for the best. I've gotten used to ignoring my instincts. Bad habit. Krannert was amazingly supportive and generous during this uncertain time. And I have to say, though for years I'd relied more on credit cards than grants, the arts community rose to this occasion and supported artists, including me, in a way I couldn't have imagined. I was honored to be a part of this coterie. Truly.

Since we didn't yet know the end or near end of this pandemic, Krannert moved ahead with the thirteen-hour premiere of *One Boy's Day*. Working with Tammey Kikta has always been a joy, but now we were in horrific and uncertain times, trying to move forward. We set a premiere date for April 29, 2021, hoping that maybe this moment would pass us by. But unsettled America would make everything more complex. And as the unraveling happened, I only felt grateful. Not grateful that this seven-year journey might not reach completion. But grateful to know people who care. Mike Ross, Emily Laugesen, Sam Smith, Tammey Kikta, everyone in the Urbana school system. C'mon! No one is more jaded than me. But here are folks who care about their world and the families in it. And they'll actually humor me. My gratitude knows no bounds. Krannert decided to honor their 2020–2021 season by making their season brochure, even though most of the events wouldn't be happening. An immensely thoughtful gesture to all the artists, producers, and technical people who worked so hard to keep the faith. *One Boy's Day* has a page in this brochure, and it's both surreal and oddly comforting at the same time. Kinda like life these days.

"I'm still waiting to become the man that I made." I'm awake in bed. I'm either seven or sixty-five. I've survived the tumult of rage in rural America and I've survived a pandemic. I'm filled with loss and hopelessness. I'm frozen in time. I have a Braille libretto. I have peripheral neuropathy, or my first real pet is licking my feet. I'm a believer in big ideas. More than ever, I'm that strange kid from Missouri, fumbling through life. Wondering what's next. And they say you can't go home again . . .

Acknowledgments

I'd like to say thanks to a few who helped along the way. I didn't always listen, but I did hear. Rob Shepperson. I've met some wonderfully talented people, but few geniuses. He's one. A great artist and drummer of Tirez Tirez and early Mikel Rouse Broken Consort. But so far beyond that, everything he touched became art. I also learned a ton from Jeff Burk, the original bass player for TT. A melodic player and the solid rock of the early band when I was still learning guitar. Those early days in Kansas City were complemented by great artists and friends. Jim Bourgeois was and is a constant delight. It's an honor that someone so special thinks I'm special. James Gleespen was the star of my first film. He was always inspiring. Peter Keenan and Ted Dibble provided the early inspiration for my video wanderings. Cliff Baldwin would become a trusted collaborator over many years. Mike Stoughton, Christine Inukai, and Tim Steele helped the transition from cows to culture. LeRoy Pogemiller (conservatory) and Ron Slowinsky (painting instructor) provided much needed contrasts that left a mark. Also, designer and teacher Steve Sidelinger.

Landing in New York added to the list, and of course I'm afraid I'll miss someone here. Tom Lee and Arthur Russell were the first people I met. How lucky is that? Musicians and lifelong friends start with James Bergman, Bill and Rave Tesar, Phillip Johnston, Ellery Eskelin, Dale Kleps, Davo Bryant, and Mark Lambert. Mark was my next-door neighbor in Hell's Kitchen as we climbed in and out of the Reagan '80s. I hope

I helped him as much as he helped me. I want to acknowledge a few who acknowledged me: Jon Pareles at the *New York Times*, Mark Swed at the *Los Angeles Times*, and composer and writer Kyle Gann. Along with a bunch of writers too numerous to include here, these folks gave me my first breath of hope as I struggled to find my artistic path. I was lucky with Kyle, becoming close friends and confidants for over thirty years. It's always advisable to have someone like Kyle who understands what you're up to more than you do. I'm filled with gratitude that he contributed the foreword to this book. John Schaefer and his program *New Sounds* created a sounding board for a couple of generations of artists. Steve Smith, who probably saved *The End of Cinematics* with his *Time Out New York* feature. Thanks to Jim Fouratt and the early years at Peppermint Lounge and Danceteria.

Cheers to Jaqueline Davis, who gracefully guided me into my archive at the New York Public Library for the Performing Arts. Jonathan Hiam, also at LPA, has been a great supporter and friend. Along with George Boziwick, he made the archival process more artful. Gratitude to Barbara Cohen-Stratyner, Amy Russell, and Caitlin Mack at LPA. I'm indebted to Brent Reidy for insight, support, and friendship. Unimaginable kudos to the Luminato Festival and the family of Janice Price, Martha Haldenby, Trevor Haldenby, Clyde Wagner, Chris Lorway, and Mitchell Marcus. A visionary group if ever there was one. Grace to Adrienne Clarkson and John Ralston Saul, artistic inspirations who became valued friends.

The Krannert Center for the Performing Arts has been a home away from home for over twenty years. Director Mike Ross is a trusted friend and a leading light for the arts. The world that he brings to the Urbana community is breathtaking. Rebecca McBride, the senior associate director of Krannert Center for twenty-four years, has been a force in my life, along with her partner, Betsy Bachmann. In fact, it was Bec's prompting that got this book off the ground. Tammey Kikta, the assistant director of artistic services, always managed to keep a welcoming smile on her face, even when juggling the impossible. Karen Quisenberry ran Level 21 with a grace and aplomb I'll always treasure. Thanks, Emily Laugesen and Sam Smith, for all things community. Thanks, Terri Ciofalo and Maureen Reagan, for so many supportive ideas. Ditto to Nathan and Julie Gunn. Props to Michael W. Williams for keeping the lights on. And through Krannert, I stole some of the best talent in the world. Carolyn Cubit Tsutsui was the original stage manager for *Dennis Cleveland* and would be a hard act to follow. But follow I did with Valerie Oliveiro, who not only was a great stage manager, but as a photographer, a great collaborator to boot. And then there's Jenny Goelz, a soul like no other. Through many trials and tribulations, she kept an inspirational outlook on life, unintentionally but helpfully shaming me when I had a narrow view. It feels good just thinking of her now. Finding soundman Chris Ericson through Krannert was like finding the younger brother you didn't know you needed. His unrelenting smile and optimism are infectious. You must give in. Through Mike Ross, I also met Donna Cox, Robert Patterson, Jeff Carpenter, and the team at the National Center for Supercomputing Applications, all valued friends and collaborators.

Thanks to Joseph V. Melillo, Karen Brooks Hopkins, and Alice Bernstein at BAM; I'll always remember Joe's kindness and support when he took me and my work to Harvey Lichtenstein. Jon Nakagawa and Jane Moss at Lincoln Center held fast after 9/11, supporting the *Dennis Cleveland* revival when mere mortals might have balked. I'm forever grateful to them. Dean Corey was also a brave leader in introducing the work to audiences and presenters alike. To Chad Herzog for always fighting the good fight. And Jay Weigel, a great friend and composer who also served his community at the Contemporary Arts Center in New Orleans. To Séan Doran, who made so many things possible: I raise a pint to him. And in quick succession, presenters Richard Wakely, Graham Sheffield, David Sefton, Neil Murray, Emil Kang, Paul Fahy, F. John Herbert, and Mel Andringa. Something many of these folks have in common is Michael Mushalla, my agent for a good fourteen-year run. This book's title is taken from a song written for Michael, a friend and confidant; his wanderlust wasn't always easy, but it was always interesting. I'm grateful for our extended run. To Laura Kuhn and the John Cage Trust for so many memories, opportunities, and good will. We had some adventures. Thank you, Anthony Creamer, for the friendship and support. To Sue Devine, as she frantically tore through Post-it notes, trying to grasp *Dennis Cleveland*, and later saved the day with Pink's Hot Dogs. Veanne Cox, my Tony-nominated HK neighbor who played such a big part in my work. Thanks to Mary Anne Lewis: How Was Your House?

The list of artists and friends would take a book. But special thanks to Matthew Gandolfo, the best music director I could have hoped to con into working with me. Jeff Sugg, video designer and all-around artist. Richard Connors and his keen camera eye. Hideaki Tsutsui, a master of light and space. William Knapp, whose calm demeanor made every load-in seem like a breeze, even when it wasn't. And Brad Hepburn, a stalwart fellow if ever there was one. Claire Kenny, Christina Pawl, Penelope Thomas, Ryuji Noda, Levensky Smith, and Robert Arthur Altman. Thanks, Ben Neill, for being a great friend, sounding board and collaborator. Frank J. Oteri, Marla Hamburg, Stuart Leaf, Claire Silberman, the Gregory Brothers' Andrew, Evan, Michael, and Sarah, Jean Vong, Olwen Fouéré, Peter Witte, UMKC Conservatory of Music and Dance, Andrew Granade, David D. McIntire, Jack Fortune, Leslie Wayne, and Don Porcaro. A special thanks to Scott Hull, Matt Agoglia, Kyle Kelso, Dave O'Donnell, Randy Merrill, Jeff McErlain, and Masterdisk NYC for the studio camaraderie at 321. To Hal Willner and Sallie Sanders. Thomas Barefoot, Paul Katz, JB Moore, Gregory McNally, Marit Brooke-Kothlow, Liz Burritt, Joe Goode, Curtis Smith, and Sue Threlkeld. Melissa Madden Gray and the magic shoes. Margarete Roeder, Mark Kingsley, Katie O'Donnell, Mario Juarez, Raymond E. Van Cott, Joey Di Gregorio, Victor Borg, Steve Knutson, Susana Ribeiro, John Margolis, Claire Karoly, Valda Witt and Jay Hatfield, Nancy Cook, Bernard Gann, Shankari Srinivasan, Bart and Lynda Grooms, and Brett Trach at AtoZ. Thanks to Bryan Gibson and Anne Hurst for being compadres above and beyond, and to John, Edith, and Szilvia Juhasz. And to the never-ending swing shift that is Rudy's: Danny DePamphilis, Yolanda Pelaez, Genevieve Kirby, Nils Hagstrom, Melissa Marino, and Marlon Cherry. Cheers to Peter Malfatti and Preston Boyd. And cheers to Susanna Minous, Ciera Coyan, Daniel Sterling, Margo Masi, and Dan McLaughlin. Thanks to Maria Perroni and the wonderful Lutteroth family, who invited me to the eightieth anniversary of the Arena Mexico Lutteroth and helped me jump out of an airplane. Twice. Thanks especially to Glenn Kenny and Michael Azerrad, amazing writers and friends who gently guided me through this book. Thanks to Ryan Fox for his assured counsel. Gratitude to Ann Powers and Meg Handler for their investigative skills. Special thanks to Laurie Matheson at University of Illinois Press for her steady hand and support of this book, and to Gary Smith for his guidance and kind support. Thanks to Jennifer Argo for her help coordinating the editorial stages and production of this book. And thanks to Natalie Reitano for copyediting above and beyond the call of duty: her keen eye is only matched by her kind support and enthusiasm.

And finally, to my family: matriarch Martha Sue Rouse, sage sister Cindy Ponder and her spouse Jill Holly, my nephew and inspiration, Brennan Ponder, his partner Julianne Wise, Steven Ponder, Morgan Ponder, my niece Katie Ponder Israel, her husband Will Israel, and their son Hudson. They have all been wonderfully supportive, and I'm reminded that when Katie was ten, she asked me, "What is it exactly that you do?" I can imagine they've all wondered that at one time or another, but they've never wavered in their belief in me. And where are those girls? That's another book. But love inspires, and never more so than with Lisa Boudreau, my wife, companion, and soul mate during the "rise and fall" years. And to Kathy Valentine and my extended family of Steven and Audrey Weisburd: thanks for years of love and compassion from Austin to LA. Home is where you're lucky enough to make it. And last but certainly not least: Ildiko Juhasz, a fortune teller and sage who walks the walk. Her resilience, faith, and caring through these trying times is worthy of Flaubert: "Love is a springtime plant that perfumes everything with its hope, even the ruins to which it clings."

Illustration Credits

Cover: Steve Walters

Dennis Cleveland: Photo by Stephanie Berger, Chris Brown photo: chrisbownphoto.com

Dennis Cleveland sketchbooks: Mikel Rouse Archive

Quorum patterns and LinnDrum brochure: Mikel Rouse Archive

Vespers performance: © Pierre Wachholder

Failing Kansas: Roger Woolman

Failing Kansas libretto and sketch excerpts: Mikel Rouse Archive

The End of Cinematics: Dan Merlo

Food sketches and cartoons: Mikel Rouse Archive

Gravity Radio: Photos by Stephanie Berger

The Demo: Valerie Oliveiro

One Boy's Day film still and music still: Mikel Rouse Archive

One Boy's Day set design: Model design by Jim Findlay and Jeff Sugg

Index

Note: *Italicized* page numbers indicate figures.

Academy of Arts and Letters, 13
"Active Denial," 168
"Actors with Guns (Sleepwalk through the Mantra)," 179
Against All Flags (1988), 35–38, 39–40, 180
Agnès B., 98, 156
Agoglia, Matt, 132, 161, 166, 169, 173, 194
AIDS, 38, 52, 53
Ailey, Alvin, 51
Al Attrach, Farid, 175
"Albany Handshake," xix
Albee, Edward, 6
Albritton, Sarah, 160–61, 192
"All Around the World," 166
Allen, Woody, 99
"All That Time," 166
Alphabet. See James Joyce, Marcel Duchamp, Erik Satie: An Alphabet (John Cage radio play)
Alstrom, Ed, 123–24
Alstrom, Maxine, 123–24
Alternative Museum (New York City), 48
Altman, Robert Arthur, 87, 156, 157
Alvin Ailey American Dance Theater, *Vespers* (Ulysses Dove ballet), x, *47*, 48, 50–53, 73, 136
Amazeen, Lauren, 5, 7
"America's Belief," 158
"America's Secrets," 166

Amram, David, 131
Anderson, Laurie, 13, 78, 131
"And Now We Are Not," 179
Andringa, Mel, 60
"Another World," 29
"Answer," 43
"Anthems for a Seventeen-Year-Old Girl" (Broken Social Scene), 119, 121
Archer, Robyn, 85
archives of MR: Big Fish Audio Sample Library (John Cage works), xiii–xiv, 64–66, 129; John Cage Prepared Sample library, 80; at the New York Public Library for the Performing Arts (New York City), 129–30, 136–37, 174; of Arthur Russell's work, 38–39, 65
Arthur Bryant's Barbecue (Kansas City), 102–3, 109
Ashley, Robert, xii, xv, 7–8, 27, 44, 57–58
Ashley, Wayne, 191, 194
Atlas, Charles, 71
Audika Records (label), 29
Australian Broadcasting Company (ABC), 16–18
Automat (New York City), 105
Autorequiem (1994), 38, 39–40, 42

Babbit, Milton, xxi
Baby Doll Lounge (New York City), 48
Baldwin, Cliff, 12–13, 37–38, 42, 43, 57, 132, 155, 156
Bang on a Can, 41–42

Bank, Mirra, 110
Baptiste, Jules, 27
Baracz, Jan, 6
Bar de l'X (Paris), 72–73
Barker, Jonathan, 189–90
Barker, Roger, 188–91
Barrueto-Cabello, Felipe, 164
Baryshnikov, Mikhail, 78
Batali, Mario, 105
Bates Method, 155
Batzner, Jay, 167
BC Studio (Brooklyn), 31, 33, 35, 49
Beach Boys, 5
The Bears (band), 35
The Beatles (band), 83, 85, 96, 97, 178
Beaudreau, James, 173
"Beautiful Murders," xvii
Becco (New York City), 111
Beer Culture (New York City), 111
Belafonte, Harry, 157
Belew, Adrian, 35
Bell, Clive, 175
"Be More Really," xv, 98
Berger, Mark, 129
Bergman, James, 28, 32, 35, 36, 40–41, 48, 49
Berry, Chuck, 177
Bette's Too (Kansas City), 25
Bey, Richard, 3–4
Big Fish Audio Sample Library, xiii–xiv, 64–66, 129
Billy's Topless (New York City), 104
Birch, Raymond, 188–89
Bisi, Martin, 31, 33, 35, 49
Biss, Rod, 61–62
Bither, David, 26
Blachly, Michael, 96, 157
Black Watch (National Theatre of Scotland), 118, 120
Bleecker Bob's (New York City record store), 26
Bley, Carla, 50, 78
"Blow Dried Bodies," 172
Bogosian, Eric, 13
Book 1 (MR string quartets), 154
Boost | False Doors (2012), 171–74
Borg, Victor, 111, 124
Boudreau, Anita (sister-in-law), 116, 139
Boudreau, George (father-in-law), 116
Boudreau, Lisa (former wife), 78–80, 109–13, 116, 182, 183; at fiftieth anniversary of Canadian Governor General

position, 20, 115; marries MR, 110; meets MR, 53, 83; with Merce Cunningham Dance Company, 2, 17, 21, 53, 69, 73, 74, 78, 83–84, 103, 118, 123; MR works and, 83–84, 88, 92, 95, 97–98, 118, 120, 123, 155; separation from MR, 138, 172; "staycation" (2008), 110–11, 123–25; tax audits, 95, 137–38; World Trade Center terrorist attacks (2001) and, 69; as yoga teacher, 118
Boudreau, Mark (brother-in-law), 116, 123, 139
Boudreau, Roe-Enid (mother-in-law), 116
"Bounce to Disc," 157
Bourdain, Anthony, 106
Bourgeois, Jim, 102, 103, 179
Bowie, David, 174
Boziwick, George, 136
Bradlee, Ben, 133
Bradshaw, James, 121
Braga, Sônia, 9, 104, 110
Brakhage, Stan, 155
Branca, Glenn, 27
Brassard, Marie, 117
Brezhnev, Leonid, 32
Broken Consort/Mikel Rouse Broken Consort (MRBC, band), x–xi, 5, 27–28, 31, 32, 35–38, 40–42, 48–50, 56, 57, 108, 112, 123, 129, 135, 154
Broken Social Scene (band), 119, 121
Brook-Kothlow, Marit, 164, 165
Brooklyn Academy of Music (BAM), 82; *The End of Cinematics* at, 83, 84, 89, 93–96, 142; *Gravity Radio* at, *126, 127,* 132, 136–38, 142, 167, 171; Merce Cunningham Dance Company benefit (1997), 53, 83, 84
Brooks, Richard, 56
Brown, Earle, x, 65
Brown, Michael, 176–77
Brown, Steven, 30
Bruno Ravioli (New York City), 106
Bryant, Arthur, 102–3
Bryant, Davo, 35
Buckner, Thomas, 7–8
Buena Vista (San Francisco), 152, 164
Burk, Jeff, 24, 25–26, 50, 104, 182, 195
Burns, Martha, 120
Burritt, Elizabeth, 164
Buscemi, Steve, 5
Bush, George W., 19, 97, 166
Bush, Vannevar, 146

"Busy Humanist," 168
Byrne, David, 20, 24–25, 26–27, 50

Cage, John, 64–71; Big Fish Audio Sample Library, xiii–xiv, 64–66, 129; "Cage's Satie" (Musée d'art contemporain de Lyon), 80; *The City Wears a Slouch Hat* (stage film), 80–81; Foundation for Contemporary Arts and, 94–95; *4'33"*, 81, 144; *James Joyce, Marcel Duchamp, Erik Satie: An Alphabet* (radio play), 14, 19, 59, 66–70, 80, 157–58; John Cage Prepared Sample library, 80; prepared piano works, xiii–xiv, xx, 64–65, 80, 165; *Roaratorio* (Cage/Rouse sound installation), 59, 70; *Sonatas and Interludes,* xiii–xiv, 64–65. *See also* Cage Trust/John Cage Trust
Cage Trust/John Cage Trust, xiii–xiv, 13, 64–81, 93, 129
Calbi, Greg, 34, 37
Caldicott, Helen, 32
Cal Performances (Berkeley), 70
Cameraworld (2001), 85, 87, 96, 132, 156–58
Cameron, James Edward, 119
Capote, Truman, xii, 40, 55, 56
Carl's Drive-in (St. Louis), 102
Carmon's (Urbana, Illinois), 77, 92
Carnegie Deli (New York City), 107–8
Carpenter, Jeff, 84, 86, 143, 145
Carroll Music Studios (New York City), 137, 157
Cavallero, Paul, 178–79
Cavern Club (Liverpool), 97
CBGB (New York City), 26–27
Cedar Tavern (New York City), 105
Center for Electronic Music, 42, 56–57
Cerveris, Michael, 20
Chance, James, 27
"Change for My Baby," 161
Chang in a Void Moon (serial play), 5
Chatham, Rhys, 41
Chez Napoléon (New York City), 51
Chiao, Raymond, 128–29
Citizen DJ project, 182–83
Citron, Paula, 122–23
City Center (New York City), 48, 50–52, 53, 73
"Clarion Hotel," 166
Clark, John, 101
Clarkson, Adrienne, 8–9, 20, 115–18, 120, 122
Club Soda Music (label), 32

Cochran, Tom, 25, 26
Coffee Shop (New York City), 104
Cohen, Leonard, xxiii, 117, 119, 161
Coleman, Anthony, 131
Collapsable Hole (New York City), 147–48, 193
Collom, Wayne, 159–60
Colorado Suite (1984, with Blaine Reininger), 8, 30–31
"Come from Money," xix, 172
Connors, Richard, 19, 86, 93
Conservatory of Music, University of Missouri, x, 24–25, 102, 115–16
Contemporary Arts Center (CAC, New Orleans), 134, 177
Copeland's (New York City), 109
Corbo, Georgina, 88
Corey, Dean, 14, 15–16, 77, 99
"The Corner," 43
Corner Loading (Volume 1, 2010), 136, 167–69, 171
La Côte Basque (New York City), 55
counterpoetry, xii–xiii, 39, 40, 56–57
"Court Packing," 179
Court Street Grocers, 107n
Covid-19 pandemic, xiii, xix–xx, 60, 105, 106–7, 111, 178–79, 181–83, 195–96
Cowell, Henry, x
Cox, Donna, 84, 143–44
Cox, Veanne, xviii, 44, 83–84, 130–31, 132, 133, 155, 182
Crammed Discs, 30, 32
Creamer, Anthony, 83, 110, 173
Crew, Robert, 120, 121–22
Crivello, Stefano, 165
Crown Candy Kitchen (St. Louis), 102
Cuba, Alex, 121
Cubit-Tsutsui, Carolyn, 18, 59–61, 87
Cuneiform Records, 36
Cunningham, Merce, 20, 65–66, 115; birthdays, 67, 71–72; death, 78–80, 173; *James Joyce, Marcel Duchamp, Erik Satie: An Alphabet* (John Cage radio play), 14, 19, 59, 66–70, 80, 157–58; MR tribute for NewMusicBox, 79. *See also* Merce Cunningham Dance Company
Cunningham Trust/Merce Cunningham Trust, 76–77, 79–80
Cupcake Cafe (New York City), 117
"Cutting Class," 170
Cyr, Mike, 65, 67
Czaplinski, Lane, 161–62

Dadaism, xvi, 26
Dafoe, Willem, 14
Dallas Black Dance Theatre, 51
"Dammit Bikini," xiv
Damski, Paul, 77, 92
Dana Tana's (Los Angeles), 178
Danceteria (New York City), 27, 51
Dance Theater Workshop (New York City), 14, 37
"Darling Be Home Soon," 177
Darrow, Clarence, 32
Dave's Luncheonette (New York City), 105
Davis, Jacqueline, 136–37, 152
Davis, Peter, 21
Davoy, Napua, 9, 15
Dayton Contemporary Dance Company, 51
Deer Run restaurant (Poplar Bluff, Missouri), 101
Dell'Orto, James, 106
Dell'Orto, Sal, 105–6
DeMiceli, Michael and John, 107
The Demo (2015), 142–50, 188; cast and crew, 142, 143–49, 151–52, 174; original Engelbart demonstration film, 142–46, 148, 153; performances of, *140, 141,* 143–44, 146, 149–52; press coverage, 150–51, 177; SRI International and, 142–46, 150
Dennis Cleveland (1996 opera), 1–21, 52, 142, 156; cast and crew, 5–8, 9, 12, 14–19, 21, 86–87, 116–17, 134–35, 147, 157, 161; documentary by Australian Broadcasting Company, 16–18; New World Records release, 7; performances of, xii–xiii, 2–3, 5–9, *10, 11,* 12–21, 67, 82–84, 86–87, 89, 99, 114–20, 157; press coverage, 9, 12, 15–16, 20–21, 44, 120; recording process, 43–44; researching, xii–xiii, 3–4, 43; sketchbooks, *22, 23*; as talk show opera, xii–xiii, xvi–xvii, 2–3, 58; in trilogy, xiii, 8, 42–45; and *Voltaire's Bastards* (Saul), xvi–xvii, 3, 115
Descarfino, Charles, 37
"Designing Women," 170
Devine, Sue, 13, 15, 77
Di Gregorio, Joey, 111, 124, 168
Diliberto, John, 33
Dirt, Johnny, 2–3, 7, 21, 173
Dirt Club (New Jersey), 2
Les Disques du Crepuscule (Belgium), 28–29, 30–31

The Distinguished Wakamba Cocktail Lounge (New York City), 104–5
Dobson, Ray, 86, 93
"Dolls & Dreams," 170
Donohue's Steak House (New York City), 148
Doran, Séan, 16, 61
Dorsey, Henry, 159–60
Double M Arts & Events, 16
Dove, Ulysses, 44; *Dancing on the Front Porch of Heaven* (Royal Swedish Ballet), 52–53; *Vespers* (Alvin Ailey ballet), x, *47,* 48, 50–53, 73, 136
Downtown Sound studio (New York City), 25–26, 180
Driscoll, Kermit, 37
"Drop the Ball," xv, 83
Duchamp, Marcel, 67, 68
Duckworth, William, 7, 42
Duval, Michel, 28
Dylan, Bob, 168–69

Eataly (New York City), 105
Eatock, Colin, 120, 123
Eclectic Orange Festival (California), 14–16, 67, 70, 77, 99, 155
"The Edges of Entertainment," xvii–xviii, 180
Edinburgh International Festival (Scotland), 67–68, 158
eDream Institute (National Center for Supercomputing Applications, Urbana, Illinois), 81, 84–85, 143–47
Edward Albee Foundation grant (Montauk), 6, 9
Egoyan, Atom, 122
Eisenberg, Monus, 106–7
Eisenberg's Sandwich Shop (New York City), 64, 81, 106–7, 107n
Ellington, Duke, xxi
"The Eloquent Dissenter," 32
Emley, Sarah, 135, 138
Empire Diner (New York City), 9
The End of Cinematics (1998 opera/film), xv, 14, 82–99, 129, 154, 156, 163, 195; cast and crew, 19, 44, 73, 83, 85–89, 92–96, 98, 99, 116–17, 119, 121, 131, 132–35, 143; CGI and, 83–86; editing process, 59; as film opera, xiii (*see also Funding* [2001 film]); performances, 18, 44, 83, 84–89, *90, 91,* 92–99, 114, 116–19, 121–22, 142, 149; press coverage, 95–96, 98, 121–22;

recording process, 44–45; sign language in, 88–89, 121; in trilogy, xiii, 8, 42–45

Enfield, Cynthia, 87–88, 119, 135

Engelbart, Douglas, 142–46, 148, 153

English, Bill, 143–46

Eno, Brian, 31

Ericson, Chris, 86–87, 89, 92, 93–94, 98, 99, 117, 118, 120, 122, 134, 137, 143, 146, 149, 150, 162, 191–93

Esca (New York City), 107, 110–12, 123–25, 171

Eskelin, Ellery, 36, 37, 48

Essig, Linda, 133

Etudes (1980), 24–28, 180

Europadisk, 50

Evans, Gil, 27, 37

Everett, Mark, 138, 167

ExitMusic Recordings (label), 7, 36, 136, 154–56, 157, 166–71

eyeSpace iPod score (for Merce Cunningham Dance Company), xxiii, 73–78, 84, 92–94, 96, 129, 131, 169–70

Fable, Lili, 106

Fable, Paul, 106

Factory Benelux (Brussels, Belgium), 28

Fahy, Paul, 162

Failing Kansas (1995 opera), 55–62, 82–83, 102, 142; cast and crew, 122–23, 155; counterpoetry, 39, 40, 56–57; excerpts, 63; film footage, 42, 57, 60, 132, 181–82; New Tone Records release, 7, 43, 57; performances, xxi–xxii, 54, 57–62, 77, 85, 99, 116, 117, 122–23, 162, 181–82; press coverage, 13, 21, 43, 55, 57–62, 122–23; recording process, 42–43, 57; researching, xii, 4–5, 40, 55, 56, 57; in trilogy, xiii, 8, 16, 42–45

Falcon Club (Kansas City), 25

False Doors (2012), xix, 171–74

False Films (2010), 137

Farrell, Nora, 42

Fearn, D. W., 130

Feldman, Mark, 37–38

Feldman, Morton, 37, 65

Ferry, Bryan, 79

Fibonacci series, xi

Findlay, Jim, 142, 147–48, 152, 191

Finkelman, Jason, 192

Finkelstein, Eric, 107n

Finley, Karen, 3

Flanagan, William, 6

Fleming, John, 173

Florent (New York City), 124–25

Florida State University (Gainesville), 96, 157

Fogerty, John, 167

Foo, Brian, 182–83

Fortune, Jack, 118

Foundation for Contemporary Arts, 94–95

Fouratt, Jim, 51

Fox, Katrina, 162

Frank's (New York City), 109–10

Freeman, Betty, 76–77

Freeman, Denny, 177

Frontier Booking, 35

Funding (2001 film), xiii, xvi, xviii–xix, 70, 154–56; cast and crew, xviii, 2, 83–84, 130, 155; at the Eclectic Orange Festival (California), 155; at the Perth Arts Festival (2002, Australia), 59, 155; press coverage, 155–56

FuturePerfect, 191, 193, 194

Galapagos Art Space (Brooklyn), 132, 166–67

Gallagher, Billy, 111–12

Gallaghers Steakhouse (New York City), 16

Gandolfo, Matthew, 87–88, 117, 131–34, 148, 151

Gann, Kyle, ix–xxii, 2, 3, 19, 21, 39, 41, 55, 155, 166, 194

Gateway Mastering, 161

"Gaza Strip Mall (Get Happy)," 166

Gebhard, Matt, 111

Gelb, Peter, 14, 89

Gem Spa (New York City), 105

Gene's (New York City), 177

Georgie's Pastry (New York City), 109

Gerald W. Lynch Theater, John Jay College (New York City), 19–21

Gershwin, George, x

Gershwin, Ira, 40

Ghomeshi, Jian, 118–19

Gibson, Bryan, 182, 193

Gilberto, Astrud, 2

Gill, John, 31

"A Girl Named Jesus," 166

Glass, Philip, 13, 27, 38–39, 65, 117

Gleespen, James, 155

Goelz, Jenny, 77–78, 86–87, 89, 96, 98, 99, 116, 149

Go-Go's, 178, 179

Goldberg, Ron, 56

Gomes, Joe, 114
Goode, Joe, 164–66
Gordon, Peter, 131
Górecki, Henryk, 13
Gotham Bar and Grill (New York City), 32
Gotovac, Mike, 178
Governor's Conference on the Arts (New York City), 42, 57
Grace (2004), 92–93, 96, 130, 164, 165
Gramavision (label), 50
Grant, William H., III, 50
Graves, Robert, 89
Gravity Radio (2009), xiv, 99, 128–39; cast and crew, 73, 130–39, 143; ExitMusic release, 166–67; instruments and equipment, 129–30; performances, *126, 127,* 131–39, 142, 166–67, 171; press coverage, 136, 138, 166–67, 171; sound/film triggering, 80–81, 132–33, 135, 177
Gray, Melissa Madden, 17, 138–39, 147, 162
"Great Adventure Jail," 136, 168, 169
Gregory Brothers, 137
Grimaldi's Pizzeria (Brooklyn), 109
Grimm, Mark, 26
Gross, Paul, 120
Gulf Course (2016 film), 176
Gunn, Nathan, 89
Guthrie, Woody, 168–69
Gwiazda, Henry, 39

"Habibi Lossless," 174, 175
Hafez, Abdel Halim, 174, 175
Haines, Matt, 65
Hair, Julie, 25
Haldenby, Martha, 114–15
Hancock, Herbie, 31
"Hardfall," 32
Harrington, David, 66
Harris, Barry, 29
Harry's Bar (Venice), 78
"Harvest Moon" (Neil Young), 119, 121
Hatfield, Jay, 192
Hatzis, Christos, 117
Hausam, Wiley, 146, 149–51
Hawthorne, Karen, 121
Hayden Drive-In (Popular Bluff, Missouri), 101
Hebbel Theatre (Berlin), 68–70, 158
Hebron, Kameko, 156
Hemisphere (2017), 138, 151, 174–78
"Hemisphere," 176–77
Hepburn, Brad, 77–78, 87, 120
Herbert, F. John, 60

HERE (New York City), 42
Herman, Lisa, 44
Hero Boy (New York City), 106
Hertzman, Stan, 35
Herzog, Chad, 134–35
Hiam, Jonathan, 136
"High Frontier," 36
Hill, Dave, 130
Hinton, David, 52
hip-hop, 42, 49, 56–57, 87, 156
Hobbs, John Maxwell, 5, 7
Hockney, David, 77
Holland, Rosemary, 14
Holland Bar (New York City), 1
Hollander, Marc, 30, 32
Holley, Jill, 118
"Hollywood & Sons," xvii, 178, 179, 180
Honoré, Annik, 28
honors and awards of MR: Academy of Arts and letters nomination, 13; Center for Electronic Music grant, 56–57; Conservatory of Music (University of Missouri) Alumni Award, 115–16; Edward Albee Foundation grant (Montauk), 6; Foundation for Contemporary Arts award (2001), 94–95; grant from Change (Rauschenberg organization), 71; Jumbotron appearance (New York Yankees, 2008), 123–24; Margarete Roeder Gallery exhibit (New York City), 136, 137; Meet the Composer Residency (MTC), Louisiana Tech University, 18, 66, 92–93, 157–59, 160–61, 164; National Center for Supercomputing Applications (NCSA) visiting research artist status, 81, 84–85, 143–45; New York Public library exhibition of sketches and watercolors, 136; New York Public Library for the Performing Arts (New York City) "living" archive, 129–30, 136–37, 174; *Underemployed* (comic strip) exhibit at CSPS Art Gallery (Iowa), 175, 183
Hooker, John Lee, 168
Hope, Larry, 155
Horvitz, Wayne, 34
Hose, Anja, 193
Hotel Del Capri (Los Angeles), 14–15, 66–67, 163–64
Hourglass Cafe (New York City), 112–13
House of Fans (2006), 92–93, 131, 164, 166
"Housewife," 164
Houston Ballet, 51
Howard, Rachel, 165

Howard Johnson restaurants (New York City), 108
Hull, Scott, 169
Hunt, Calvin, 51–52
"Hurdle Rate," 172–73

"I Broke," xx, 183
"I Changed My Mind," 166
ICP Recording Studios, 30
"I Loved that Too," xvi
"I Might Never Give Up," 40
In Cold Blood (Capote), xii, 55, 56
"Inside the Waste of Time," 176
Interferences (Brussels, Belgium), 30
International Cloud Atlas (2006), 164–66; cast and crew, 77–78, 164–66; as commissioned work, xiii, 76–77; *eyeSpace* iPod score (for Merce Cunningham Dance Company), xxiii, 73–78, 84, 92–94, 96, 129, 131, 169–70; performances, 74, 77–78, 94; press coverage, 74
International Society for the Performing Arts (ISPA), 85
Interpretations music series, 7–8
I.R.S./Copeland group, 35
I.R.S. Records, 34
Island Records, 28
Israel, Hudson, 182
Israel, Katie Ponder (niece), 35, 76, 118, 182
Ivan (San Francisco bon vivant), 152
Ives, Charles, 32, 115

Jade Tiger (1984), x, 28–29, 31, 36, 48, 50
James Joyce, Marcel Duchamp, Erik Satie: An Alphabet (John Cage radio play), 14, 19, 59, 66–70, 80, 157–58; cast and crew, 67–70; performances, 67–70, 158; press coverage, 68
Jamison, Judith, 51
Jazz Cultural Theater (New York City), 29
Jensen, Clarice, 136
Jesurun, John, 5, 13, 15, 17, 83
Jezebel (New York City), 112
Joe Goode Performance Group, 92, 96, 130, 164–66
Joe Jr's (New York City), 104
John Lurie and the Lounge Lizards, 38
Johns, Jasper, 65–66, 67, 71, 77–79
Johnson, Mimi, 58
Johnston, Matt, 95
Johnston, Phillip, 28, 36
Jones, A. M., x
Jones, Chuck, 72

Jones, Jenny, 8
Jones, Quincy, 56
Joyce, James, 67
Joyce Theater (New York City), 74, 94
Juarez, Mario, 110–11, 112, 124
Jumer's Castle Lodge (Illinois), 18
Juniata College (Pennsylvania), 134–35

Kallenberg, Gregory, 177
Kamins, Mark, 28
Kamm, Thomas, 85–86
Kang, Emil, 93–94
Kansas City Art Institute (KCAI), x, 24, 65–66, 102, 155
Karoly, Claire, 151–52, 174–76, 182
Keenan, Peter, 179
Keens Steakhouse (New York City), 70, 106, 109
Keller, Allison, 182, 183
Kelly, John, 59, 67
Kelso, Kyle, 169
Kenny, Claire, 133–36
Kenny, Glenn, 33, 133
Key, Phillip, 98
Kikta, Tammey, 18, 196
Kingsley, Mark, 7, 9, 136–37, 157, 159
"Kiss Him Goodbye," 41, 42
The Kitchen (New York City), 27, 28; *Dennis Cleveland* (1996) premiere, xii–xiii, 2–3, 5–9, 12–15, 20, 82–83; *Failing Kansas* (1995) premier, 57–58
Kitsch Studio, 30–31
Kleps, Dale, 38, 154, 155
Knapp, William, 73, 92, 114, 137, 191, 194–95
Knelman, Martin, 121
Knitting Factory (New York City), 36–38, 42, 154
Knutson, Steve, 29
Koch, Ed, 104
Korder, Tom, 86, 93
Kozinn, Allan, 96
Krannert Center for the Performing Arts (Illinois): *The Demo* and, *140, 141,* 143–44, 149–50; *Dennis Cleveland* and, *11,* 16, 18–19, 84, 86–87, 89; *The End of Cinematics* and, 18, 44, 84–89, *90, 91, 92,* 149; *Gravity Radio* and, 133–37; *International Cloud Atlas* and, 77–78; *James Joyce, Marcel Duchamp, Erik Satie: An Alphabet* and, 70; *One Boy's Day* and, 191–96
Kriegsmann, Tommy, 147–49, 151

Kronos Quartet, 66
Kuhn, Laura, 13, 64–81, 93, 129
Kunofsky, Larry, 6
Kvitsinsky, Yuli, 32
Kwan, Derek, 152

La Bamba (New York City), 105
"LA Continental," 180
LaMar's Donuts (Kansas City), 103, 109
Lambert, Mark, 8, 9, 17, 19, 35–38, 53, 103, 104, 106, 154, 165–66
Landmark Tavern (New York City), 105, 183–84
Lang, Michael, 39
Lanier, Jaron, 146
Larson, Jonathan, 14
Larson, Larry, 65
La Rue, JJ, 30
"The Last to See Them Alive," 42, 56
Laswell, Bill, 31
Laugesen, Emily, 191, 196
Laurentian String Quartet, 154
Layton, Eddie, 124
Led Zeppelin (band), 27
Lee, Harper, 56
Lee, Tom, 27, 29, 38–39, 41
"Left in My Life," 41
Lemon, Ralph, 89
Levy, Benjamin, 164
Lewis, Mary Anne, 59–62, 69, 77–78, 94, 97–98, 122, 160–61
Lexington Candy Shop (New York City), 110
~/Library/Mouth/Congress (2020), xix–xx, 181, 183–84
Library of Congress, Citizen DJ project, 182–83
Lichtenstein, Harvey, 82, 94
Lieberman, David, 164
Lied Center (Lawrence, Kansas), 152
"Lift Your Hands," 176
"Light from a Trailer," 41
Lighting and the Design Idea (Essig and Setlow), 133
Lin, Austin, 81, 144
Lincoln, Rachel, 164
Lincoln Center (New York City), 10, 16–21
A Lincoln Portrait (1988), 35–38, 48
Lindsay, Arto, 27
LinnDrum, 31–32, 36, 47, 48–50, 182
LIVE 1987 (2021 live recording), 37
Living Inside Design (1994), xi, 40–43, 108, 132, 155; counterpoetry technique, xii,

57; fundraiser based on, 12–13, 65; in Paris, 72–73
LL Cool J, 34
Lorway, Chris, 114–15
Louis' Lunch (Gainesville, Florida), 96
Love at Twenty (2006), xi, xiv, xvi, 92, 130, 131, 164–66
Low-Rent Quartet, 135, 138
Luminato Festival (Toronto), 9, 114–23; Bymark "SeeHearFeelTaste" private dinner, 117–18, 121; Canadian Songbook, 117, 119, 120–21; "Crossing the Line" discussion, 117; Dennis Cleveland in, 10, 21, 99, 114–20; The End of Cinematics in, 99, 114, 116–18, 119, 121–22; Failing Kansas in, 99, 116, 117, 122–23; Gravity Radio, 138–39
Lurie, John, 38

Mac, Taylor, 148
MacLaine, Julia, 135
Made to Measure series, 32
"Made Up, Oh Lord," 168
Madonna, 28, 33
Mael, Ron and Russel, 173
"Make Her Won," 172
Malaspina, Sisto, 58
Malfatti, Peter, 111, 182
Mamet, David, 13
Mangan, Timothy, 16
Manganaro's (New York City), 105–6
Marcus, Mitchell, 114–15
Margarete Roeder Gallery (New York City), 136, 137
Margolis, John, 103
Mark Morris Dance Group, 16, 62, 118
Markoff, John, 150
Marseille (New York City), 112, 195
Martin, Wendy, 162
Masenheimer, David, 15, 156
Mason, Jackie, 108
Mason, James, 25, 28
Masterdisk (New York City), 32, 161, 169, 173
Max's Kansas City (New York City), 27, 104
Maya, Frank, 5
MCA, 34
McBride, Rebecca, 18, 88, 92
McCartney, Paul, 97
McCombs, Joseph, 96
McErlain, Jeff, 138, 169, 177, 192
McLaughlin, Dan, 111
McManus, Peter, 14

McManus bar (New York City), 14, 82
McSorley's Old Ale House (New York City), 16, 105
Meadows, Tom, 65
Meet the Composer Residency (MTC) in Louisiana, 18, 66, 92–93, 157–59, 160–61, 164
Melbourne International Arts Festival (Australia), 85
Melillo, Joe, 14, 82, 89, 95
Merce Cunningham Dance Company: Lisa Boudreau career with, 2, 17, 21, 53, 69, 73, 74, 78, 83–84, 103, 118, 123; Brooklyn Academy of Music benefit (1997), 53, 83, 84; Ulysses Dove and, 50–51; *eyeSpace* iPod score, xxiii, 73–78, 84, 92–94, 96, 129, 131, 169–70; studios in New York City, 69
Merkin Hall (New York City), 38
Metronome-*Community Spread* (2020), 181–83
Metronome-*Take Down* (2016), 151, 174–78, 188
Metropolitan Opera (New York City), 4, 14, 89
M&G Diner (New York City), 108–9
Microscopic Septet, 28
Mikel Rouse Sports Blog, 174–75, 179–80
Miller, Crista, 182
Miller, Graham, 178
Mill Luncheonette (New York City), 110
Miltenberger, Bill, 178
minimalism, x, xi, xxi, 29, 31–37
Mitchell, Joni, 119
Mitchell, Joseph, 56, 105
Mondavi Center, UC Davis (California), 93
Monk's Corner (New York City), 112
Monument (2017 film), 179
Moore, Stephan, 74, 76
Morozumi, Marc, 164
Morris, Mark, 62
Morton, Brian, 180
"The Movie We're In," 173
Mozart, Wolfgang Amadeus, xi, xii
MR. *See* Rouse, Mikel (MR)
Muna, RJ, 165
Murman, Eryn, 135
Murphy, Anne, 165
Mushalla, Michael: MR begins relationship with, 14, 16; MR ends relationship with, 147; MR gifts for, 59, 156; MR gifts from, 17, 122

Music for Minorities (2003), xv–xvi, 66, 85, 129, 159–64, 166
Musso & Frank Grill (Los Angeles), 178
"My Love's Gone," xi
"My Love's Gone Remix," 166
Mytnowych, Natasha, 117

Nakagawa, John, 16, 19, 21
Nancarrow, Conlon, 166
Nathan's (Brooklyn), 109
National Center for Supercomputing Applications (NCSA), University of Illinois at Urbana-Champaign, 81, 84–85, 143–47
National Sawdust *Hemisphere* retrospective (2017), 138, 177
Neill, Ben, 5, 9, 38, 39, 57, 142–48, 150, 151, 152, 174
Nelson, Caleb, 159
Neumann, Georg, 130
"Never Begin," 35–36
"Never Forget a Face," xi, 40, 43
NewMusicBox, 79
New Music Distribution Service, 50, 78
New Tone Records, 7, 38, 39, 41, 43, 57, 108
New World Records, 7
New World Symphony Centennial Celebration (2013), 81, 144
New York Public Library (New York City), 40, 56
New York Public Library for the Performing Arts (New York City), 152; MR exhibition, 136; MR "living" archive, 129–30, 136–37, 174
New York State Theatre (New York City), 53, 78
New York Yankees, 123–24
New Zealand Festival (2002), xxi–xxii, *54*, 59–62, 181–82
"The Next World," 171–72
NEXUS percussion ensemble, 80
Nilsson, Harry, 178
Nitze, Paul, 32
Nixon, Richard, 42
Noda, Ryuji, 6–7, 9, 18, 118
Nolte, Gibson, 17
NWS: 4'33" (video installation), 81

Object Music (UK label), 26
Ochs, Phil, 168–69
O'Donnell, Dave, 169, 172
O'Donnell, Katie, 80–81, 110–11, 124, 171, 182, 193

O'Donnell, Pat, 182
Off, Carol, 138–39
Oliveiro, Valerie, 77, 99, 116, 122, 149–50, 151, 161–62, 163–64, 168, 173
One Boy's Day (2014-? music/installation piece), xiii, 73, 177, 178–79, 182, 184–85, 188–96; Krannert Center for the Performing Arts (Illinois) and, 191–96; permissions, 189–90; as research study update, 188–90, 192; stage designs, *186, 187*; website, 193
O'Neill, Eugene, 14
Oneohtrix Point Never (band), 175
"One Way Down," 35–36
On the Boards (Seattle), 161–62
Original Pantry Cafe (Los Angeles), 178–79
"Orson Elvis," 173
O'Sullivan, Donnchadh, 105
Oteri, Frank, 79
Ouimette, Tim, 154

Paik, Nam June, 80
"Paper Boy," 34
Paramount Theater (New Zealand), 60
Pareles, Jon, 12, 33, 34, 138, 171
Park Avenue Armory (New York City), 148
Parks, Van Dyke, 163, 176
Pasternak, Dave, 124
Pasternak, Donna, 124
Pastis (New York City), 65
Patchen, Kenneth, 80
Patterson, Robert, 84, 143–44
Pawl, Christina, 88, 119, 131, 135
Pellegrini's Espresso (Australia), 58
Peppermint Lounge (New York City), 27, 51
Perry, Phil, 107
"Persons Unknown," 43
Perth International Arts Festival (Australia), 16–17, 59, 61–62, 70, 120, 155
Pettigrew, Henry, 118
Philharmonic Society of Orange County (California), 14–16
Philippe the Original (Los Angeles), 179
"Pick It Up, Audrey," xx, 183
Pink's Hot Dogs (Los Angeles), 15, 67, 77, 99
Pizza Giove (Staten Island), 111–12
Place, Oliver di, 168
Plan K (Brussels, Belgium), 30
"Plug Nickel," 170–71
Po' Boys (Urbana, Illinois), 92
Pogemiller, Raymond LeRoy, 115–16

Pognani, Renzo, 38, 39, 41
Po' Henry and Tookie (stage names), 159–60
Point Records, 38–39, 65
Ponder, Brennan Mikel (nephew), 76, 79, 102, 117–19, 137, 151, 152, 173, 182
Ponder, Cindy (sister), 6, 35, 38, 79, 102, 115, 118, 151, 152, 182, 183
Ponder, Katie (niece). *See* Israel, Katie Ponder (niece)
Pony Bar (New York City), 80–81, 111
"Poor God," 158
"The Pop Machine," xvii, 180
Porter, Cole, 40
Poseidon Bakery (New York City), 106
post-minimalism, 36, 37
Pottorf, Darryl, 71
Powers, Ann, 55
The Pretenders (band), 33
Price, Janice, 114–15, 117–18
Prime Burger (New York City), 107
Primitive Man Recording Company (PMRC), 34, 36
"Professional Smile," 173
"Prosperity Gospel," 172
Putsch's Cafeteria (Kansas City), 103
Pyramid Club (New York City), 5, 28

"Quick Thrust," x–xi, 36, 42
Quisenberry, Karen, 18, 86–87, 144
Quorum (1984), 13, 31–33, 40, 48–53, 78; LinnDrum and, 31–32, 36, *47,* 48–50; master patterns, *46;* press coverage, 50; and *Vespers* (Alvin Ailey American Dance Theater ballet), x, *47,* 48, 50–53, 73, 136

"Radiation Dance," 25–26
The Ramones (band), 33
The Ranch Mastering (Agoglia), 161, 169, 177
"Random Forests," 183
Raoul's (New York City), 65
Raphael, Sally Jessy, 20
Rasbury, Michael, 66, 67–68
Rauschenberg, Robert, 65–66, 71, 75–76, 129
Reagan, Ronald, 30, 32
Reaves, Keanu, 20
Recess (2010), 136, 166, 169–71
Record Plant (New York City), 132, 135, 169
Redman, Dewey, 37
Reed, Lou, 78, 105, 131, 184

Reich, Steve, 13, 20, 50, 159
Reininger, Blaine, 8, 28, 30–31
The Reliable (New York City), 109
Rent (Larson), 14
Return (1999), xiv, xvi, 85, 154–55
"Reverend," 183
Ribeiro, Susana, 19, 83–84, 155, 165
Ribeiro Lampariello, Julieta, 165–66
Ribot, Mark, 131
Rich, Alan, 163
The Richard Bey Show (WWOR-TV), 3–4
Richards, Fran, 13, 65
Richmond, Jonathan, 27
Riesman, Michael, 39
Rivera, Geraldo, 4
Roadfood (Stern and Stern), 113
Roararatorio (Cage/Rouse sound installa-
    tion), 59, 70
Robinson, Mike, 34
Rockwell, John, 74
Rose, Jonathan, 50
"Roseland," xvi
Ross, Matt, 107n
Ross, Mike, 16, 18, 84, 85, 88–89, 95, 134,
    137, 149, 191, 193, 196
Rough Trade, 34
Roulette (New York City), 35
Roundhouse (London), 31
Roundtable (1977 film), 155
Rouse, Martha Sue (mother), 9, 38, 58, 93,
    102, 115, 118, 151, 152, 176, 190, 193, 195
Rouse, Mikel (MR): archives prepared by
    (see archives of MR); birth (1957), ix,
    102, 189; in Brussels, Belgium, 8, 30–31,
    32, 62; carnival work, x, 58–59, 130,
    193; in Chang in a Void Moon (serial
    play), 5; Club Soda Music label, 32;
    early years/family background, ix–x, 6,
    101–2, 128–29, 189, 190, 191–96; educa-
    tion, x, 24, 65–66, 102, 115, 155, 193,
    195; ExitMusic Recordings label, 7, 36,
    136, 154–56, 157, 166–71; father, ix, 101,
    111–12, 124, 189, 190, 195; at fiftieth anni-
    versary of Canadian Governor General
    position, 20, 115; financial challenges,
    2–3, 7–8, 12–14, 37–38, 42, 44, 55–56,
    71, 82, 112–13, 147–48, 149, 158, 194–96;
    honors and awards (see honors and
    awards of MR); in Interpretations music
    series, 7–8; marriage (see Boudreau,
    Lisa [former wife]); in "Meet Me in the
    Middle" (YouTube video), 137; Mikel
    Rouse Sports Blog, 174–75, 179–80; at

Minnesota State University, 39; move
    to New York City (1979), x; and the
    National Sawdust Hemisphere retro-
    spective (2017), 138, 177; NewMusicBox
    tribute for Merce Cunningham, 79; in
    Palladio, 142; in Paris, 72–73; perfect
    pitch by hypnosis training, 27–28; at the
    Rally for Nuclear Disarmament (1982,
    New York City), 32; sketchbooks, 22,
    23, 72, 76, 113; solo benefit concert at St.
    Clement's Episcopal Church (New York
    City), 12–13, 65; spelling/pronuncia-
    tion of name, ix–x; "staycation" (2008),
    110–11, 123–25; studio in Alabama,
    157–58, 176; studios in New York City,
    6, 8, 30, 38, 42–43, 49, 57, 86, 112, 132,
    135, 147, 169, 174; tax audits, 95, 137–38;
    Underemployed (comic strip), 175, 183
Rowell, Mary, 155
Royal Court Theatre (Liverpool), 96–98
Royal Lyceum Theatre (Scotland), 67–68
Rubnitz, Tom, 104
Rudy's Bar & Grill (New York City), xxi,
    1–2, 21, 108
Ruggiero, Angelo, 111
Russell, Arthur, 27, 29, 34–35, 38–39, 41,
    52, 65
Russell, Ben, 136

Sam's Grill (San Francisco), 152, 164, 165
Sancimino brothers, 164–65
Sanders, Sallie, 131
Sanderson's Lunch (Kansas City), 103
Sandow, Greg, 29, 31
San Giovanni, Susan, 7, 38, 105
Santoro, Gene, 33
Sarah's Kitchen (Ruston, Louisiana),
    160–61
Satie, Erik, 67
Saul, John Ralston: at Dennis Cleveland
    premiere, 8–9, 20; at fiftieth anniversary
    of Canadian Governor General position,
    20, 115; Luminato Festival and, 115–18,
    120, 122; Voltaire's Bastards, xvi–xvii, 3,
    4, 115
Schaefer, John, 137, 154
Schillinger, Joseph, x
Schillinger System of Musical Composi-
    tion, x–xi, xiv, xx, 28
Schoenoff, Jon, 86–87, 143
Schroeder, Ernie, 1–2
Schubert, Franz, 167
Scopes, John, 32

Sears Fine Foods (San Francisco), 164
Sebastian, John, 177
Secret Sound Studio (New York City), 28
"See My Problem," 34
"See the Living," 180
"See You," 182
Sefton, David, 163
Sélavy, Rrose (Marcel Duchamp female alter ego), 67
Selby, Margaret, 13, 14, 15, 52–53, 72
Sellars, Peter, 17
Seren, Xander, 191, 194
serialism, xiv, xxi, 31–32
Setlow, Jennifer, 133
"Set the Timer," 33–34
Set the Timer/Uptight (1986), 33–34, 35
Sexsmith, Ron, 121
Shagwong restaurant (Montauk), 6
Shamberg, Michael, 28
"Share the World," 179, 180
Sharp, Sylver Logan, 19, 21
Sharrock, Sonny, 27
Sheffield, Graham, 117
Shepperson, Rob, 8, 24–25, 26, 28–29, 30, 66, 103, 104, 171–72, 195
Shield '81 (unused album title), 28
Sidelinger, Stephen, 65–66
"Side Myself," 176
Simon, Lizzie, 173–74
Simpson, Doug, 168, 171
Sire Records, 33
Skinny Dennis (New York City), 147–48
"Sky Sprites," 172
"Sleep," 30
Smith, Eric, 9, 15, 156
Smith, Levensky, 9, 15, 120, 157
Smith, Sam, 191, 196
Smith, Steve, 95, 136, 169
Smothers Brothers, 178
"Snowball Earth," 183
Social Responsibility (1986), 33, 34–35, 36–37
Soderbergh, Steven, 133
Sontag, Susan, 82–83
Soul Menu (1993), x, 38–39, 57
"Soul Train," xii, 43–44
Southam, Andrew, 104
Spencer's Grill (St. Louis), 102
Spinale, Guy, 165
"Spin Your Wheels," 35
"Spokecard," 183, 184
SRI International, 142–46, 150

Stannard, Joseph, 175, 180
Stark, Stacy, 94–95
St. Clement's Episcopal Church (New York City), 12–13, 65
Steele, Tim, 32, 37
Stein, Gertrude, xvi
Stein, Seymour, 33
Steiner, Leo, 107–8
Sterling Sound, 34
Stern, Jane and Michael, 113
Sting, 37
Stone, Carl, 39
The Stone (New York City), 131–32, 135, 166
Story of the Year (1983), 28–29
Stoughton, Mike, 103, 104
Stroud's Chicken (Kansas City), 103
Studies in African Music (Jones), x
Studio Coffee Shop (New York City), 44
Studio X (New Jersey), 39–40
Sugg, Jeff, 19, 21, 86, 92, 134–35, 137, 142, 146–49, 191
Sullivan, Kate, 15, 161
Supreme Macaroni Co. (New York City), 105
Sutcliffe, Stu, 97
Suzara, Imelda Ortega, 122
Suzuki, Dean, 29, 43
Swan Oyster Depot (San Francisco), 152, 164, 165
Swed, Mark, 44, 58–59, 155–56, 163, 164
Swingers Castle (2019), xvii–xviii, 178–81, 183
Sydney Opera House (Australia), 58, 162

Talking Heads (band), x, 24–25, 33
Tandon, Shaun, 150–51, 177
Taylor, Walter, 165
"Tennessee Gold," 154
Tesar, Bill, 35, 36, 48, 49, 123, 129, 135
Tesar, Rave, 35, 36, 39–41, 157
Test Tones (2005), 66, 85, 158–59, 161
"That's My Universe," 160
Théatre de la Ville (Paris), 76, 84
"(I'm Thinking about You Every Minute that I'm Not) Thinking about Myself," 40
39th Street Music Studio (New York City), 28
"This is the Best," 159
Thomas, Michael Tilson, 81, 144
Thomas, Penelope, 87, 99, 119, 131, 135
"#3," 36
Thrun, Sebastian, 146

"Thumb Skills," 172
Tilles, Nurit, 64–65
Tirez Tires (band), x, 24–28, 33–37, 39–40, 49, 50, 56, 66, 78, 104, 108, 112, 129, 171
Tod and John's (Brooklyn), 89
Tommy's Joynt (San Francisco), 164
"Tomorrow Never Knows," 175–76
Tom's Restaurant (Brooklyn), 110
Tong, Winston, 30
"Top This Ride," 166
"To Serve Man," 183
totalism, x, xxi, 2
Totonno's Pizza (Brooklyn), 109
The Townsend (Austin), 177
Toy Specialists, 35, 49
TR3 (New York City), 27
Travis, Geoff, 34
"The Treatment," 44–45
Trenchant, Jean, 30
The Troubadour (Los Angeles), 178
Tsutsui, Hideaki, 85, 132–33, 137, 149, 150, 156, 162
Tuxedomoon (band), 30
twelve-tone, x–xi, 36, 42
21CC, 150–51
Twigs, FKA, 174
"#2," 36

"The Uncanny Valley," 176
Underemployed (comic strip), 175, 183
"Under the Door," 30
Under the Door/Sleep (1983), 30–31
University of North Carolina, Chapel Hill, 93–94
"Uptight," 33–34

Valentine, Kathy, 177–83
Van Zon, Carla, 62
Vaughn, David, 68–69
Le Veau d'Or (New York City), 148
Verlaine, Tom, 104
Vertical Fractures (band), 37
Vespers (Ulysses Dove ballet), x, *47,* 48, 50–53, 73, 136
Vesta Lunch Restaurant (Toronto), 116
Vesuvio Cafe (San Francisco), 152
Voltaire's Bastards (Saul), xvi–xvii, 3, 4, 115
Vong, Jean, 53

Wagner, Clyde, 114, 115, 119
Wagner, Richard, 95, 167
"Wait for Me," 99

A Walk in the Woods (1985), 31–33
Wallace, David Foster, 173, 180
Walls, Seth Colter, 173, 175, 184
Walman, Jerome, x, 27–28
Walton Art Center (Arkansas), 133
Wang, Kenny, 135–36
Ward, Artie, 107
Warner Bros., 33
Waronker, Lenny, 33
WATCHOUT multi-display software, 86
Waters, Sylvia, 48
Weber, Andrea, 9, 15
Weigel, Jay, 134, 177
Weinberg, Howie, 32, 50, 169, 173
Weisburd, Audrey, 178, 183
Weisburd, Steven, 177, 181
Weymouth, Tina, 25
What the Doormouse Said (Markoff), 150
"When Pilots Came," 35–36
"When This Side Is Empty," 166
"When You Turn Your Face On," 157
"Where Are Those Girls," xv–xvi
"Where the Lights Are On," 166
"WhiteBlackYellowBat," 88
White Castle hamburgers, 1, 20, 21
Whitehead, Kevin, 33
"Why!," 183
Williams, Ann, 51
Willner, Hal, 131
Wilson, Brian, 159
Wilson, Robert, 85–86
Wilson, Tom, 171
Winners Circle (New York City), 70
Witt, Valda, 192
WNYC, *New Sounds,* 137, 154
Wolf Burgers (Kansas City), 103
Wooster Group, 14
"Words Are Missing," 171–72
World Trade Center terrorist attacks (2001), 68–69, 158
Wright, Herbert, 188, 190

Yes We Kant (2016 film), 176
"You Know Why I'm Here," xiv
Young, Neil, 119, 121
Younge, Michael, 105
Youngman, Henny, 107–8

Zevon, Warren, 107
Zimmerman, Melissa, 138
Zollo, Fred, 13–14
Zorn, John, 131

MIKEL ROUSE is a New York–based composer, director, performer, and recording artist. His works include 40 records, 7 films (including *Funding* and *Music For Minorities*), and a trilogy of media operas: *Failing Kansas, Dennis Cleveland,* and *The End Of Cinematics.* His work has frequently appeared on Top Ten lists around the country. He has received commissions from the Brooklyn Academy of Music, the Mary Flagler Cary Charitable Trust, and the Meet the Composer/Reader's Digest Commissioning Program. Rouse's compositions have been performed at Lincoln Center, the New York State Theater, and Alice Tully Hall, and throughout the United States and Europe. More information is available at www.mikelrouse.com.

Mikel Rouse's music is available on iTunes.

The University of Illinois Press
is a founding member of the
Association of University Presses.

———————————————

Composed in 11/14 Minion Pro
with Avenir LT Std display
by Kirsten Dennison
at the University of Illinois Press
Manufactured by Versa Press, Inc.

University of Illinois Press
1325 South Oak Street
Champaign, IL 61820-6903
www.press.uillinois.edu